INTRODUCTION

Welcome to the world of digital publishing ~ the book you now hold in your hand, while unchanged from the original **1967** edition, was printed using the latest state of the art digital technology. The advent of print-on-demand has forever changed the publishing process, never has information been so accessible and it is our hope that this book serves your informational needs for years to come. If this is your first exposure to digital publishing, we hope that you are pleased with the results. Many more titles of interest to the classic automobile and motorcycle enthusiast, collector and restorer are available via our website at **www.VelocePress.com**. We hope that you find this title as interesting as we do.

NOTE FROM THE PUBLISHER

The information presented is true and complete to the best of our knowledge. All recommendations are made without any guarantees on the part of the author or the publisher, who also disclaim all liability incurred with the use of this information.

TRADEMARKS

We recognize that some words, model names and designations, for example, mentioned herein are the property of the trademark holder. We use them for identification purposes only. This is not an official publication.

INFORMATION ON THE USE OF THIS PUBLICATION

This manual is an invaluable resource for the classic **Porsche** enthusiast and a must have for owners interested in performing their own maintenance. However, in today's information age we are constantly subject to changes in common practice, new technology, availability of improved materials and increased awareness of chemical toxicity. As such, it is advised that the user consult with an experienced professional prior to undertaking any procedure described herein. While every care has been taken to ensure correctness of information, it is obviously not possible to guarantee complete freedom from errors or omissions or to accept liability arising from such errors or omissions. Therefore, any individual that uses the information contained within, or elects to perform or participate in do-it-yourself repairs or modifications acknowledges that there is a risk factor involved and that the publisher or its associates cannot be held responsible for personal injury or property damage resulting from the use of the information or the outcome of such procedures.

It is important that the reader recognizes that any instructions may refer to either the right-hand or left-hand sides of the vehicle or the components and that the directions are followed carefully. One final word of advice, this publication is intended to be used as a reference guide, and when in doubt the reader should consult with a qualified expert.

PORSCHE

OWNERS HANDBOOK AND SERVICE MANUAL

SPECIAL SECTION ON
INCREASING POWER
AND PERFORMANCE

Published by

FLOYD CLYMER PUBLICATIONS
*World's Largest Publisher of Books Relating to Automobiles,
Motorcycles, Motor Racing, and Americana*
222 NO. VIRGIL AVE., LOS ANGELES, CALIFORNIA 90004

REVISED EDITION
COPYRIGHT ©1967
FLOYD CLYMER PUBLICATIONS

THE DYNAMIC DR. FERDINAND PORSCHE
AND HIS UNUSUAL MOTOR CARS

In every field of endeavor seldom does one man dominate his profession as did Dr. Ferdinand Porsche in the automotive field. Not because Dr. Porsche designed cars that were to outsell all others or designed the cars that changed basic thinking of automotive design and construction, but because of the uniqueness of cars that were his ideals.

Long before Volkswagen or Porsche cars were heard of, Dr. Porsche, who was born in 1875 in Maffersdorf, Austria, was designing unique automobiles in Austria. He developed the Electromobile Car, carrying the name Porsche-Lohner-Chaise. A gas engine powered the generator, which was a source of power for electric motors mounted in each of the four wheels. This was only one of the many revolutionary ideas that Dr. Porsche was to develop in the years to follow.

In 1906 he became technical director of the firm that manufactured the famed Austro-Daimler. In 1907 he designed light engines suitable for airplanes and industrial use. In the spring of 1923 he joined the factory of Daimler-Benz as Technical Director and Member of the Board. His outstanding engineering ability had much to do with the development of these famous cars.

Later on he designed the Auto-Union and these rear-engined racing cars were highly successful against Mercedes-Benz, Alfa Romeo and all other makes of racing cars.

When he designed the Volkswagen few ever dreamed that it would reach the tremendous popularity that it enjoys today. Dr. Porsche stuck with certain basic ideas in which he strongly believed, such as the rear engine, air cooling, and torsion bar suspension. While many of his other ideas became popular, these three basic engineering features have revised the thinking of many automotive manufacturers throughout the world.

He later founded his own company to manufacture the Porsche Sports Car — which now enjoys a fine sale throughout the world to customers who enjoy owning and driving a thoroughly different type of motor car. Using the basic Volkswagen engine, Porsche engineers, through special tuning of this engine, developed one of the outstanding performance cars of the world. The remarkable ability of the Porsche to operate at sustained high speeds over treacherous and winding road racing courses has been one of the outstanding characteristics of this car.

Driving a Porsche is fun — on city streets, on the high speed turnpikes and highways, in the mountains, or over any type of road racing course.

Fortunately, Dr. Porsche had a son who was intensely interested in continuing the good work and honorable business principles and manufacturing techniques established by his father. Ferry Porsche is to be commended for the businesslike way in which this company has continued building a fine reputation. Responsible Porsche dealers and distributors are located throughout the world, and the Porsche owner is assured of good service wherever automobiles are driven, regardless of where he may reside.

We thank Dr. Porsche and his excellent organization for all the technical and press information that they have supplied to Clymer Publications during their period of existence.

This book will give the layman tremendous and valuable information. We do not recommend that the average Porsche owner do any major work on his car. If such work is required it should be taken to an authorized Porsche dealer who has the necessary special tools and trained mechanics to do the job properly. The book does, however, give full information on the various models, and it is also a sales catalog that is valuable to prospective buyers. It likewise is a book for collectors and enthusiasts, who do not own a Porsche but who just want to understand the basic design and features that make this unusual car "tick."

Floyd Clymer

Contents

	Page
Family Tree	6
What Is It?	14
Pushrod Engine	24
Fuel System	27
Solex Carburetors	31
Zenith Carburetors	42
Ignition	49
Engine—Remove/Refit	52
Oil Circulation & Cooling	60
Cylinder Head & Valves	66
Cams & Followers	73
Crankshaft	76
Cylinders & Pistons	82
Carrera Engine	85
Weber Carburetor	97
Clutch	99
Transmission/Differential	107
Brakes	118
Front End	127
Steering	134
Rear Suspension	139
Shocks	142
Heater & Exhaust	144
What To Do Till The Doctor Comes	145
Maintenance	149
Tires	158
Driving	160
Electrical Diagram	163
More Push	166
Competition	183
Weber Carb	198
Solex Carb	199
Electrical Diagram 356 A	200
Electrical Diagram 356 C	201
Engine Specs	202

Family Tree

Every Porsche owner who has taken delivery on a shiny new car knows the thrill of the first few hours of possession . . . the minute examining of detail, re-exploring of features and most of all, digesting the maintenance manual. It is probably the restrained but prideful statement of background in the preface to this little handbook which firmly convinces the Porsche buyer that he has a singular automobile. Aside from the other considerations of beauty, finish, design or performance—that may have brought him to the purchase of the Porsche, the owner can take justifiable satisfaction from knowing that his car is the product of a unique organization. And, the enthusiast who feels that competition breeds competence knows he has an **able** tool at his command.

The Dr. Ing. h.c.F. Porsche K.G. of Stuttgart-Zuffenhausen, Germany, a development center without precedent in the annals of automobile and engine designing, has, for over 20 years, been engaged as an independent research and development bureau with the aim of advancing the automobile and its engine. Many productions of this firm have acquired fame and reputation of international significance.

The latest creation, the Porsche Model 356 sports touring car is a product of the long experience of our construction staff and has been developed by the pick of our developing department. It has established itself an unrivalled record for performance in the fastest European class.

The Porsche torsion-bar suspension, the engine and transmission in one unit in the rear, the low center of gravity and the steering arrangement have been adopted in principle from the Auto-Union racing car, another famous Porsche creation.

The beautifully designed body is an improved version of the service-tested Auto-Union world record car which had been designed on the results of months of wind tunnel testing.

The air-cooled engine, the torsion resistant frame and the sturdy wheel suspension are backed by the abundant experience gained by the Volkswagen which was subjected to severest trials during the war in climates ranging from the glowing heat of North Africa to the ice and snow of the far north, under the worst possible conditions in regard to terrain and temperature.

With the knowledge gained fom this unique background we are in a position to offer our clientele a supreme combination of speed, driving safety and high quality workmanship.

. . . this car has been produced in limited quantity for discriminating drivers.

So goes the factory introduction in the manual issued with the first export models of the 356 . . . and there is no reason to change a word except to add that American victories in racing have also produced an "unrivalled record".

Two references in the above paragraphs catch the eye more than any other: Auto-Union and Volkswagen.

To have been the 'father' of one of the world's fastest and most renowned Grand Prix automobiles and one of the world's most 'practical' and use-tested sedans is a unique achievment for one man. To begin with, most automobiles are the product of many minds, but there is no doubt that these two designs, so widely separated in application were the brain-children of that singular person; Dr. Ferdinand Porsche.

The Porsche story, at least many parts of it, is probably quite familiar to owners of the cars that bear his name, but, since the qualities that induced us to buy the vehicle in the first place are so typical of and dependent on the prior designs, we should examine this background at least briefly. Pride of ownership too, if nothing else, dictates that we should be adequately informed on a car that has such an ancestry.

Dr. Porsche was born in Austria and reached maturity at a time of great industrial development; the late 1890's. As a young man he was fascinated by electricity which, at the turn of the century, occupied the same relative position as 'electronics' in the mid-fifties. His first designs for Lohner in 1900 were of electric-powered automobiles, driven by individual motors in the wheel hubs with a power source of an engine generator in the chassis. This principle is basically employed today by the "Diesel" locomotives at the head of freight and passenger trains.

The automobile, in a relatively infantile state as far as production went in 1905 (when Porsche joined the Austro-Daimler firm, had already been exposed to nearly all the concepts that we find in a 'modern' car. Since that time we have benefitted mainly from 'improvements', but Porsche managed to come up with several innovations in the next few years that can be tabbed as original, culminating in the designs for the 'Peoples Car' and the 'P-Wagen'.

Having established his own Engineering firm in 1930 at Stuttgart, Porsche speculated on a couple of ideas that he had toyed with while heading the design staffs at Daimler-Benz (now Mercedes as we know it) and Steyr, an Austrian automotive concern.

The 'P-Wagen' was a pure and simple race car: A Grand Prix machine to compete in the then new Formula 1 which placed a weight limitation of 750 kg. (approximately 1,650 lbs.) on the car without fuel, water, oil or tires, but no ceiling on displacement. This type of restriction was made to order for Porsche who had long been an advocate of the use of light alloys, aluminum and magnesium and formed-steel shapes that provided strength without excess weight.

THE AUTO-UNION G.P. CAR

About this time the German government decided to encourage national participation in GP racing by offering a $200,000 subsidy to firms who competed successfully in such events. Auto-Union, a newly-organized concern made up of the independent marques, Horch, Audi, DKW and Wanderer, enticed by this bonus and convinced that race-bred publicity would be good for sales, bought Dr. Porsche's design for the competition machine and retained his services. Thus the 'P-Wagen' (which it was at first called) became the Auto-Union A-Type.

The Auto-Union record during the 750 kg. formula period is outstanding. Victories in the French GP, German GP (2), Swiss GP (2), Italian GP (3), Belgian GP, Tunis GP, Eifel GP and the Vanderbilt Cup Race plus innumerable hill climbs attest to the soundness of Porsche's design and the thoroughness with which the cars were prepared. In fact, the 'tryout' of the first model produced a new world record for 100 miles (134.46 mph) on the Avus track near Berlin.

The car, regarded as highly unconventional, placed the engine at the rear, used transverse torsion bars to suspend the front wheels, employed the swing axle principle and made much use of light alloys. Its 16 cylinder powerplant developed 295 bhp at 4500 rpm and the car was capable of close to 200 mph. Modified and developed, with various bodies, the Auto-Union eventually attained speeds of nearly 270 mph. In photos taken at Montlhery, France, where the Auto-Unions made their debut in 1934, there is a historic shot showing Dr. Porsche with the team manager and driver Hans Stuck. Clearly evident in the photograph is the torsion bar suspension with twin trailing arms identical to your present Porsche. The only difference is that friction shock absorbers were used at that time in place of the later hydraulics.

One outstanding difference, of course, was the use of a supercharged V-16 water cooled engine at the rear rather than an air cooled type. The engine, of 4.3 litres displacement, used a single camshaft to operate valves in both banks of cylinders in a highly developed and weight-saving arrangement of rocker arms and pushrods.

As Dennis May says in his article TURNABOUT TORNADOS in the July, 1958 **Sports Cars Illustrated;** "The fewness and simplicity of the modifications to the original concept that proved necessary

Above — The V-16 cylinder 6000 cc supercharged Auto Union racing car. Driver Rosemeyer is cornering during 1936 German Grand Prix.

Left — Dr. Ferdinand Porsche, famous German engineer who designed the Auto Union Racing cars and the Volkswagen.

The 1937 6000 cc V-16 cylinder Auto Union Race Car engine. Photo taken during world's speed records and after the "Internationales Eifelrennen" in 1937.

during the life of the 750 kilogram formula are their own testimony to Porsche's remarkable foresight. So far as the running gear was concerned, they amounted to little more than the substitution of longitudinal torsion bars for the original transverse leaf spring at the back and revisions to the shock absorbers. In the engine department, a three-stage growth in swept volume was achieved without altering the original cylinder centers. The first of these increases marked the A to B transition, brought the capacity to 4950 cc and the power to 340 bhp at 4700 rpm. The C type successor, operative during 1936/37, displaced 6000 cc, developed 520 horses at 5000 rpm. Finally there was the 6300cc R-Type, prepared for records, which gave 545 bhp at 5000."

So, in competition with the worlds finest machines through six strenuous Grand Prix seasons, (and actually halted only by the outbreak of World War II) Dr. Porsche's winning race car was refined basically by merely adding cubic inches to the engine. A remarkable bit of foresight, indeed.

That the production Porsche is based on the concepts employed in this car——and other race-bred vehicles——is probably a large part of the reason that it gives such a feeling of assurance on the road. The other side of the coin is equally intriguing. Given the leeway, any successful competition car builder can put a race car on the road in dress suitable for town and country. But, to make it untemperamental, long-lived and demanding no special service is another story, And, here is where the Volkswagen or 'People's Car' comes in.

As far back as 1930 Dr. Porsche was trying to promote interest in a cheap, light, easily made and maintained sedan that could be used anywhere in the world. The visionary Doctor, knowing that export was life blood to Germany, wanted to build a car that could be sold in Africa, South America and the north of Europe where water, strangely enough, is sometimes more of a problem than gasoline. His design called for an air-cooled engine, transmission/differential integral with it and swing axles/torsion bar suspension.

The first attempt to market the car was made by the German motorcycle firm of Zundapp whose familiarity with air cooling of powerplants made them a natural choice. The depression and other factors, however, did not let this effort get off the ground and it was not until after NSU had given it a whirl and Hitler seized upon this ideal to extract extra **Reichmarks** from his minions that further progress was made. Then, the political shenanigans of the Nazi government prevented any big realization of the premise.

There is no need to go into the VW story which is a modern industrial drama with few counterparts, but, just as Auto-Union found it necessary to make substantially no changes in their race cars except for power requirements, so has VW found it practical to stand by Dr. Porsche's original concept.

More remarkable foresight.

The Porsche, too, first of all his designs in a 50 year career to bear his name, is a sort of 'timeless' vehicle. The familiar shape and mechanical aspects of the Porsche coupe bear more than a little resemblance to the modified streamlined Volkswagen prepared 20 years ago for a projected Berlin-to-Rome race which was never held due to the war. Though this cannot be tagged as the direct antecedent of current series cars, its 40 hp hopped up VW 1100 cc engine reminds us that the maintenance manual states that the Porsche power unit is "an improved Volkswagen engine".

Porsche #1 was actually built in 1947 by Dr. Porsche's son, Ferry who had been actively assisting his father since the early 1930's. The Porsche firm, an engineering consulting service then operating out of Gmuend, Austria, had gotten re-established after the war with a design for a Grand Prix car for Cisitalia. This Italian concern commissioned the firm to produce the racer and the young members of the organization used used of the money to get the elder Porsche out of France where he had been jailed by the eager French as an enemy alien. Aside from the fact that it too made use of the torsion bar suspension and other design ideas from the Auto-Union the Cisitalia need not enter into Porsche history. Although tremendous in potential it never reached the track and we have plenty of other experimental models that did.

The number one car was a roadster that looks a great deal like the present day 'D' or Speedster. It had the engine ahead of the rear axle but otherwise was built along the same lines as the cars being produced 13 years later. A VW mill, again modified to put out about 40hp, was employed.

It took only two years to progress to the point where a production model could be offered to the public. Unveiled at the Geneva automobile show in 1949, the tiny streamlined coupe was an instant hit and a most controversial subject. Between the first "speedster" and the '356' coupe were about fifty hand-built aluminum bodied models. The show car and succeeding series models had a steel body by Reutter. Aluminum has since been used in racing coupes and, of course, the Spyder.

In another two years the Porsche name was synonymous with class victories in sports car racing all over Europe. The drivers took to the little coupe in such numbers that by 1952 the Porsche factory, now moved to Stuttgart-Zuffenhausen, was turning out six units a day and foreign trade had become a reality. Factory-sponsored cars had won the 1100cc class at Le Mans in both 1951 and 1952 and three record cars had established 17 international marks at Montlhery. The 1100 cc coupe averaged 100.72 mph for 1,000 kilometers (621 mi.) the 1500 cc coupe averaged 98.95 for 3,000 miles (!) and the Glockler-Porsche went 500 km. at 116.88.

The mention of Glockler brings up a name closely associated with Porsche during those early days and a person whose enthusiasm and efforts led to a greater participation by Porsche in competition.

Walter Glockler, a VW dealer in Frankfurt, grabbed onto an early Porsche 1100 cc engine and tweaked it up to 58 hp output on alcohol, stuffed it in a tube frame and surrounded the chassis with a light body of his own manufacture which kept the Porsche family resemblance. With this car he promptly went out and waxed everything in sight. He copped the 1950 German Championship then sold the car to fellow driver Kathrein who repeated in 1951. In 1952 the Glockler-Porsche was in the hands of a young man named Brendel who also cleaned up and took the 1100 cc title. Glockler had moved up to the 1500 class when Porsche brought out that engine and his new machine (practically a dead-ringer for the first Spyder) won him the 1951 1500 cc German Championship and was used to set the records referred to above. This car was sold to Max Hoffman, Porsche Distributor in New York, who drove it rather capably. Glockler then built a coupe version of the car that competed notably in races and rallies in Europe then found its way to the U.S. where it finally was destroyed in a highway accident that took the life of young Tom Shipman a promising actor and sports car enthusiast.

Unusual, one-off Glockler-Porsche coupe had pleasing lines

Glockler stood aside to let the factory carry racing development with the advent of the Spyder and particularly the Type 547 engine, but it can legitimately be said that he inspired the Spyder and the Speedster which, rather than the coupe so popular in Europe, captured America.

A discussion of the Spyder is not within the confines of this chapter and, since the Carrera is a hybrid, it will not be considered as an extension of the line historically. The new '90' will be taken up with the pushrod engines.

So, we have a car with remarkably little history in its tremendous "history". It is safe to say that the Porsche works has succeded within very close limits in the projects it has undertaken and has produced cars with a high degree of integrity. They are sound, well found and need only a master, as the seagoing saying has it. Now that yours has a master, lets see what adventures lie ahead.

356 B Porsche 1600 Roadster

356 B Porsche 1600 Coupe

What Is It?

Even in this enlightened era, eight years after its introduction to the U.S., the Porsche sometimes calls for an explanation. Due to self-limited production, examples of this marque will never be as thick as chiggers in Georgia yet we owners are often mildly astonished that acquaintances do not recognize our cars for what they are. Fortunately we have seemingly passed through that early period when well meaning individuals would exclaim "Oh, is that one of those Volkswagens?"

What can we tell these people? Most of us have a stock answer that satisfies the incurious and leaves the way open for a discussion if the questioner is intelligently interested. Once in a while, as can happen to anyone, a real enthusiast is encountered . . . or a quiet type who asks penetrating questions. In such an event it is well to be prepared to back up your statements with data.

Has this ever happened to you? A casual acquaintance, or some friend of your brother-in-law asks:

"Wot'tle she do?"

"Oh, about 110," you toss off, expanding the truth slightly.

"Pretty good for 55 horsepower. What's the torque rating on that little engine?"

And you gulp.

Alright, quickly now, what **is** the peak torque of your engine? What ratio is your third gear? What is the maximum spark advance and at what rpm does it occur? What is the number of the main jet in your carburetors?

If you can't answer these questions you **do** need to read farther in this book. Not so you will be able to do a snow job on by-standers but in order that you may be able to judge whether you are getting the performance from your car that you paid for and, more important to one who appreciates fine machinery, so that you can maintain the automobile yourself . . . within limits, naturally.

This volume is intended to bridge the gap between the rudimentary tips in the maintenance manual and the technical procedures of the shop manual. It will contain full instructions on all but the most intricate repairs which require professional skills. With it, you can not only tune the car for everyday driving and competition but you can make those repairs for which you are equipped.

As a basis, let us examine the various models which have been produced at Stuttgart up to now. Here are the statistics and performance data on everything except the Spyders.

1100
(Built from 1950 to 1955)

Bore 73.5mm
                               2.89 in.
Stroke 64.0mm
                               2.52 in.
Displacement 1086cc
                               66.3 cu. in.
Comp. Ratio .... 7 to 1
Horsepower .... 40 DIN
                               46 SAE
Max. Torque .... 51.8 lb./ft.
Carburetors .... Solex 32 PBI
Sparkplugs .. Bosch W 225 T 1
Wt. Dry .... 1808 (coupe)
Top Speed .... 87 mph

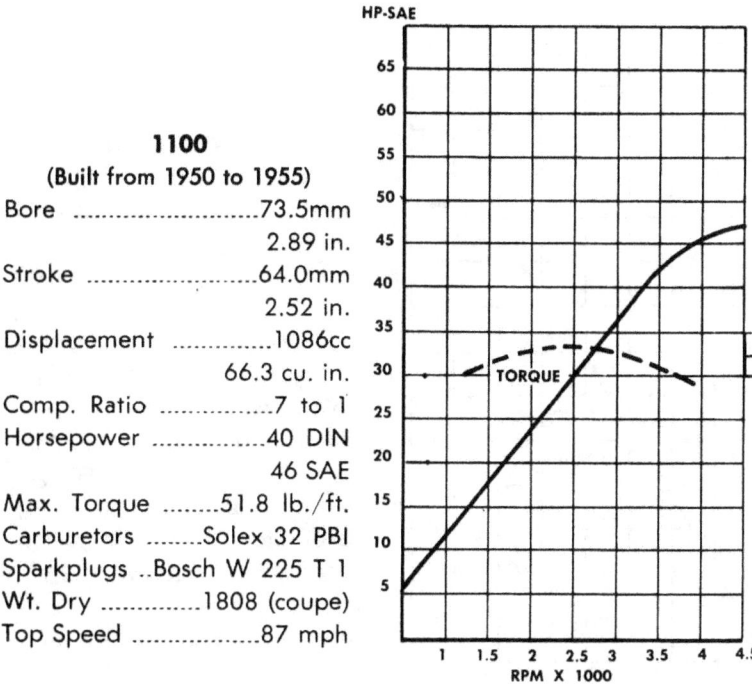

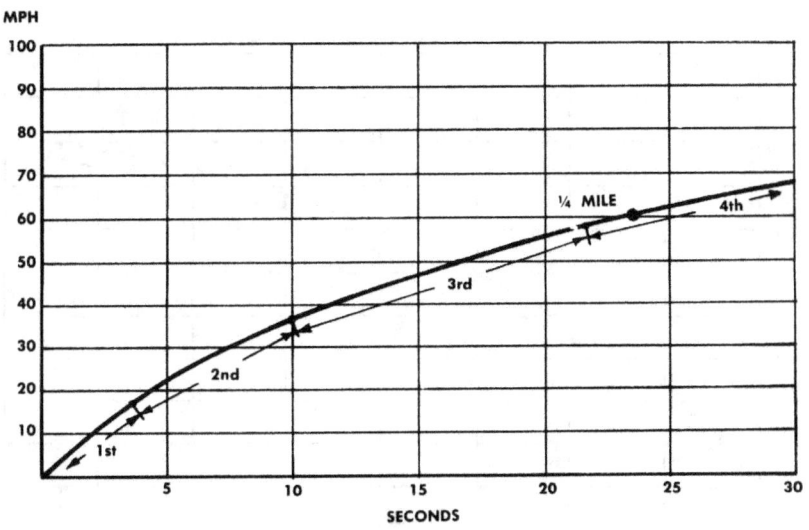

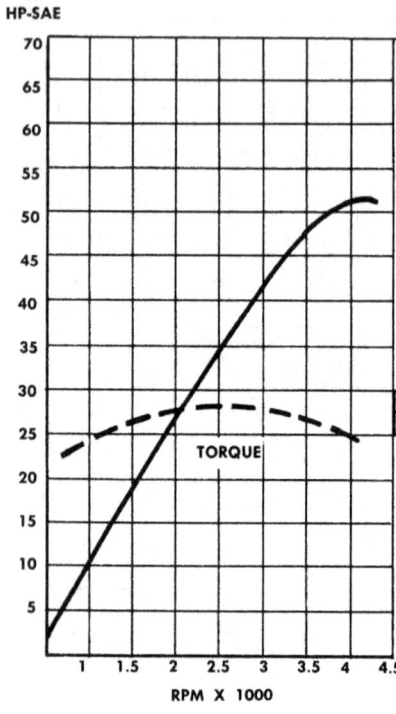

1300 Normal
(Built from 1951 to 1957)
Bore 74.5mm
                              2.93 in.
Stroke 74mm
                              2.91 in.
Displacement 1290cc
                           74.5 cu. in.
Comp. Ratio ....6.5 to 1
Horsepower ....44 DIN
                              50 SAE
Max Torque ....59.8 lb./ft.
Carburetors ....Solex 32 PBI
Sparkplugs ..Bosch W 225 T-1
Wt. Dry 1802
Top Speed ....90 mph

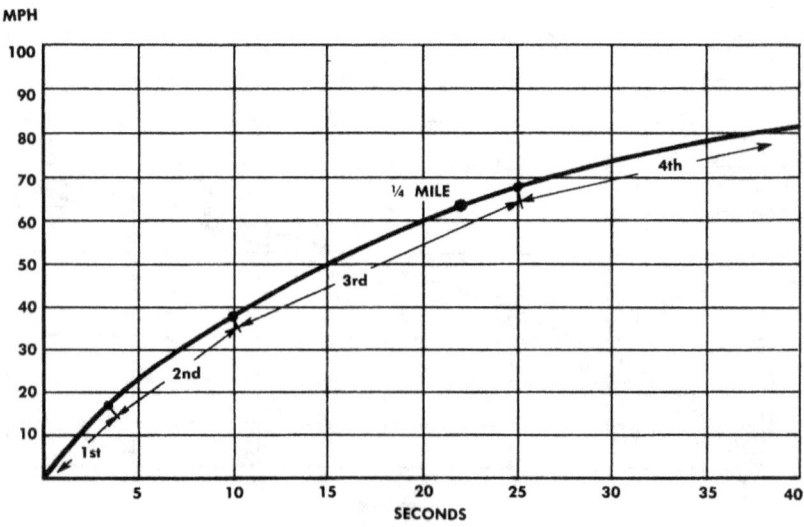

1300 Super
(Built from 1954 to 1957)

Bore 74.5mm
2.93 in.
Stroke 74mm
2.91 in.
Displacement 1290cc
74.5 cu. in.
Comp. Ratio .... 8.2 to 1
Horsepower .... 60 DIN
71 SAE
Max Torque .... 65.2 lb./ft.
Carburetors .... Solex 40 PICB
Sparkplugs .. Bosch W 240 T 1
Top Speed .... 100 mph

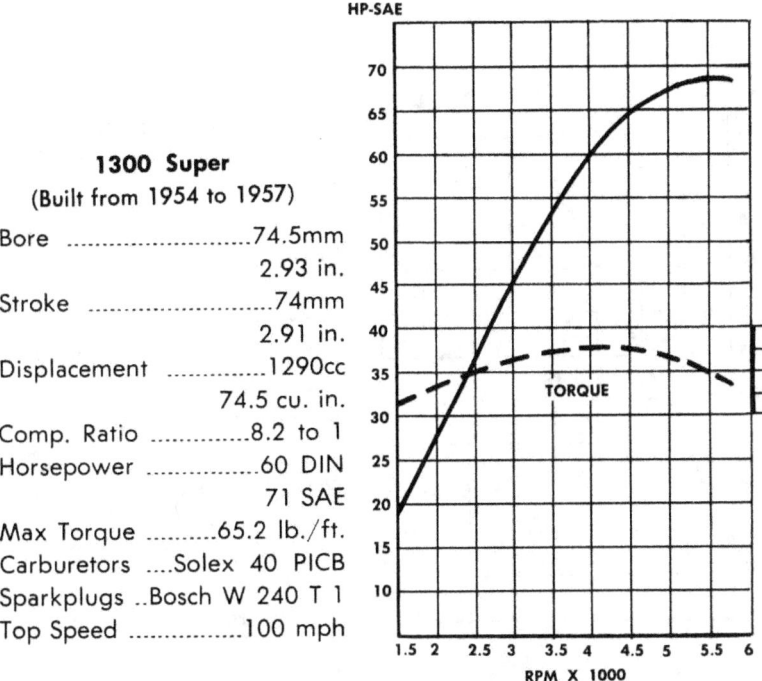

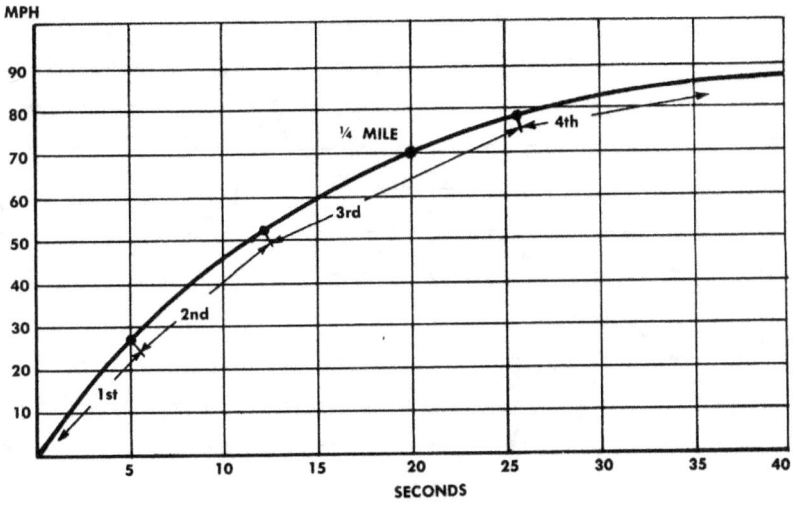

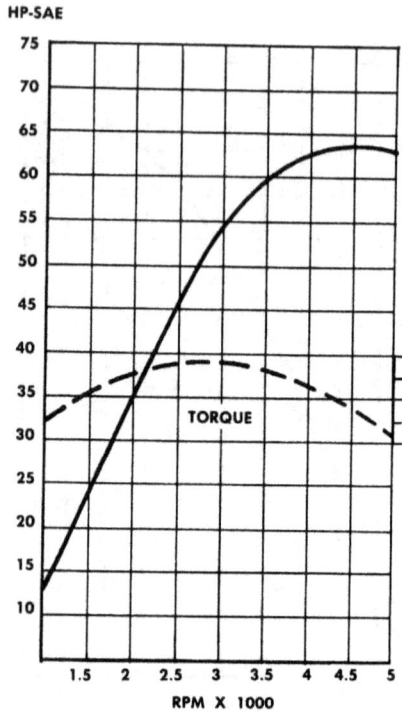

1500 Normal
(Built from 1951 to 1954)
Bore 80mm
                                       3.14 in.
Stroke 74mm
                                       2.91 in.
Displacement 1488cc
                                       90.8 cu. in.
Comp. Ratio ....7 to 1
Horsepower ....55 DIN
                                       64 SAE
Max. Torque ....78 lb./ft.
Carburetors ....Solex 32 PBI
Sparkplugs ..Bosch W 225 T 1
Wt. Dry 1802
Top Speed ....96 mph

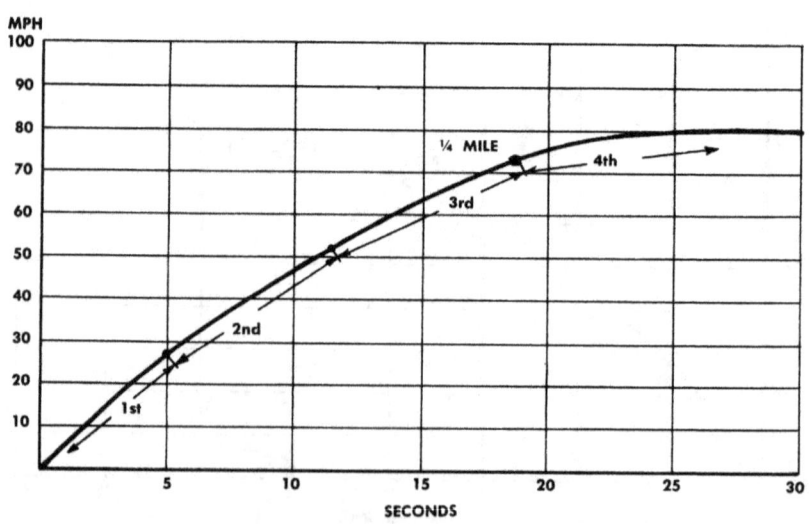

1500 Super
(Built from 1952 to 1954)

Bore 80mm
                              3.14 in.
Stroke 74mm
                              2.91 in.
Displacement 1488cc
                            90.8 cu. in.
Comp. Ratio ....8.2 to 1
Horsepower ....70 DIN
                              82 SAE
Max. Torque ....79.7 lb./ft.
Carburetors ......Solex 40 PBIC
Sparkplugs ..Bosch W 240 T 1
Top Speed ....105 mph

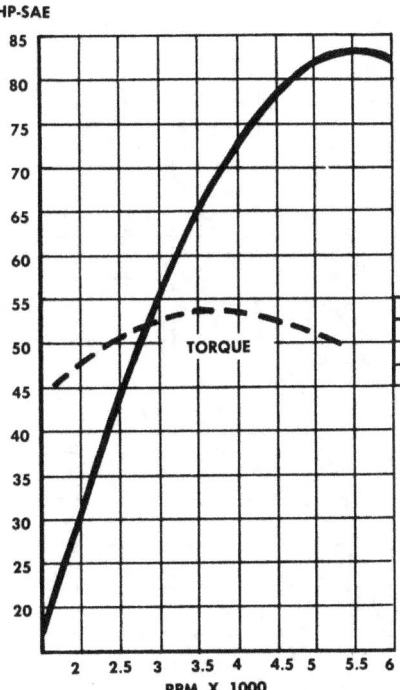

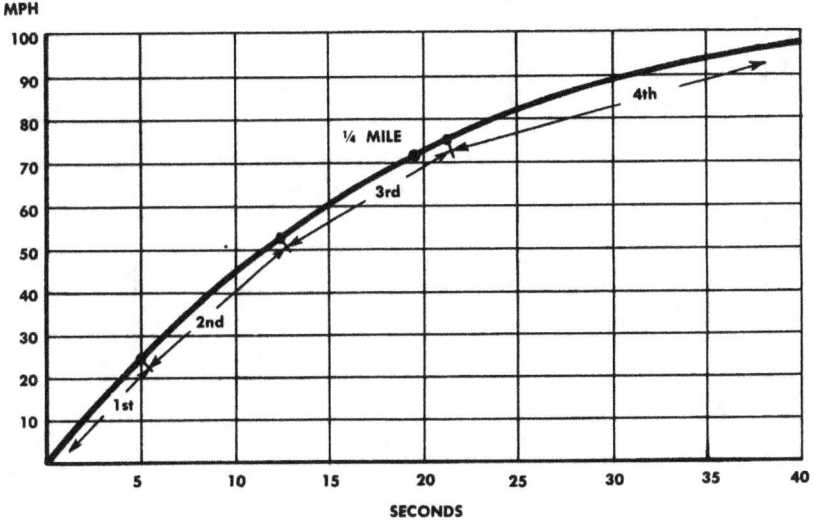

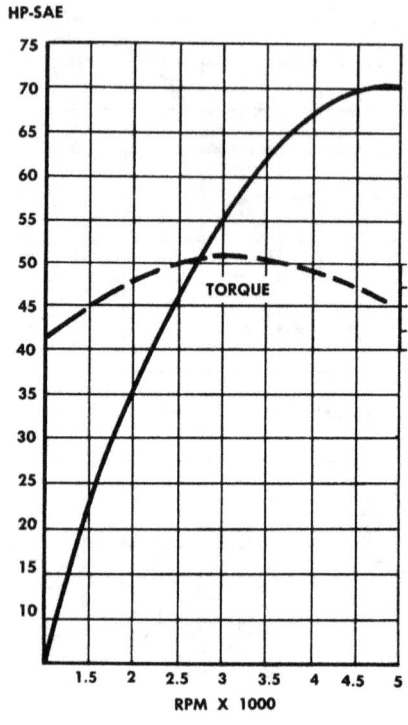

1600 Normal
(Built first in 1955)

Bore 82.5mm
                                  3.25 in.
Stroke 74mm
                                  2.91 in.
Displacement 1582cc
                                  96.5 cu. in.
Comp. Ratio ....7.5 to 1
Horsepower ....60 DIN
                                  70 SAE
Max. Torque ....81.2 lb./ft.
Carburetors ......Solex 32 PBIC
                              Zenith 32NDIX
Sparkplugs ..Bosch W 240 T 1
Wt. Dry 1820
Top Speed ....100 mph

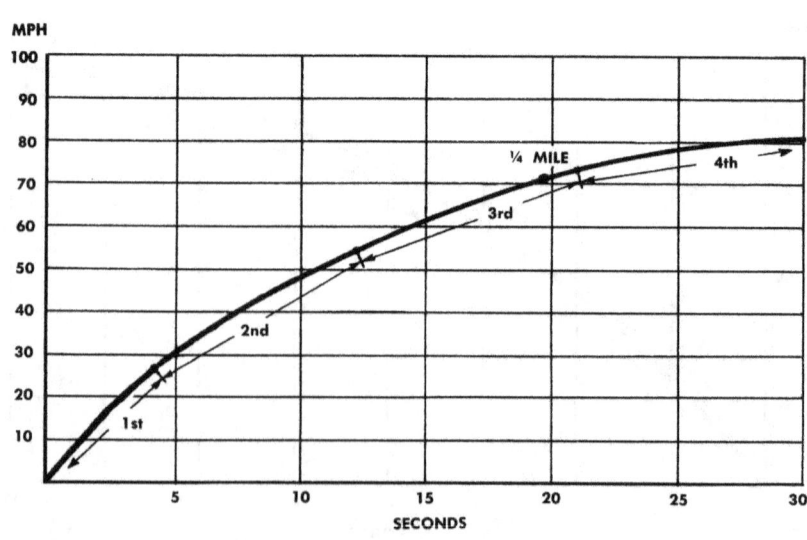

1600 Super
(Built first in 1955)

Bore	82.5mm
	3.25 in.
Stroke	74mm
	2.91 in.
Displacement	1582cc
	96.5 cu. in.
Comp. Ratio	8.5 to 1
Horsepower	75 DIN
	88 SAE
Max. Torque	87.6 lb./ft.
Carburetors	Solex 40PICB
	Zenith 32 NDIX
Sparkplugs	Bosch W 240 T 1
Top Speed	110 mph

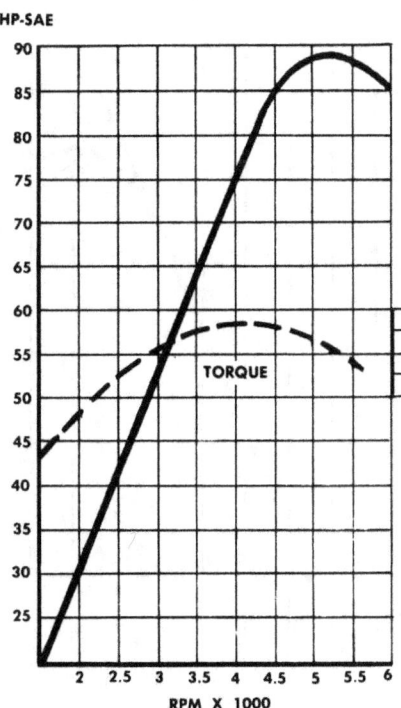

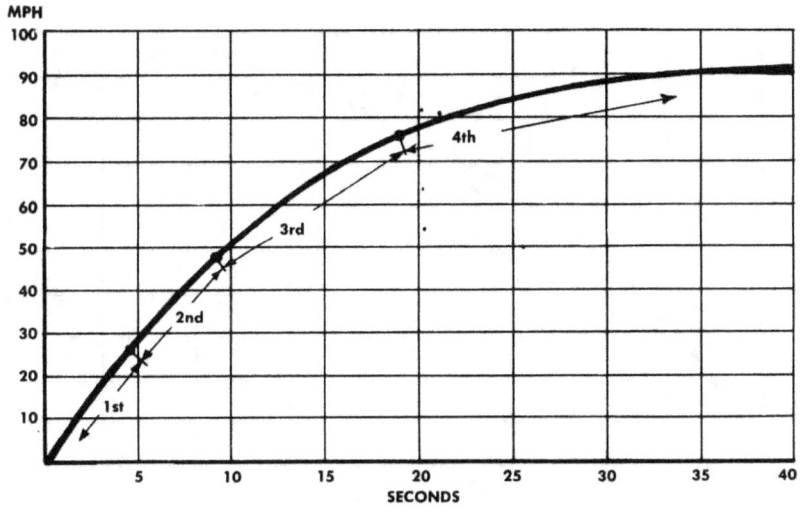

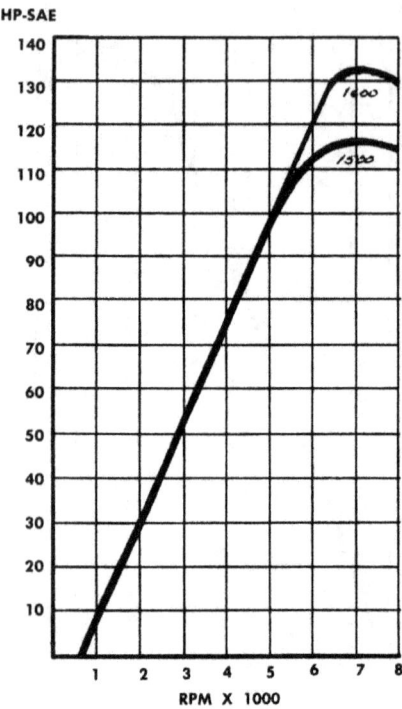

Carrera 1500-1600
(1500 introduced in 1955,
1600 in 1958)

	1500	1600
Bore	85mm	87.5mm
Stroke	66mm	66mm
Disp.	1498cc	1587cc
Comp.	9 to 1	9.5 to 1
H.P.	115	132

Carbs. ....Solex 40 PII
                    Weber 40 DCM 1
Ignition..Dual distr. & dual coil
Wt..(Coupe) GS: 2030 GT: 1918
      (Speed) GS: 1881 GT: 1852
Top Speed ....125 mph

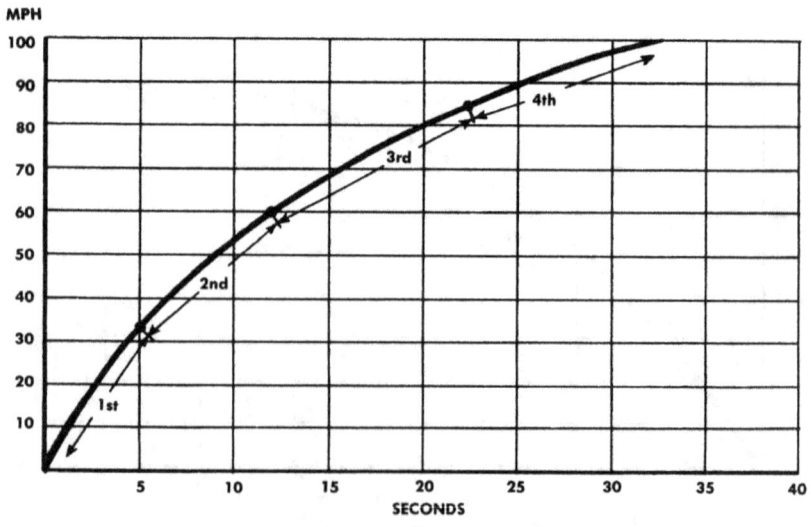

1600 Super 90*
(built first in 1959)
Comp. Ratio ....9 to 1
Horsepower ....90 DIN
                           102 SAE
Max Torque...............99 lb./ft.
Carburetors ....Solex 40 P11-4
Wt. Dry 2000
Top Speed 115

* The Super 90 features aluminum rocker arms, a lighter flywheel, larger diameter diameter main bearings, hi-dome 4-ring pistons, stiffer valve springs and a transverse leaf spring connecting the rear axles.

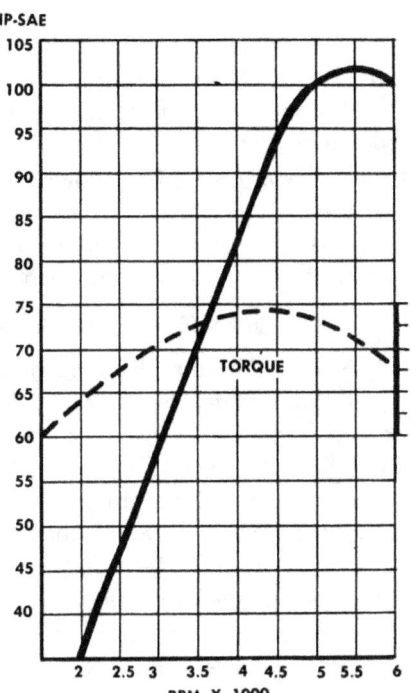

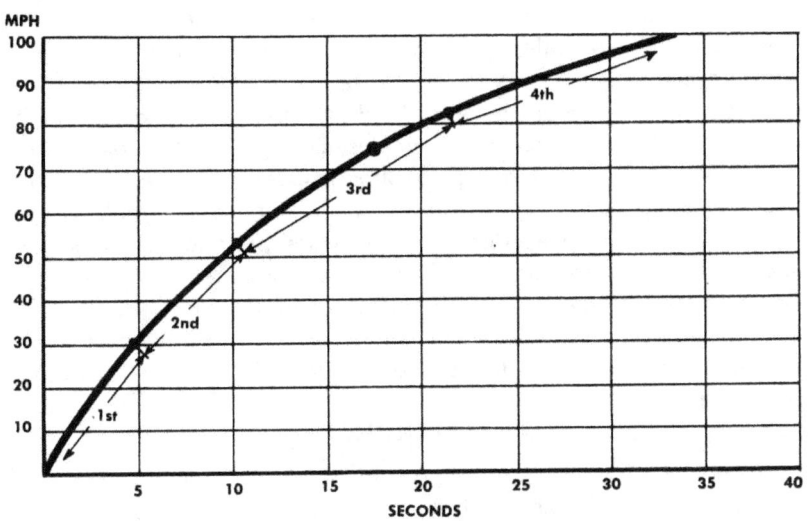

Pushrod Engine

Before getting into serious mechanical repairs or alterations it might be well to review the plan and construction of the engine.

The Porsche is a four cylinder, four stroke-cycle, air cooled, overhead valve engine. The individual cylinders are arranged in pairs horizontally opposed. The engine is mounted on rubber blocks and is secured by four bolts. Its crankcase is of split-type construction and in case of damage the entire unit must be replaced or repaired inasmuch as the pieces are factory-mated.

CRANKSHAFT AND CONNECTING RODS

All Normal Porsches have forged one-piece crankshafts running in four plain metal bearings. Supers before 1957 utilize a Hirth roller bearing crankshaft of the assembled type. Late Supers (beginning with engine #P81201) have the same crank as Normals. All bearing surfaces of the crank are hardened and Main bearing #1 (clutch end) takes the engine thrust load. The flywheel is mounted to the crank by a hollow bolt and 8 locating pins, Timing gears are secured to the crank and cam by woodruff keys, a hex bolt and woodruff key hold the V belt pulley. The crankshaft is sealed in the case by a gasket at the clutch end and an oil-deflecting ring at the pulley end.

Connecting rods on Normal Porsches and Supers using plain crank have "insert" bearings (referred to by the factory as "interchangable" which term will be avoided because it might confuse the reader into thinking that the bearings could be changed from one rod to another on the same engine) of a high grade alloy. Hirth crank bearings are roller type. Rods are weighed at the factory and color-keyed.

At this point it might be explained that the reason for abandoning the Hirth crank on the Super is simply that the factory no longer considers it as a competition model and feels that the average buyer will not treat it as such. The roller crank, useful in sustained high speed operation, is also subject to galling at low speeds or "lugging" and can suffer from improper lubrication if not correctly warmed up. Plain metal bearing cranks, as built by Porsche and other competition-minded firms are fully safe at upper rpm limits if correctly installed and maintained. They are also much less expensive.

PISTONS

A chart farther on in the book will show the various types of pistons used in Porsches. They are all alloy aluminum with full-floating piston pins secured by lock rings at either end.

CYLINDERS AND MAIN BEARINGS

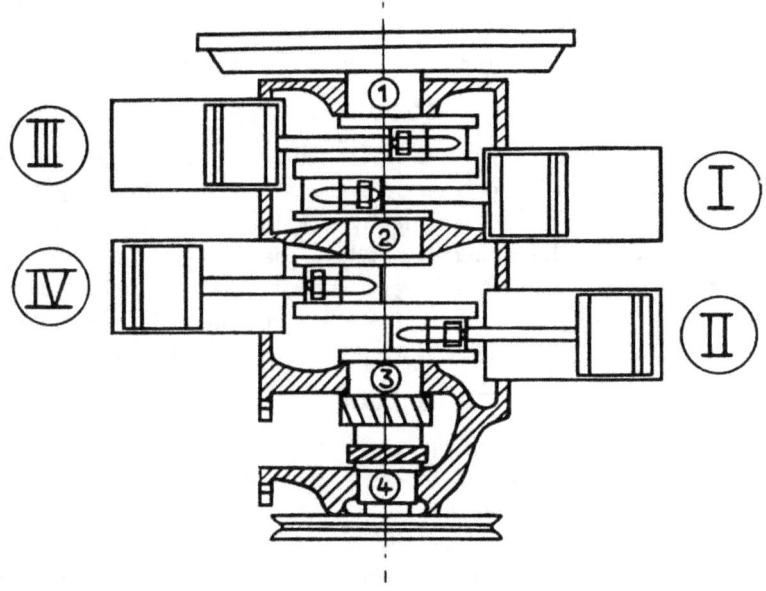

Cylinder I: flywheel side right   Main Bearing 1: with shoulder, solid
Cylinder II: pulley side   right   Main Bearing 2: split
Cylinder III: flywheel side left   Main Bearing 3: solid
Cylinder IV: pulley side   left   Main Bearing 4: solid (pulley side)

CYLINDERS

All engines, except 1100's which used VW cylinders, have aluminum alloy cylinders with chromed bores. Pistons are mated to bores by selection to very small tolerances (not to be confused with clearances) and are sold as paired units. Cylinders cannot be rebored by ordinary methods.

HEADS

Each pair of cylinders supports a common head of aluminum alloy. No head gasket is used, the walls of the cylinders protrude into head bores. Steel valve seats, valve guides and spark plug thread inserts are pressed into the head. Valves are inclined in a V and operated by pushrods and rocker arms from a cam running in the crankcase.

CAM

The cam rides in three plain metal bearings and is driven by a helical-cut gear of Elektron alloy. (early models used a pressed-fibre type that can be replaced with the alloy model.)

COOLING

Forced air cooling is by means of a fan mounted vertically above the engine. The fan is mounted on a common shaft with the generator and is driven from the crank by a V belt. Adjustment for belt tension is within the generator pulley. The fan sucks air through an intake hole in the housing and directs it downward over the heads and cylinders which are finned for greater heat dissipation. Metal shrouds contain the airflow and guide it properly.

OIL CIRCULATION

Lubrication is maintained in a pressurized system. Oiling in the Porsche plays a greater part in heat-dissipation than it does in the conventional water cooled engine and it is controlled more rigidly. The oil pump is in the crankcase and is driven from the driving end of the cam. Oil is taken from the lowest point of the crankcase and is forced into the lines by way of the oil cooler. Part of the lubricant is forced into the crank bearings, through the hollow crank and into the connecting rod bearings. Another part goes to the cam bearings, a third portion enters the hollow pushrods and flows up to lubricate the rocker arms and valve stems. Cylinder walls and pistons are splash-lubricated. Oil returns to the crankcase where it is cleaned by a strainer and magnetic filter before renewing its journey. A replaceable-cartridge filter is also in the system.

OIL COOLING & PRESSURE

The oil cooler is mounted on top of the engine and is under draft from the fan. Oil goes directly from the pump to the cooler through a by-pass valve. Regulated by pressure (viscosity) the valve either permits oil to be cooled or not, according to need. A warning light on the instrument panel is activated by a pressure-sensitive device installed in the line between pump and cooler. If pressure drops below 6 to 8 lbs. per square inch, the light will glow.

Further information on the specifications and operating conditions of these various parts will be found under suitable headings. The main point to remember is that this is an internal combustion engine utilizing the same principles and parts that conventional powerplants employ. It is not mysterious and once the nuances are understood any owner so inclined can easily care for it himself.

THE FUEL SYSTEM

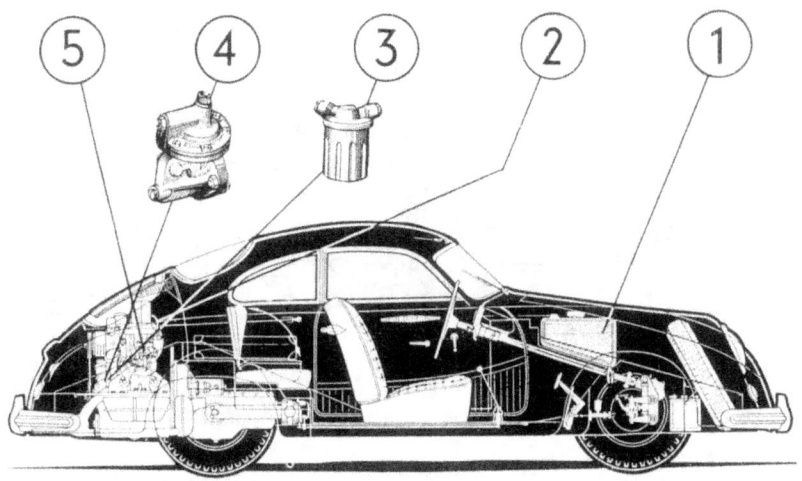

Elements of fuel system include (1) tank, (2) lines, (3) filter, (4) pump, (5) carburetors. Not shown is water trap, valve

FUEL TANK AND LINES

The fuel tank with a capacity of 13.7 gallons, including a reserve of 1.3 gallons (in all models except Carrera GT which has a 21 gallon tank) is under the front decklid. The three-way fuel cock : AUF-ON, ZP-OFF RES-RESERVE, (operated from a lever under the instrument panel) with its water trap is attached to the tank and is removable with it. Cleaning this trap every 5,000 miles is sound maintenance procedure. Cleaning the tank after 50,000 miles of operation to remove accumulated rust and sediment is simple enough to be well worthwhile:

Close the fuel cock and remove the cotter pin from the end of the operating rod. Withdraw rod and disconnect fuel hose. At the tank, remove flexible vent hose and disconnect fuel gage. Unbolt straps (on early models, unscrew bolts on tank flaps) and remove from car. Examine strainer inside tank for intact state and cleanliness, flush out and blow out with compressed air, Refit in reverse of above procedure.

FUEL FILTER

The filter at the fuel pump should be removed and cleaned every 5,000 miles. The bowl unscrews and a filter cartridge inside can be rinsed in cleaning fluid or white gas. Be careful not to lose the small spring in the bottom of the bowl and that the gasket is sound when replacing.

FUEL COCK

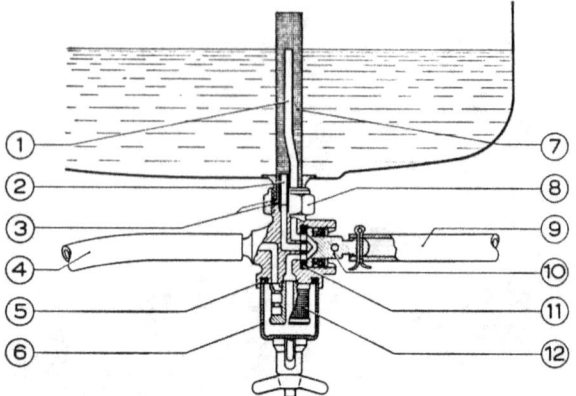

① Drain line with the cock set at "open".
② Drain line with the cock set at "reserve".
③ Gasket.
④ Fuel hose.
⑤ Gasket.
⑥ Filter bowl.
⑦ Filter in tank.
⑧ Fuel cap nut.
⑨ Operating rod.
⑩ Three-way tap.
⑪ Three-way tap gasket.
⑫ Filter.

Fuel Pump Description

Fuel is fed to the carburetors by a diaphragm type pump which operates from the distributor shaft. An eccentric on the shaft forces a pushrod against a rocker arm in the base of the pump. The rocker arm transfers this lateral movement into a vertical down-thrust against the pressure of a spring-loaded diaphragm. This creates a vacuum in the upper chamber of the pump and fuel is sucked in through a one-way valve. On the up-thrust, the fuel which has been drawn into the upper chamber is forced out into the carburetor line and more fuel is drawn into the bottom chamber from the tank.

Two factors control the amount of fuel delivered (a) the diaphragm spring and (b) the length of the pushrod stroke. Compressing or extending the spring can, to a degree, correct over or under supply. Adding or subtracting gaskets between the pump and the engine block regulates the pushrod stroke.

The spring pressure, and therefore the delivery rate, is controlled by the float needle valve in the carburetor. As the float rises in the carburetor float bowl the needle valve closes and raises the pressure against the diaphragm and spring. Under normal operation the movement of the diaphragm is only .1 mm (.02") but the pump should deliver a minimum of 167cc per minute with the engine running at 2000 rpm.

Fuel pump is driven off distributor shaft

If pump pressure is too high, flooding of the carburetor, poor running and idling and dilution of the crankcase oil will result. Too low pressure will cause a lean mixture and handicap performance.

Commonest troubles stem from bad diaphragms or weakened springs. These can be replaced without disturbing the pushrod, but if necessary to remove the unit, replace with the same number of gaskets as originally used unless eccentric, rod or rocker is badly worn. A special gage VW328b is used to measure the pushrod stroke.

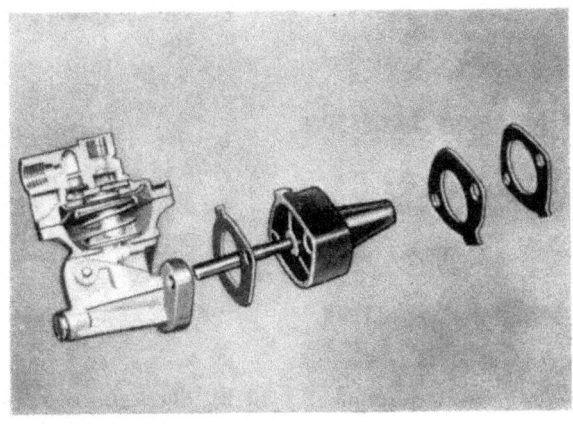

Cutaway of fuel pump shows drive rod, gaskets

Fuel Pump Troubles, Causes and Remedies

1. LEAKY PUMP AT JOINING FACES

- a) Slotted screws insecure
- b) Diaphragm cracked

- a) Tighten screws
- b) Replace diaphragm

2. DIAPHRAGM LEAKS AT RIVETS

- a) Diaphragm damaged in assembly

- a) Replace diaphragm

3. DIAPHRAGM MATERIAL LEAKY

- a) Material damaged by solvent in fuel

- a) Replace diaphragm

4. EXCESSIVE PUMP STROKE OVERSTRAINS DIAPHRAGM

- a) Pump incorrectly installed, gasket too thin

- a) Increase gasket thickness

5. PUMP PRESSURE LOW

- a) Pump incorrectly installed, gasket too thick
- b) Spring pressure low

- a) Remove gaskets to correct thickness
- b) Replace spring or stretch coils apart

6. PUMP PRESSURE EXCESSIVE

- a) Gasket too thin
- b) Spring pressure excessive

- a) Add gasket
- b) Replace spring or bring intermediate coils closer together

7. FUEL PUMP INOPERATIVE

- a) Valves leaking or sticking
- b) Broken rocker arm spring

- a) Renew valves and valve seats
- b) Check rocker arm spring, replace if necessary

Solex Carburetion

For many years the 32 PBI and 40PBIC (or PICB) were standard equipment on Normal and Super types respectively (except the 1954-55 1300 S which mounted the 32 with a strange assortment of jets). The carburetor types are identical in design but the 40 is somewhat larger as befits a more powerful higher revving engine. An accompanying table lists the normal factory-installed venturis and jets commonly found in these carburetors. Not always, mind you, but generally.

The Solex is a fine carburetor, easy to understand, capable of being adjusted to a fine degree and relatively trouble-free. The home workshop tuner need ordinarily concern himself with two elements: Idling speed and idling mixture, should his car come to him correctly jetted for his locality and the type of driving he prefers. If the second condition is not met, there are many happy hours in store (if he is the experimenting type) or possible avenues of frustration.

The first step in tuning is the simple one of adjusting the idling speed and mixture—balancing the two carburetors. We will begin with this, and for those who have passed this stage, it can be skipped over until the level you are currently operating on has been reached.

With the engine warm and idling:
1. Loosen the linkage between the two carburetors (a few turns on each nut will suffice)
2. Tighten **idling adjusting** screw on each carb slightly to bring engine up to fast idle (1,000 rpm)

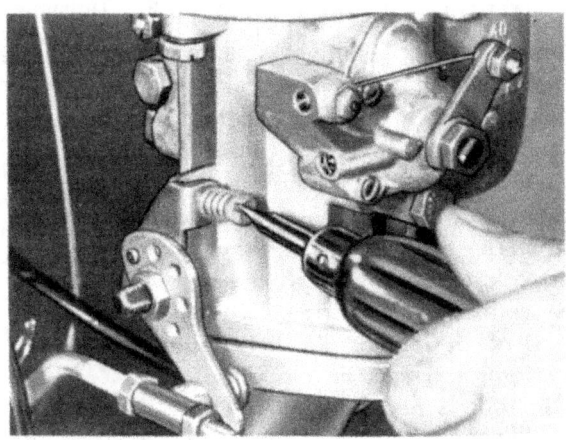

Idling Adjusting screw regulates idle speed

Volume control screw regulates idle mixture

3. Close **volume control** screw fully on one carburetor, then back it out 1½ turns
4. Repeat on second carb.
5. With this idling mixture as a starting place turn the volume control screw on one carb back and forth until the engine attains its best speed. If you don't trust your ear have someone watch the tachometer.
6. Repeat on second carburetor.
7. Back off each idling adjusting screw until both carburetors are "sucking" the same amount. (With air cleaners removed place the ear close to each carburetor in turn, the sound each makes is a guide) and engine is idling at 600-800 rpm.
7a. Use a Unisyn or vacuum gage to determine airflow through each carburetor. The instructions in the Unisyn box cover the use of this simple but valuable instrument.
8. Tighten adjusting nuts on carburetor linkage.

The idling mixture on the Solex (determined by the size of the idling jet and the volume control screw) carries well up the rpm range—to 3,000 rpm or so. Therefore it is an important function of performance. After you have set the idling mixture in the above manner run the engine up, either in free revs or by driving around the block, to clean it out. Then rev it up to 3,000 and release the throttle suddenly. The engine should drop to idling speed smoothly and not sputter or die. If it hesitates or runs poorly, run the volume control screws in (clockwise) ½ turn to lean the mixture slightly. If it is necessary to run the volume control screws closed or within a half-turn of being closed to attain best speed the idling jet is too rich. With the proper setting and pump stroke correct, the engine will not falter on sudden application of throttle.

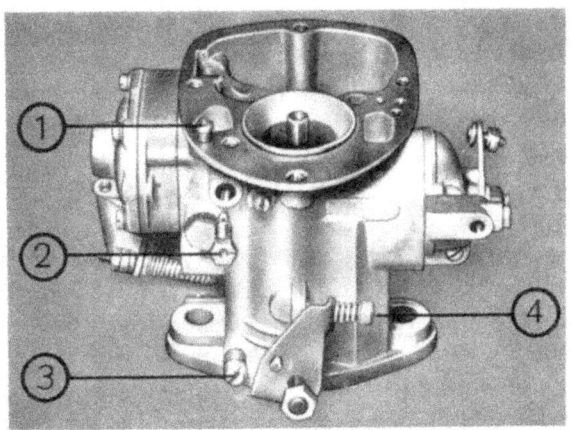

These components influence idle and performance to 3,000 rpm: (1) Idling air jet, (2) Idling Jet, (3) Volume control screw, (4) Idling adjusting screw

The carburetor serves two purposes: it is a metering device to provide the right amount of fuel and it is an emusifier which breaks the liquid into a fine mist for better mixing. The carburetor must also be versatile. At low rpm, where residual exhaust gases dilute the mixture, a richer than normal condition must prevail and at high rpm additional fuel is needed to provide extra cooling. (Actually; to absorb more heat and prevent detonation.) This versatility is provided by jets or other mixture controls within the carburetor body.

Before beginning a discussion of jets, let us review the principle of carburetion: The internal combustion gasoline engine operates on 80-90 octane gas—most efficiently on an air/fuel ratio of a little more than 12 (air) to 1 (fuel) by **weight.** Since the **weight** of atmospheric air varies with temperature, humidity and altitude but the engine requires a fixed **volume,** because of fixed bore/stroke, we can only vary the weight (or volume) of the fuel by varying the jets that admit the fuel.

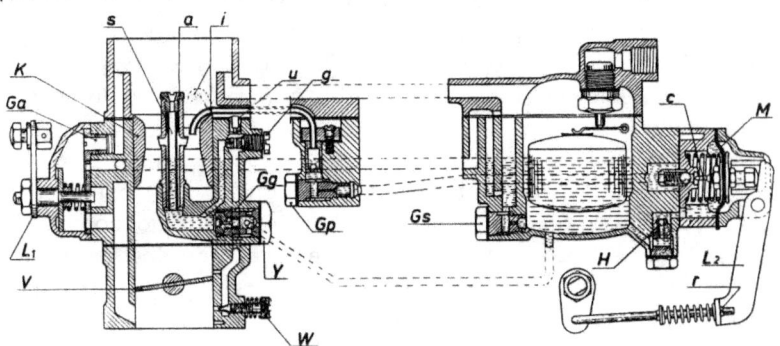

The Solex embodies the following jets to control fuel volume through different ranges.
1. Main jet (Gg on chart and cutaway)
2. Air correction jet (a)
3. Idling jet (g)
4. Idling air jet (u)
5. Pump jet (Gp)

Two other adjustable units, not properly classified as jets, enter into the picture: The volume control screw (W) and the pump operating rod with its adjustable nuts. The choke (called "starter" on the diagrams) and its jets need not concern us since it is seldom used and then only for a brief period.

The **Main** jet controls the fuel air mixture over the entire range, is **Air Correction** jet combined with the **Mixture** (or **emulsion) tube** (s) makes the mixture leaner with increasing vacuum in the venturi. The **Idling** jet and its volume control screw companion take over when the throttle is only partly open and negative pressure in the venturi is not sufficient to draw a good mixture from the main jet. The **Pump** jet richens the mixture on acceleration and also corrects for high speed leanness. The high vacuum opens it at about ¾ throttle.

As can be seen from the diagram and explanation, two variations are possible at each jet except the pump . . . air and fuel . . . this means a most precise adjustment of the ratio can be made.

Without going into myriad combinations which can be covered under "tuning" let us familiarize ourselves with the components and specifications. The jet **numbers** have no meaning other than to show a size relationship . . . they do not represent millimeters, inches or ells, but they do increase and decrease arithmetically: The higher the number the larger the cross section. A grand selection of jets is available from Porsche dealers or parts houses that handle Solex carburetors. The two you will probably be most concerned with are the Main Jet and the Air Correction jet. Their designations run from around 100 to 130 (Main) and 150 to 260 (Air). The Main jet is reached by removing the Jet Holder in the side of the carburetor body adjacent to the pump. The Air Correction jet can be reached by removing the air cleaner. It is positioned in the center of the venturi.

The Idling jet is directly above the volume control screw, it has no cover. The slot in the head is at right angles to the orfice in its tip. When replacing it, be sure that this slot is horizontal. The Idling air jet is reached by removing the cover from the carburetor. It will be found above the Idling jet.

All jets are marked on the heads.

Solex Carburetor Specifications

Engine	1100	1300N		1300S	1500N
Year*	'50-54	'51-54	'55-57	'53	'54-57	'52-55
Carb.	32PBI	32PBI	32PBI	40PBIC	32PBI	32PBI
Venturi	23mm	24mm	23mm	26mm	24mm	24mm
Main jet	110	115	125	105	160	120
Air Corr.	230	240	220	150	160	260
Idling jet	60	60	50	50	55	55
Idling Air	1.0	1.0	1.0	2.0	1.0	1.0
Pump jet	50	55	60	50	80	55
Needle	1.5	1.5	1.5	2.0	2.0	2.0
Mixture Tube #	23	23	31	28	0	28
Float Wt.	12.5g	12.5g	12.5g	21g	12.5g	12.5g

*Note: Many cars with the factory designation 1954 were delivered here into 1956, '57s in '58 and so on. Generally the 1955 (as we bought it) was the last of the 1500 series.

Solex Carburetor Specifications

Engine	1952		1500S 1953		1954-55 40PBIC (PICB)		1600N 1956-1957	1600S
Year								
Carb.	40PBIC		40PBIC				32PBI	40PBIC
Use	City	Comp.	City	Comp.	City	Comp.	Normal	Normal
Venturi	26mm	29mm	26mm	29mm	26mm	29mm	26mm	29mm
Main jet	117.5	135	107.5	117.5	085	*	110	130
Air Corr.	160	160	160	160	160	160	200	200
Idling jet	55	55	50	50	55	55	55	55
Idling Air	2.2	2.2	1.0	1.0	2.0	2.0	1.0	2.0
Pump jet	60	60	85	110	80	90	60	80
Needle	2.0	2.0	2.0	2.0	2.0	2.0	2.0	2.0
Mixture Tube #	23	23	28	28	28	28	28	28
Float Wt.	21g	21g	21g	21g	21g	21g	21.5g	21g

*Factory admonition. "Try jets #97.5 to 102.5, find out correct jet by testing."

FLOAT LEVEL

Proper level of fuel in the float bowl is important and the condition of the float needle valve often determines whether performance is good or ragged. Checking the fuel level with the carburetors on the car is not the easiest task in the world because of their position in the engine compartment, but the alternate method of removing them from the car and filling the bowl by running fuel in from a tank held above the carburetors is cumbersome, to say the leas. However it can be done either way.

Remove the carburetor air cleaners and the bowl covers after having shut off the engine at the idle. With a depth gage or a narrow pocket rule of the sort that has a spring clip, gage the height of the fuel in the bowl at the **meniscus:** the point where the fluid creeps up the side of the bowl. The distance from the top of the bowl to this point should be .63" in the 32 PBI and .79" in the 40PBIC. Tolerance is .06" and .04" in the 32 and 40 respectively. (Some factory workshop manuals list this as plus or minus 0.6 and 0.4 which is a misprint.)

To change the float level, bend the float toggle, The toggle bears on the needle valve in an upward direction . . . the valve being in the top section.

The needle valve in its chamber unscrews in a conventional manner.

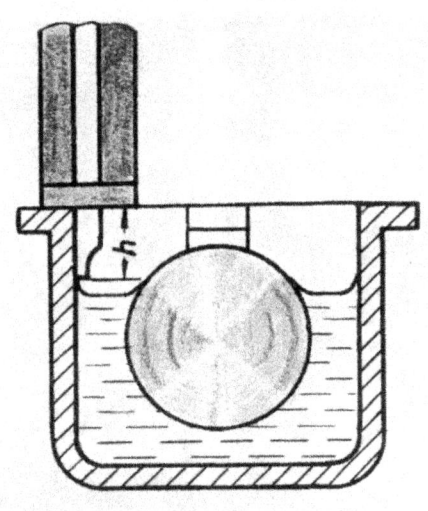

'h' = .63" (32 PBI) or .79" (40 PBIC)

ACCELERATION PUMP DELIVERY

Performance in the Zero to 30 mph range is much affected by the volume of the charge delivered by the acceleration pump. The amount discharged at each stroke should be .5 to .7cc in the 32 PBI and .7 to .9cc in the 40 PBIC and both carburetors should deliver an identical amount as closely as can be determined.

In the absence of "liquid measure P25" used by the factory, seal the small end of an eyedropper of the glass variety by holding in a gas stove flame for a few minutes. Then take another dropper and put 10 drops of ethyl gas (it's red and easy to see) into the first dropper. With the edge of a file, scribe a line at this level. This is .7cc. (Add 3 drops and you have .9cc.) The average dropper is too long for our purposes, so cut it off with a glass cutter or hot wire to about ½" above your mark, loop a piece of wire around it for a handle and you have your own "liquid measure P25".

With the engine idling and air cleaners removed, work the throttle a couple of times to clean out the jets then make a full stroke of the pump with the throttle rod holding the "liquid measure" under the delivery tube that curves above the venturi. Do this several times until consistent results are obtained. If the amount in the dropper does not come up to the .7 or .9 level (depending on the carburetor) unscrew the adjusting nuts with an 8mm wrench and set the stroke until this ideal is attained. Clockwise lengthens the stroke, counter clockwise shortens it.

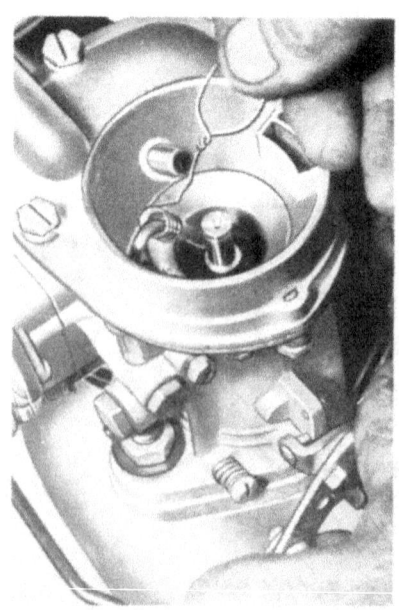
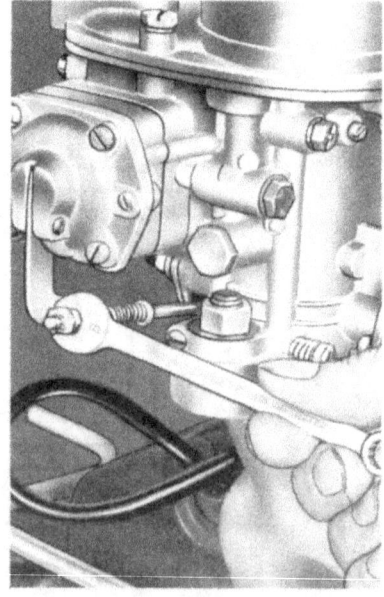

DISASSEMBLY AND CLEANING

After using our domestic highly leaded and dyed gasolines for a while, the carburetors become unsightly and are suspected of having the same sort of internal appearance. To clean them they should be disassembled and washed thoroughly in cleaning solvent, unleaded gas or carburetor cleaner. This is the sequence:

1. Remove carburetors from manifold.
2. Unscrew hex screws that hold cover, remove carefully, watching for sticking gasket.
3. Screw float needle valve out of cover.
4. Take out float toggle pin and float.
5. Remove air correction jet and mixture tube.
6. Remove main jet cover, main jet.
7. Take out idling jet and idling air jet.
8. Release venturi retaining spring and take out venturi.
9. Unscrew adjusting nut on pump lever.
10. Remove pump chamber cover, take out diaphragm and spring.
11. Screw out discharge nozzle plug (alongside discharge tube) and remove tube.

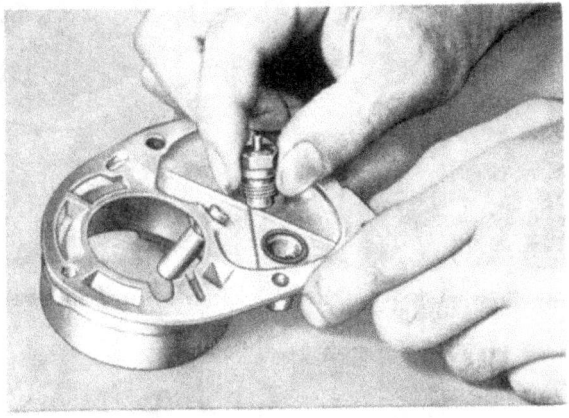

Remove float needle valve after top is off

After cleaning, blow compressed air through all orfices. Do not use wire to unplug a jet because you may roughen the bore. Check the following items before re assembly: **Float.** Hold it near your ear and shake it, if there is fluid inside it must be replaced. As a double check immerse it in hot water, air bubbles rising to the surface are a giveaway. Do not solder a leak, this will change the weight which is critical.

Solex 32 PBI with cover removed

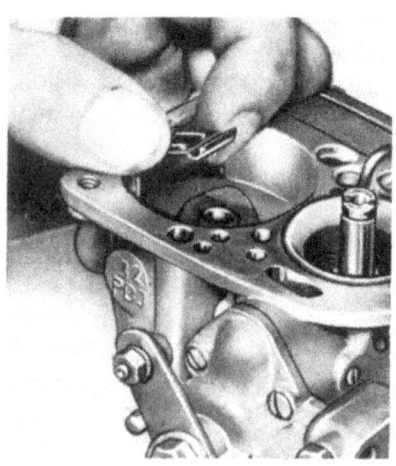

Removing float, step 1

Removing float, step 2

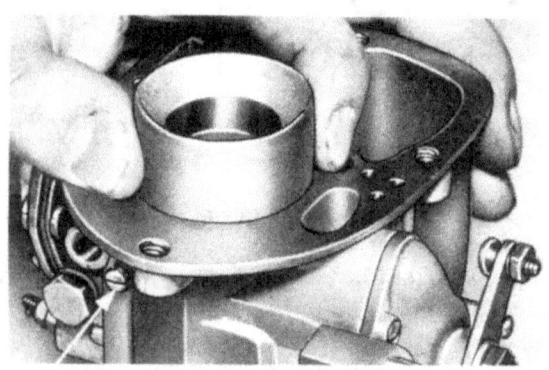

Release venturi retaining spring, lift venturi

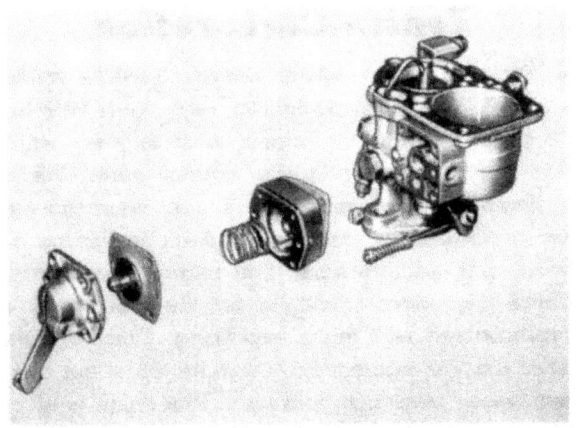

Exploded view of accelerator pump assembly

Pump diaphragm: Should be firm, flexible and whole.
Pump spring: Check these against each other, they should be equal in resistance.
Volume control screw: Be sure tip is tapered, not blunted.

To re-assemble, follow the above pattern in reverse, of course, paying attention to these points: **Venturi;** Be sure that the venturi is in the bore right side up. The restricted "waist" of the venturi is offset toward the top. **Throttle valve (butterfly) shaft:** The clearance between shaft and carburetor body should be minimal. If this is a loose fit, outside air can be drawn in to ruin the mixture. **Toggle lever:** The word "OBEN" is stamped on the upper side of the toggle in the 32PBI; replace it this way.

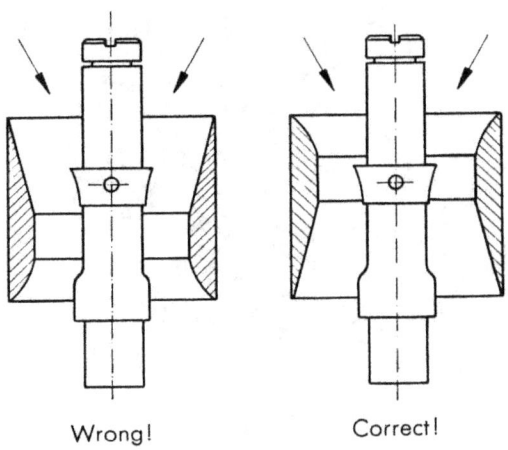

Wrong!   Correct!

Zenith Carburetion

In 1957 Porsche began fitting Zenith 32NDIX carburetors to all models and Porsche pushers had to learn some new facts of life. The main fact was that they had about twice as many adjustments to play with in order to bring it into normal tune. The dual-throat Zenith (or **doppelfallstromvergaser,** if you want to amaze your friends) has a number of personality traits including a tendency to leak, flood over and to spray the engine compartment on the overrun. These jugs were touchy about the float level and if improperly synchronized will cause backfiring. One Porsche specialist when quizzed on the subject of "what to do about Zeniths" said "throw them away and get Solexes". This may only have been prejudice, but it is a temptation until you learn a few things about them.

With the Zeniths, a life can be made easier by beginning right away to show them who is master. This calls for setting the accelerator pump, the float level and the idling mixture. Remember, these cars are set at the factory to run on local German gasoline and are driven around for a number of miles as a final checkout. The Works people feel that the owner or his mechanic, no matter where in the world he may be or what fuel is available, has the common sense to adjust the carburetor to conditions that prevail. If you live in Washington D.C. the jet requirements will be quite different from those if you lived at the top of Mount Washington

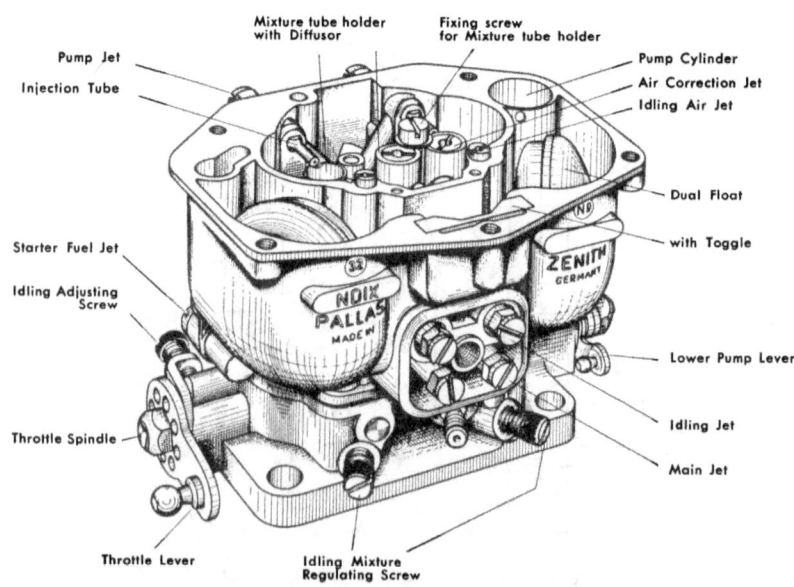

or Seattle, Washington, so we won't go into jets here. But we can standardize a couple of other items because the type of fuel we have in the United States does run pretty true to form everywhere.

To save repetition on the printed page, if haven't read the chapter on Solex carbs, check it briefly as regards air/fuel ratio. We can add one thought here that wasn't expressed in that discussion, however: U.S. gasolines are compounded from lower fractions in the distilling process and made less prone to detonation by adding patented chemicals whereas European fuels are brought up in octane rating by including the upper fractions. 100 iso-octane, the standard by which gasolines are rated, here is reserved for aviation fuels (for piston engines, that is).

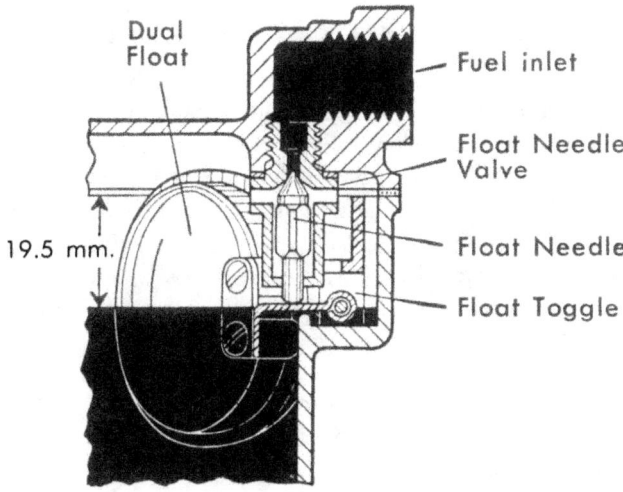

Float system

To get back to the original subject, a fuel of a different specific gravity such as a German blend will support the carburetor float at a different level. This level is critical in that it furnishes the correct pressure and supply within the carburetor system. Your dealer may have set the float levels for our gas as a routine "get ready" chore, or he may not. To do it yourself, warm up the engine and shut off the ignition at an idle. Then:
1. Remove air cleaners.
2. Remove covers of float chambers.
3. Measure from top of chamber to meniscus of fluid (where fuel touches wall of chamber) This should be .77" A depth gage or one of those thin, narrow pocket rules graduated in 64ths should be used. .77" is about the next line above the ¾" mark.

If you have a millimeter depth gage, fine: This is 19.5 mm. If you get within a 64th, you'll be doing great.

It should be obvious that the car and the carburetors must be level to accomplish this task.

Altering the float level calls for making small brass washers from shim stock and inserting them between the float needle valve housing and the bowl cover. The ratio here is 4.2 to 1. In other words a shim cut from .025" stock will **lower** the float .105" if it is interposed. **Removing** a washer of the same thickness would **raise** it a corresponding amount. The factory washers are fibre and should be replaced anyway.

Getting the float down where it belongs will help the flooding and spewing situation.

ACCELERATOR PUMP DELIVERY

The pump delivers less volume than its Solex counterpart because of the carburetor design but it remains a critical factor in low acceleration. Each delivery tube should put out .2 to .3 cc for every two strokes. This is such a small quantity that it is hard to measure, but acquiring the factory instrument "liquid measure P25a" is also difficult and bothersome. Make your own by following the tip in the Solex discussion but only put 4 drops in the sealed dropper, then make the scribed mark. This is as close as you can get to .3cc. Hold the "measure" under the delivery tube and work the pump twice. Repeat the process with all four tubes, and bring them into alignment by changing the linkage.

Unscrew the lock nuts and screw the center section either clockwise to decrease the amount of delivery or counter clockwise to increase it. Then snug up the nuts.

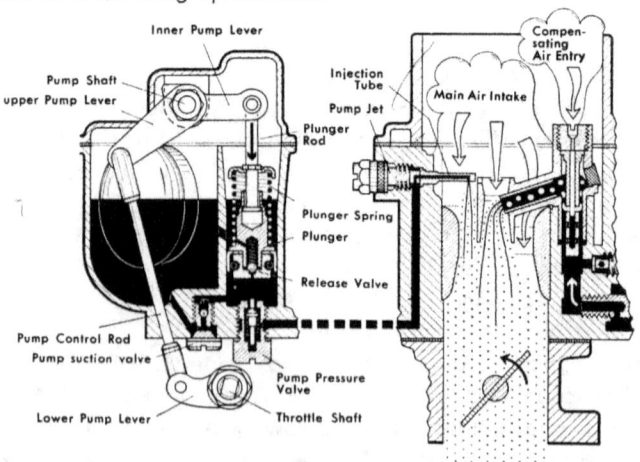

Operation of accelerator pump

Synchronization of these jugs in accomplished in the same way as with the Solexes. Use a Unisyn or Vacuum gage if you have one or want to lay out $9.95 . . . a worthwhile investment in the opinion of most owners. This device (Unisyn) gives a visual indication of the amount of air each carburetor is pulling and enables you to set the throttle (by means of the idling adjusting screw) exactly. If you are without one, listen closely at the air intake (with cleaner removed) the hiss will tell you its story. Go through this routine with the engine warm and idling:

Use of Unisyn in adjusting carburetors.

1. Disconnect throttle linkage (cross link between carburetors).
2. Run up the idling adjusting screws on both carbs equally so that the engine is turning about 1,000 rpm.
3. Screw the volume control screws (idling mixture) on one carburetor in until they seat. Then back them each off an equal amount to where the engine is running smoothly about 1½ turns).
4. Repeat on the other carburetor.

5. Begin adjusting the volume control screws until maximum rpms are attained by playing with each one. Go from one carburetor to the other. Have a friend watch the tach if necessary.
6. Using the Unisyn or ear method back the idling adjusting screws off until the carburetors are balanced and the engine is turning at 600-800 rpm.
7. Go back to the volume control screws and turn them in and out individually until best engine speed is attained once again.
8. Reset idle adjusting screws as necessary to bring idling speed to 600-800 (as you prefer) and carburetors are drawing an equal amount.
9. Run the engine up to 1500 by holding the throttle open and set the unisyn atop the carburetors once more or listen closely to each air intake. If unbalanced at this speed, re-connect linkage use one idling adjusting screw to maintain this speed and go through the routine with the volume control screws once again.

When this has been completed, rev up the engine in the garage or in a short trip of a few blocks to clean it out then check by revving up to 3,000 rpm and suddenly releasing the throttle. If the engine dies or falters the idling mixture is too rich and the screws should be turned in a tiny amount to lean it. More than likely the mixture will be on the lean side of normal under these conditions but plugs are less likely to load up in traffic.

ZENITH CARBURETOR SPECIFICATIONS

Engine	1600 N	1600 S
Carburetor	32NDIX	32NDIX
Venturis	24mm	28mm
Main Jet	115	130
Air Corr.	230	220
Mixture Tube #	1-S	1-S
Idling Jet	50	50
Idling Air	120	140
Pump Jet	50	40
Float Needle Valve	150	150
Float Wt.	5.2g	5.2g

DISASSEMBLY AND CLEANING

To properly care for carburetors it is necessary occasionally to subject them to a thorough cleaning. In the absence of the powerful "gunk" that garages use for this task, ordinary cleaning solvent and a little elbow grease with a brush will suffice. Compressed air for blowing out jets and orfices helps. Never clean a jet or opening by passing a wire through it. This is an invitation to ruin. Here are the steps in sequence for disassembly of the Zenith NDIX 32:

1. Remove carburetor from manifold.
2. Remove spring clip and spring at accelerator pump linkage and disconnect pump.
3. Loosen screws and remove cover, watch for sticking gasket.
4. Remove float toggle lever and take out floats.
5. Take out retaining screw on mixture tube holder.
6. Loosen air correction jets.
7. Pull out mixture tube holder.
8. Screw out air correction jets and remove both mixture tubes.
9. Remove idling air jets.
10. Take out pump jets.
11. Remove injection tubes by prying gently with screwdriver A small block of wood should be used to protect venturi.
12. Release venturi clamping screw and take out venturi.
13. Take off jet chamber cover.
14. Remove main jets and idling jets.
15. Remove idling mixture screws.

In reassembly, the reverse of the above procedure should be followed. Pay particular attention to these things:
1. The float needle valve seat should be concentric and smooth.
2. Sealing surfaces of carburetor should be clean and true.
3. The cover gasket is secured by two rivets. The old rivets can be removed with a knife. New rivets must be used with a new gasket.
4. Be sure the tip of the idling mixture screw is tapered and has not been blunted.
5. Be sure that restriction of the venturi faces upward.
6. Do not over-tighten clamping screw that holds venturi.
7. Check floats for leaks and proper weight (see table).

Carburetor Troubles, Causes and Remedies

1. **ENGINE WILL NOT SPART WITH IGNITION IN ORDER, FUEL IN TANK**

   a) No fuel in system

   a) Check in order:
   Release main jet holder. If fuel comes out, the main jet is obstructed. If no fuel comes out, disconnect line to fuel pump and turn engine with starter. If there is a well-defined spurt with each pump stroke, the float needle valve is clogged. If no fuel is ejected it may be pump valve sticking, worn pump mechanism or dirt in shut-off cock.

   b) Carburetor floods over

   b. Check and clean float needle valve. Check gasket and float.

2. **FLAT SPOT AT IDLING SPEED**

   a) Idling adjustment wrong
   b) Idling jet or airbleed clogged
   c) Intake manifold leaking
   d) Volume control screw damaged

   a) Re-adjust idling speed
   b) Clean idling jet or idling air bleed jet
   c) Check gaskets at flanges. Check balance tube.
   d) Replace volume control screw

3. **POOR ACCELERATION**

   a) Idling mixture too lean
   b) Incorrect pump injection
   c) Intake manifold leaking

   a) Re-adjust iding speed and check jet
   b) Check injection of pump
   c) Check flanges, gaskets and balance tube

4. **ENGINE STALLS WHEN ACCELERATOR IS REALEASED SUDDENLY**

   a) Idling adjustment wrong

   a) Re-adjust idling speed

5. **ENGINE RUNS UNEVENLY, MISFIRES OR CUTS OUT**

   a) Fuel surplus
   b) Fuel starvation
   c) Manifold leak

   a) Check pump pressure, needle valve, float and fuel level in float bowl
   b) Clean main jet, fuel lines Check float level
   c) Check manifold flanges, gaskets and balance tube

6. **EXCESS FUEL CONSUMPTION, POOR MILEAGE**

   a) Float needle valve flooded
   b) Float sunk
   c) Float needle valve does not close

   a) Check pump pressure
   b) Check float for leak
   c) Check needle valve

Ignition

The Porsche ignition is highly conventional and never seems to give any trouble. Owners have reported picking up performance by fitting a magneto but this is a pretty expensive way to gain a few RPMS. The stock coil-distributor set up is adequate for the capacity of the pushrod engine.

The elements of the system are; battery, coil, distributor, breaker points condenser and sparkplugs. The battery provides the electrical energy (The generator merely replaces the charge in the battery) which flows into the coil when the points are closed. When the points open a magnetic field which has been set up in the coil breaks down and induces a momentary overload in the secondary coil winding. This flood of electricity rushes to a sparkplug via the distributor rotor and the ignition wiring, where it arcs across the space between the center electrode and the grounded electrode thus igniting the charge of fuel in the cylinder. The function of the condenser is to take up the flow of electricity from the battery for the brief time the points are open to prevent arcing.

What can go wrong? The connections, first of all. Be sure that all electrical connections are clean and tight, beginning right at the battery cables. Loose wires or wires hanging by one or two strands are an invitation to poor performance or failure.

Old wiring is another common cause of poor starting or running. Wire corrodes, insulation breaks down, dampness penetrates and causes the juice to "leak" out before it ever gets to the plugs.

The coil seldom causes any trouble but it can be suspected if the car refuses to start and there is no fire at the points. After the ignition has been "on" for some time the coil should feel warm to the touch. If it stays cold, try replacing it.

Oftener, the condenser can be faulty. If this happens, the coil is not allowed to build up a charge because it is drained right out to ground. Sign of a condenser going bad can often be detected if points pit quite rapidly. If you have fire at the points but none at the plugs and the wiring is not suspect, replace the condenser.

Points seldom disintegrate so rapidly that they are completely useless should the car be suffering from ignition troubles. Generally if a car is hard to start the gap has closed up or the points are making very bad contact and a few minutes spent with a point file and screwdriver will get you underway. Points should be set to break when the OT mark on the crank pulley is 19/64" to the left of the split in the crankcase (Normal) or 13/32" (Super). A better way of putting it: Make a timing mark 19/64" or 13/32" to the right of the OT mark, when it lines up with the split, the points should be opening.

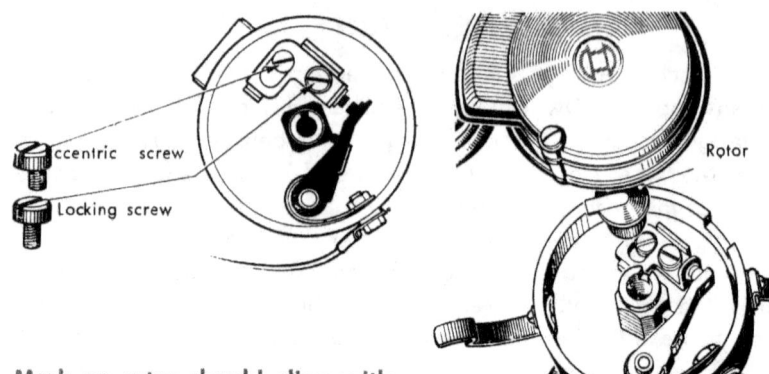

Mark on rotor should align with mark on distributor housing when points open.

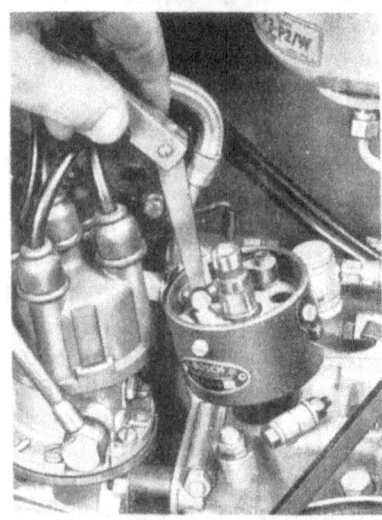

.016 feeler gage is slip fit between points.
Point file is used to remove roughness from contact area.

Always use the recommended plugs. Under normal driving they are of the correct heat range. It is possible that constant use in heavy traffic could call for a hotter plug to avoid fouling or long trips at high speed could require a colder type. To check, run the engine up to "clean it out" and remove the plugs, one at a time for a visual inspection. A tan colored center insulator is normal, dark brown or black, too cold, white or blistered, too hot. If the rim and electrodes have a lot of soft "soot" or a "wet" appearance this points at too rich a fuel mixture; fried or overheated electrodes, too lean. Oil, of course or heavy carbon deposits reveal the presence of lubricant in the firing chamber from some source.

Under severe operating conditions, or after compression has been raised, it is necessary to use a plug that is colder than normal. An alternative is to fit a platinum tip plug with a wide heat range.

Normal pushrod engine plugs are 14mm, ½" reach Bosch W225 T1 for the Normal types, W240 T1 for the Supers, gapped at .025 to .027. Equivalent Champions are: L-10S and LA-10 respectively, KLG; F 70 and F 80 while the Lodge HNP platinum point serves both heat ranges. Equivalent to the colder Bosch W260 T1 sometimes required by the Super are Champion LA11, KLG F100 and Lodge 3HN.

The Lodge chart is sometimes confusing to the uninitiated because they have very logically designated the plugs with letters that do not have anything to do with the application. H, for example denotes a cold plug, B is a hot plug and C a normal range. N, which might be expected to refer to Normal means non-detachable! On the other hand P does refer to Platinum and R to Racing.

If you haven't already discovered it, the plug wrench that the VW factory gives away with its cars is a lot better than the plug wrench Porsche gives away. Get one of these if you can and make changing #1 and #3 a lot easier. There is always an admonition to seat the plugs against the gasket with a specified amount of torque. Keen, if you can get the wrench in the proper perspective. If you haven't had any experience in changing plugs, there is only one answer: learn the feel of a gasket being crushed. Get a handful of these compression rings from a service station and practice putting a plug in. Run the plug up tight then learn to sense that ½ turn that properly crushes the compression ring and puts the plug in just tight enough. An uncrushed gasket results in poor heat dissipation and causes plug overheating, detonation and poor performance.

Losing the gasket before you get the plug into the hole is a hazard. A dab of heavy grease helps. Lodge gaskets are particularly easy to drop, get some Bosch gaskets and use them with the British plugs (only one to a plug, however).

Engine: Remove and Refit

The pushrod engine can be removed and replaced by one person but it is a big help, particularly to the amateur enthusiast, to have an assistant. The tools necessary, in addition to socket wrenches, end wrenches, etc., are floor stands (or substantial wooden blocks) and a floor jack. This sequence of operations is recommended:

1. Disconnect ground cable from battery.
2. Close fuel valve (ZU).
3. Open rear deck.
4. Remove rear cover of engine.
5. Disconnect cable at generator, ignition coil and oil-pressure switch.
6. Remove accelerator linkage and cable.
7. Jack up car to height of approximately 24". Generally a 4" block of wood atop the floor jack will be of help. Put the car on stands or blocks, remove jack.
8. Remove heater cables and linkage as well as heating ducts at engine.
9. Slip off fuel hose.
10. Remove tach drive cable.
11. Remove two nuts on bottom engine-fastening bolts.
12. Pull choke cable out of sleeve.
13. Place jack under engine, raising the jack until a slight pressure is exerted.
14. Hold upper bolts firmly and have a second man remove the nuts.
15. Raise jack slightly, rock engine to break adhesion, lower and withdraw rearward to clear car.

REFITTING

Refitting the engine is accomplished by generally reversing the above process but special attention should be paid to these details:
1. Leave rear cover of engine off until replaced in car.
2. Test driving shaft of transmission for excessive play.
3. Check clutch bearing.
4. Fill nipple on hollow bolt of flywheel with graphite grease.
5. Check gears and journal of transmission shaft, bushing for starter shaft, starter pinion gear and flywheel gears for worn or broken teeth, grease with graphite grease.
6. Clean transmission housing and engine housing flanges.
7. Positioning of engine and sliding onto drive shaft should be done with care to avoid damage, particularly to hollow bolt of flywheel. Guard against bending the drive shaft by improper alignment. Line up by rotating crank and rocking in lateral plane.
8. Insert bottom studs into transmission flange first then hold engine firmly against flange to assure all-around fit. Take up top nuts first. Apply uniform pressure to all nuts.

In replacing accelerator, choke and heater cables, examine them for worn or frayed portions.

Arrows indicate location of bolt holes and studs that secure engine to transmission-differential

ENGINE DISASSEMBLY — REASSEMBLY

When it is desired to disassemble the engine for any purpose the recommended sequence is as follows:
1. Drain oil.
2. Remove front and side engine covers.
3. Remove muffler and exhaust pipe.
4. Disconnect coil wire to distributor and remove distributor cap.
5. Remove fuel lines and carburetor linkage.
6. Take off air cleaners.
7. Remove carburetors.
8. Remove heater box.
9. Take off covers.
10. Take off V belt.
11. Remove fan and generator.
12. Remove rocker covers.
13. Remove rocker arm shafts.
14. Take out pushrods.
15. Remove cylinder heads.
16. Remove pushrod tubes.
17. Take off fuel pump and distributor.
18. Take down cylinders and pistons.
19. Unbolt oil cooler.
20. Take off clutch.
21. Remove pulley.
22. Unbolt flywheel.
23. Remove oil pump.
24. Take out oil filter.
25. Disassemble crankcase.
26. Remove driveshaft of distributor.
27. Lift out crankshaft and camshaft.
28. Detach oil-pressure control valve and pilot switch.

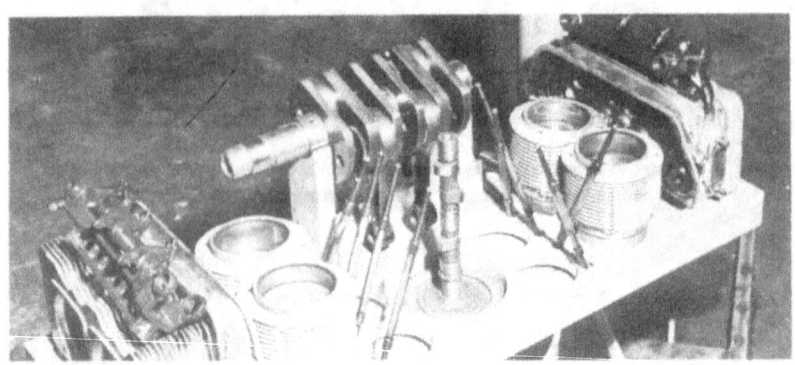

Carefully mark cylinders, pistons, valves, bearing halves, etc. so that they may be reassembled correctly. The usual shop practice of having a valve rack can be extended by laying out a "bread board" or work bench top with markings to receive individual parts.

Tools listed by the factory as essential to complete dismantling are: P4, P1, P2 (VW207), VW203b, VW215a, VW201, VW112, P18, P5, P3, P19, VW122b, VW126a. However the home mechanic will find that a complete set of metric sockets, box-end wrenches and screwdrivers will accomplish most of the dismantling. Cylinder holding strap P18 facilitates step 16. VW201 is a puller for the oil pump housing which can be made in the home workshop if desired (see illustration). P2 is a drift pin or punch for removing piston pins, VW203b is a puller for the crankshaft pulley, both can be substituted for by more common American tools.

Extracting oil pump from housing using puller

REASSEMBLY

The re-assembly of the engine is not an exact reversal of the disassembly process. Following the outlined procedure will facilitate this project:
1. Install oil pressure relief valve in crankcase.
2. Attach oil drain plug.
3. Insert locater pins for main bearings.
4. Install bearing halves in crankcase.
5. Install crankshaft & rods.
6. Install cam.
7. Insert retaining ring at pulley end and oil seal at clutch end.
8. Fasten cover for camshaft.
9. Assemble crankcase.
10. Mount flywheel.

Barrel is "offered" to case in reassembly.

11. Attach clutch.
12. Attach oil strainer.
13. Mount oil pump.
14. Fasten cover for pulley.
15. Mount pulley.
16. Attach oil cooler.
17. Attach oil pressure sending switch.
18. Install drive shaft for distributor & retaining ring.
19. Install distributor (be sure spring is in place).
20. Mount cylinders & pistons (don't forget gaskets between cylinders and crankcase).
21. Attach cylinder holding strap P18.
22. Atach deflector plate with tension strap.
23. Install pushrod tubes & gasket.
24. Remove holding strap P18.
25. Mount cylinder heads.
26. Insert pushrods, mount rocker shafts.
27. Adjust valve clearance.

28. Replace rocker covers.
29. Replace sparkplugs.
30. Attach intake manifolds.
31. Mount cylinder jacket on cylinder #3.
32. Mount fan housing & generator.
33. Attach remaining cylinder covers.
34. Mount heating boxes.
35. Attach cover for fuel pump and ducts to heater.
36. Mount fuel pump with its pushrod & connecting flange.
37. Mount side covers.
38. Strap down generator.
39. Install V belt.
40. Attach exhaust pipes.
41. Attach balance tube to intake manifolds.
42. Mount carburetor, connect linkage & fuel lines.
43. Replace carburetor air cleaners.
44. Replace ignition wires and coil lead.
45. Replace muffler.

1. rear engine duct plate
2. front engine duct plate
3. upper air channel assy
4. cylinder jacket
5. side duct plate, vertical
6. side duct plate, horizontal
7. lower air channel
8. exhaust pipe with junction box

If less than complete disassembly is required this procedure need not be followed meticulously. However, it is always well to drain the engine before removing it from the car and the order of detaching and replacing the cooling shrouds is important:
1. Unscrew rear cover of engine (before removing from car).
2. Remove front cover.

3. Remove side covers.
4. Remove muffler.
5. Remove bottom sections of air ducts.
6. Take off cylinder coverings.
7. Remove upper air channel assembly (fan housing).
8. After removal of cylinder heads, take off the deflector plates.
9. Remove pulley and cover.

In reassembling the cooling shrouds, reverse the process making sure that all connections are tight and that gaskets on rear cover plate are good. Spark plug cap gaskets, too, should be air tight and must be replaced if worn.

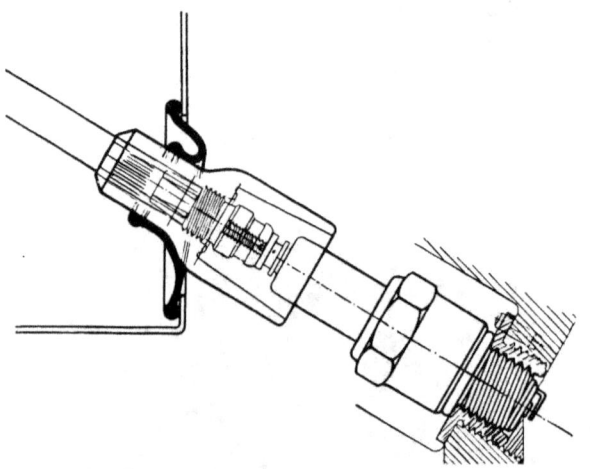

Spark plug grommets are important sealing units

Removal of upper air channel assembly as unit

BLOWER HOUSING

The upper air channel assembly, as the factory refers to the fan housing, fan and generator, is frequently removed to provide access to fan, oil cooler, etc. Here are the proper steps in that operation (engine out of car):

1. Take off V belt by removing generator outer pulley half. Hold the pulley by inserting a long screwdriver into the rim slot and bracing it against the generator, turn the nut with a 1⅜" box wrench or socket.
2. Remove spark plug wires.
3. Remove distributor cap.
4. Disconnect coil wire.
5. Remove screws on side of fan housing at cylinder shrouds.
6. Unfasten generator strap.
7. Unscrew oil filter connections.
8. Remove fuel line from pump to T.
9. Remove manifold balance tube.
10. Take off carburetor linkage.
11. Super engines with 40 P carburetors require removal of carburetors before housing can be lifted clear.

To refit the housing, reverse the procedure. Pay attention to these details: The housing must fit snugly to the cylinder head, bend the metal if necessary to insure snugness. Check the gasket in the generator support bracket and replace if necessary.

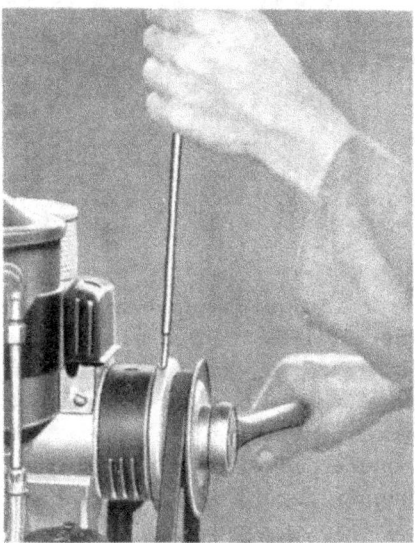

Screwdriver in notch is proper

Oil Circulation and Cooling

In any engine the circulating oil plays two roles: Lubrication and heat dissipation. We seldom think of the second function in connection with conventional water cooled powerplants. But, when we recall that all high-performance and racing engines have separate oil coolers as well as a large capacity sump or tank, we appreciate the part played by the oil radiator on the Porsche. This out-of-sight but not-out-of-mind gadget is an integral part of the engine's design and contributes much to its efficiency and long life.

OIL CIRCULATION IN WARM ENGINE WITH THERMOSTAT

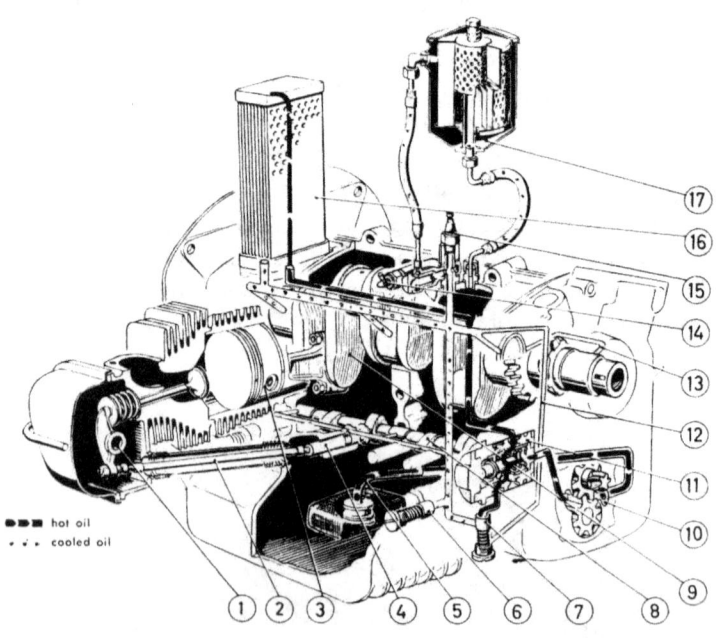

The oil reservoir of 2.5 litres (approximately 5 pints) is the crankcase. From this point the fluid is lifted by a pump, forced through the cooler and distributed to various parts of the engine (as described in the general discussion of the engine). Along the way on its round trip to the crankcase again, the lubricant encounters various mechanical and non-mechanical objects that need inspection and eventual replacement or repairs. Let us begin with the:

OIL STRAINER

At the lowest point in the crankcase lies the screened magnetic strainer. The pickup tube enters the top of the screen and extends into the magnet. All oil must pass through the screen and over the magnet before being drawn into the pump and circulated through the system. It is important, naturally, to keep this unit clean and free-flowing.

With the car on a hoist and oil drained, unscrew the hex nuts that secure the strainer cover (it is adjacent to the drain plug) remove it, the gasket, filter and filter gasket. Wash the screen and the magnetic unit in cleaning fluid, dry with compressed air.

This cover can be a source of oil leaks if the gaskets are bad or the strainer cover itself is bent so that it does not fit flush against the crankcase. Renew gaskets as necessary, be sure the surface of the case is clean and the cover not warped. The strainer should fit snugly around the pickup tube and the tube should not bottom. Be sure tube has not been bent at some previous time.

Do not tighten nuts too severely; Remember the case is aluminum and the cover is thin. Snug it up, fill with oil, run the engine until thoroughly warm and check for leaks.

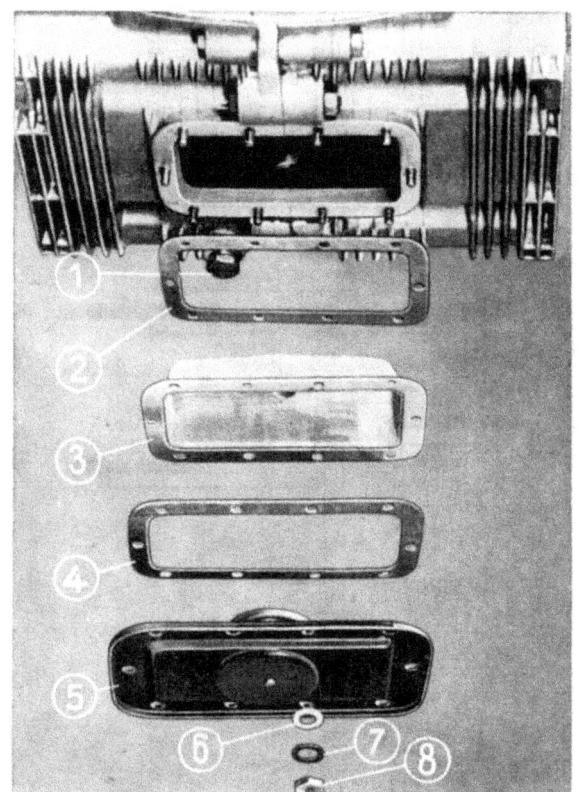

① Oil drain plug
② Gasket
③ Oil filter
④ Gasket
⑤ Cover with magnetic oil filter
⑥ Washer
⑦ Lock washer
⑧ Nut

PRESSURE RELIEF VALVE

This piece of equipment regulates the flow of oil through the cooler. In effect, when oil pressure is high because of low temperature the valve is forced open and permits a flow directly to points of lubrication as well as the cooler. In case of extreme pressure it allows a direct return to the sump. When the oil warms up and 'thins out' pressure is reduced so that the oil is directed entirely through the cooler. The accompanying schematic drawing illustrates this operation.

The valve is reached by unscrewing the plug that lies to the left of the oil pump housing (on the pulley end of the engine). Problems arise when the spring becomes weak, the piston jams in the bore because of contaminated or varnished oil or extreme overheating.

Normal oil pressure, or rather normal operating pressure for this spring-loaded piston, is around 45psi. Anything above this should force the piston down and by-pass the cooler. The Porsche, having no pressure gage, is usually somewhat of a mystery in this regard. However, the correct spring lengths and tensions are these:

Without tension—2 3/64" to 2 3/32".
Installed (bypass closed) 1½" 4 lbs. 3oz. tension.
Compressed (bypass open) 13/16" 61 lbs. 13oz. tension.

Later 1600 engines with the oil temperature thermostat still depend on on the relief valve. The thermostat opens at approximately 176° F but prior to that time the valve is in operation. In the warm engine a counter pressure line helps balance the piston.

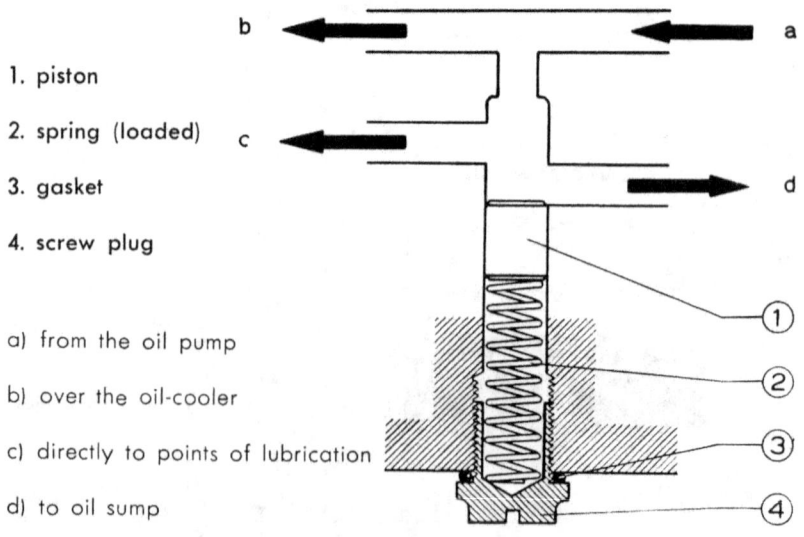

1. piston
2. spring (loaded)
3. gasket
4. screw plug

a) from the oil pump
b) over the oil-cooler
c) directly to points of lubrication
d) to oil sump

OIL PRESSURE WARNING LIGHT SWITCH

For a long time the sensing and sending unit was the bane of some Porsche owners existence. Leaking, faulty operation, failure to operate and so on. I personally had a series of four of these little devils that lasted from one day to two weeks. A bad batch, no doubt, but a discouraging situation. The unit is located to the left of the distributor and screws into the oil line leading to the oil filter.

When pressure is below something like 6 lbs. psi the diaphragm in the sender is relaxed and electrical contact is made causing the green light on the instrument panel to glow. It will glow when the sender goes haywire too, and if this happens when you are cruising somewhere between Helena Montana and East Clambake North Dakota it also results in a prickling sensation in the scalp.

There is no cure for a defective part, Throw it away. A spare is always nice to have in the tool kit and, it is good to know that Nash Dealers stock an almost identical sender that is an exact replacement. Cheaper, too, if memory serves me.

Assuming normal operation, the green light should glow when the ignition is on before the engine is started and at a slow idle. If it comes on at speed, stop as soon as practical and check the engine for oil leaks. If oil temp stays down, the dipstick level does not drop an there is no visible evidence of a gusher, accuse the sender.

OIL PUMP

The pump is driven off the pulley end of the camshaft. It is remarkably trouble free and long lived. In older cars which have been patched several times, the pump may never have been inspected or replaced and the gears bearings or housing could be

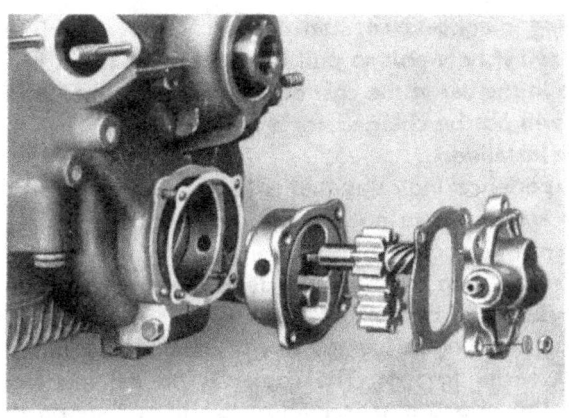

Oil pump components. Gear lash is critical

worn. The sympton is consistent low pressure and high oil temperature under fairly normal operating conditions.

This is the inspection method:
1. Take off rear engine cover plate and cover between lower sections of air ducts.
2. Remove V belt pulley and V belt.
3. Remove cover plate under pulley.
4. Take off tach drive cover.
5. Pull out oil pump gears.
6. Take out housing using tool VW201 (or a suitable puller).

There should be minimal clearance between housing and gear bearings, any looseness here means loss of pressure. Worn gears are indicated by excessive backlash.

Specifications: Gear backlash of .001" to .003" permissible end play (without pressing) .0025" to .007".

When re-installing use only new .003" gaskets and no gasket compound. Be sure both crankcase and cover surfaces are clean and parallel.

OIL COOLER

Located atop the engine under the fan housing where it will receive the benefits of the coolest air blast, the oil cooler stands in finny glory. This erection can be a most expensive adjunct if you fall into the hands of a dissoulute, dishonest or otherwise unscrupulous mechanic. Why? Well, not all oil cooler leaks **are** oil cooler leaks, if you understand. Anytime one of this breed (and not all VW/Porsche specialists are as pure as the driver) sees oil dribbling from under the fan housing the diagnosis is "blown up oil cooler" and the "remove-refit" charges begin. (The shop practice is to remove the engine to gain access to this part . . . and lets face it this is the quickest simplest method.)

The home diagnostician, can inspect remove and replace the cooler himself if he wants to pull the engine, or it can be done with the engine in the car at the cost of a little more time. What he gains is that he will not be charged for a new cooler when it has actually never been installed.

Wide experience indicates that a high percentage of "defective" oil coolers are defective only in the rubber grommets or seals that lie between the cooler and the engine.

A leak in this area can be suspected when the oil appears below the fan housing and cannot be accounted for from any other source. If you keep the engine compartment clean at all times, this sort of thing is easier to spot. The cooler is on the left side, straight back from the pressure senser and oil will appear on this side of the shrouds first.

Before tearing down (if you have decided to go into it) warm up the engine thoroughly until you are sure oil is passing through the cooler and leaking, shut the engine off and wait for it to cool a bit. Then remove the powerplant as described under the heading **Engine, Remove and Refit.**

With the engine steady and level (on blocks):
1. Take off fan belt.
2. Remove sparkplug wires and distributor cap.
3. Disconnect coil wire.
4. Remove screws on side and cylinder covers of fan housing (upper air channel).
5. Remove generator strap.
6. Detach oil filter hoses.
7. Remove fuel line between pump and carburetors.
8. Take off carburetor balance tube.
9. Dissassemble linkage between carburetors.
10. Super engines with 40PBIC carburetors require removal of these units.

Now you can lift off the fan housing with fan and generator etc. attached, to expose the cooler.

Inspect the cooler closely to determine if it is leaking from the tubes or if the oil is issuing from the base. It is necessary to use an offset 10mm wrench to get under the cooler and the two bolts on the left side. This is listed as VW 109 but a 7/16" "bent" box wrench procurable at any parts house is a good substitute.

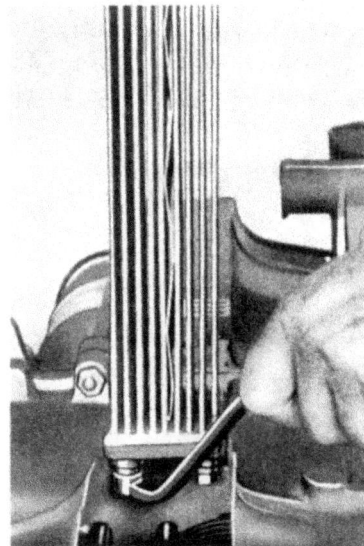 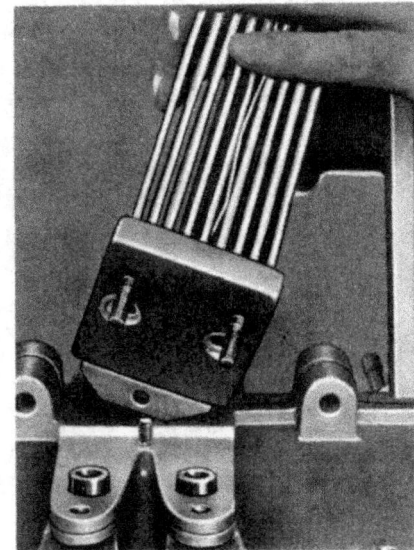

"Bent", offset box wrench is necessary tool here

With the cooler removed you can determine if the seals are "gone" and leaking. Should they be perfect and dry, give up and go get a new cooler. If deteriorated, check the cooler anyway by draining it, washing in solvent, blowing air through it and then dunking it in hot water with both inlet and outlet holes plugged. This is a crude test but small air bubbles will often reveal a leak. A well-equipped VW/Porsche agency may have a tester that will apply the factory specified 85 lbs. of pressure. Mostly a suspected cooler is thrown into the trash can or traded to a rebuilder without resorting to such a test.

As mentioned previously, the upper air channel assembly can be removed with the engine in the car if you take off the engine compartment hood and the carburetors in addition to the steps 1 through 9 listed above. Throttle linkage and choke wire which lead forward must also be disconnected and don't forget to shut off the fuel at the tank.

Incidentally, Porsche and VW oil coolers are not identical. The Porsche cooler is a copper brazed type whereas the VW part is tin soldered. There is also a difference in the size of the orifices in the base. Be sure to give your engine number, as well as year and type if you have occasion to order this part from a dealer and are installing it yourself. There are subtle differences in certain cars.

Cylinder Head and Valves

The enthusiast may be interested in performing a major tuneup which includes "de-coking" or removing carbon and grinding the valves. Porsche tool P7 for compressing valve springs is handy but not mandatory. If you have never removed valve springs from any car and you can take the heads to a friendly mechanic, do so the first time.

Removal and refit of cylinder head technique

With the engine out of the car, remove the cylinder heads:
1. Take off side cover plates.
2. Remove intake manifold.
3. Remove rocker cover.
4. Take out hex screws on rocker arm shaft.
5. Detach shaft & rocker arms.
6. Take out cylinder head nuts (Allen type).
7. Pull cylinder head off, tapping all around with wooden mallet—gently—to loosen it.
8. Repeat process on opposite head.

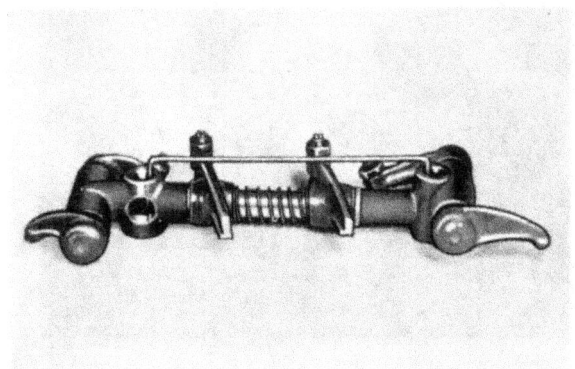

Assembled rocker shaft showing holding clamp

We will outline here the refitting and discuss valve grinding in a following paragraph.

Reverse the above steps but with emphasis on the following points:
1. Note that there is no gasket between barrel and head.
2. Use new gaskets at top and bottom of pushrod tubes.
3. Oil the gaskets (round profile type) between head and head nuts before installing.

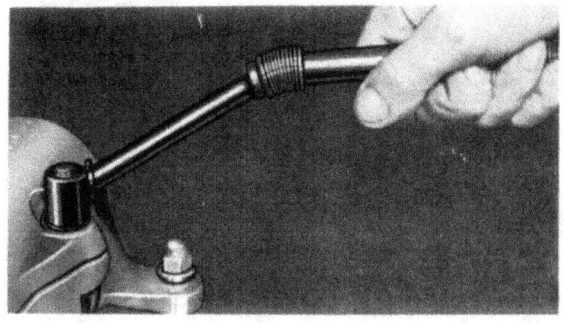

Stretching "bellows" on pushrod tube is wise

4. Use graphite on threads of head studs.
5. Expand the "accordion" on pushrod tubes with box wrench or suitable bar (a socket drive extension works well) See Illustration.
6. Tighten head studs in sequence shown on chart lightly (7 lb./ft.) then torque to 22 lb./ft. in sequence.
7. Tighten rocker shaft bolts to 36 lb./ft.
8. Final step before replacing rocker cover is adjusting valves.

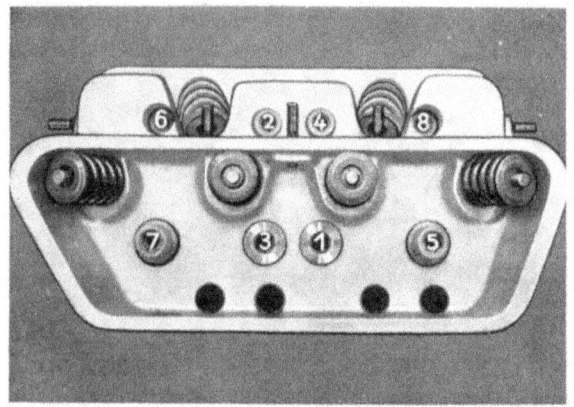

Tightening sequence of cylinder head nuts

REMOVAL AND GRINDING OF VALVES

1. With combustion chamber side of head on flat, clean firm surface, apply pressure to spring seat. Push it far enough down on stem to allow removal of keeper.
2. Take out valve, mark it according to intake or exhaust and

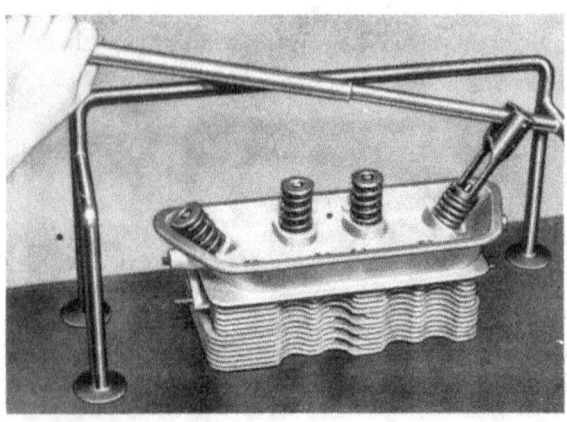

Special valve spring compressor, Porsche P-7

cylinder.
3. Repeat on all valves.
4. Inspect for excess carbon, stem wear, burned faces, pitted or burned seats, bent stems, worn guides, bad springs, keepers etc.

Badly worn or burned insert seats too severely damaged for lapping-in, can be re-surfaced by hand milling but this is best left to an expert. If damage is too extensive the head must be replaced since the seats are not replacable. Proper angles for beveling are given in the workshop manual.

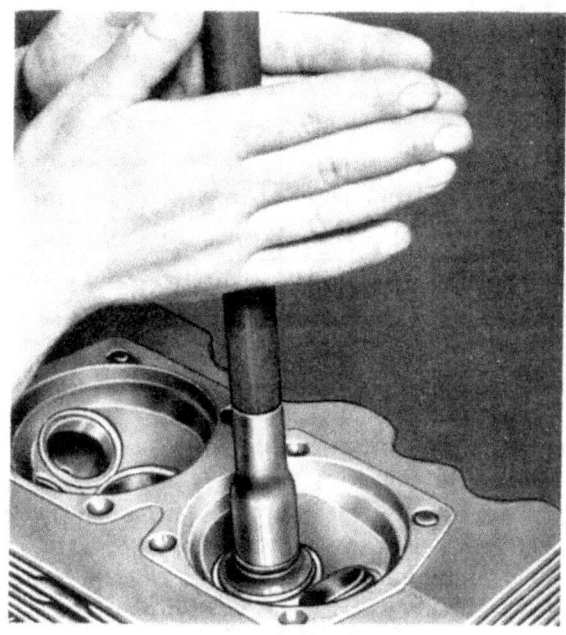

Valves can be refaced in seats using hand tool

Hand lapping is a matter of exercising care that just enough is done to assure a good seat. Apply a small amount of paste, drop the valve in the seat, and work the plunger. Examine it at frequent intervals and avoid forming rings or grooves. Thoroughly remove paste when finished. Drop the valves into their seats, fill the combustion chamber with water and note any leakage. The valves should seat under their own weight sufficiently to contain the fluid. A further check, with valves under spring tension, is to fill the intake and exhaust passages with gasoline.

Hand grinding, or compound-lapping, using the suction-cup plunger and a good paste is satisfactory for most jobs. If the valve is bad but not far enough out to require replacement, take it to a machine and use the following table for dimensions.

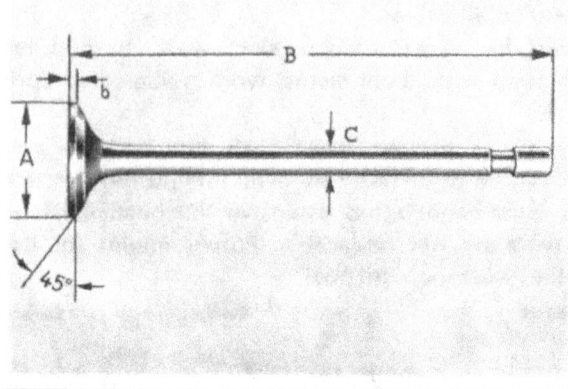

	5/16″ stem (8 mm ⌀)		25/64″ stem (10 mm ⌀)	
	intake	exhaust	intake	exhaust
A	1.49606 - 1.5000″	1.21653 - 1.22441″	1.49212 - 1.500″	1.2165 - 1.2244″
B	4.7007 - 4.70865″	5.1377 - 5.14565″	4.7007 - 4.70865″	5.1377 - 5.1456″
C	0.31318 - 0.31362″	0.31279 - 0.31318″	0.3929 - 0.3933″	0.39212 - 0.39251″
b	0.06692 - 0.09055″	0.070866 - 0.09448″	0.06692 - 0.09055″	0.07874 - 0.09055″

VALVE STEM CLEARANCE

The proper clearance is indicated on the fan housing or distributor cap of each engine. Inasmuch as there is a difference between the clearance requirements of steel and alloy pushrods, always follow this factory reference. In reworked engines alloy rods may have been substituted, if so follow the chart for clearances appropriate to that type.

VALVE CLEARANCES

STEEL PUSHRODS:	1100	1300	1500 N	1500 S
Intake	.008	.004	.004	.006
	.2mm	.1mm	.1mm	.15mm
Exhaust	.006	.004	.004	.004
	.15mm	.1mm	.1mm	.1mm
ALLOY PUSHRODS	1300 N	1300 S	1500 N	1500 S
Intake	.008	.008	.008	.008
	.2mm	.2mm	.2mm	.2mm
Exhaust	.006	.006	.006	.006
	.15mm	.15mm	.15mm	.15mm

Newer 1600 and 1600 S-90 engines have different clearances. But again, these will be indicated on the individual engine.

SETTING VALVES

Align OT and case split for TDC

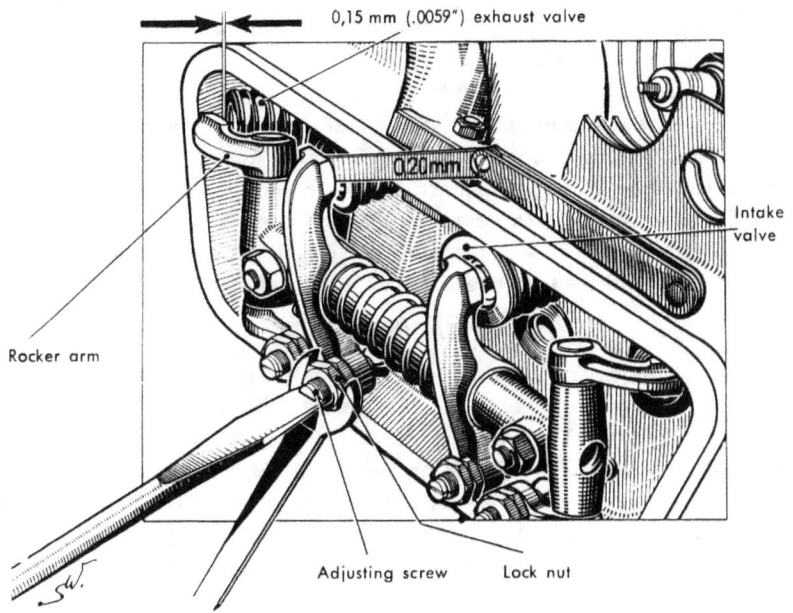

Adjustment is always made on a cold engine. Let it cool overnight if possible.

With the piston at top dead center on the compression stroke both valves for that cylinder will be closed and adjustment of stem clearance can be made. Turn the V belt pulley so that the timing mark is in line with the crankcase split and the distributor arm indicates that #1 cylinder is firing. Loosen the safety nut on the pushrod end of the exhaust valve rocker arm. Screw the slotted adjusting screw until a .20mm or .006" feeler gage blade is a tight sliding fit between the valve stem tip and the pushrod. Tighten nut carefully. Repeat with #1 intake valve. Turn the crank to the left until #2 cylinder is in firing position and repeat. Do the same for #3 and #4 in order.

Having run through this routine once, check all valves once more and adjust as necessary.

To accomplish valve adjustment with the engine in the car, it is necessary to remove the rear wheels and jack up the automobile to allow elbow room . . . or have it on the proper type of hoist. To save a lot of jacking around, run through the valve adjusting sequence twice on one side before moving to the other. This will assure that no errors have been made (usually) and cut the time down considerably.

VALVE SPRINGS

It is difficult for the amateur to check spring tension and length without proper tools, but if he has a reasonably well equipped shop, these figures are of some use. Particularly when it comes to making modifications.

Until recently Porsche utilized dual springs with the outer one 44.3mm not compressed and the inner 42.8mm. These compressed at 83 and 34 lbs. respectively and 31.7mm and 30.2mm in length. A new single spring, claimed to be an improvement (49mm uncompressed and 39mm compressed at 77 lbs.) is being fitted to all cars and offered as a replacement. This is a progressively wound spring and places less pressure on the seat face.

REPLACING HEADS

Should it become necessary to replace cylinder heads, be certain that the replacement unit has the same cubic capacity as the one being traded in. The volume in ccs is stamped between the combustion chambers. In doing any reworking such as "hop up" operations where the head may be altered, a uniform final combustion chamber is of the utmost importance. The factory gives 1cc as the tolerance but it is possible to come closer than this by exercising ordinary care.

Cams and Followers

Two series of camshafts have been fitted. Prior to the introduction of the 1600, this valve timing was used:

Normal: Intake opens 2° 30' BTDC, closes 37° 30' ABDC
           Exhaust opens 37° 30' BBDC, closes 2° 30' ATDC
Super: Intake opens 19° BTDC, Closes 54° ABDC
           Exhaust opens 54° BBDC, Closes 19° ATDC

Numeral 270 stamped on gear denotes Super

Late 1300's and 1600's have this timing:
   Normal: Intake opens 5° BTDC, closes 43° ABDC
                Exhaust opens 43°BBDC, closes 5° ATDC
   Super: Intake opens 15° BTDC, closes 50° ABDC
                Exhaust opens 50°BBDC, closes 15° ATDC

Four camshaft lobes serve all eight valves

Actually there have been narrow lobe and broad lobe cams, as well as large and small Super cams, plus the fact that individual cams vary appreciably when checked out with a dial indicator.

In this department two failures can occur that are cause for concern: Cam gear and followers (tappets). Early models are equipped with a pressed fabric or composition gear, later versions use an aluminum type. Both are of VW origin with the exception that the later Porsche bolts its gear to the cam whereas VW uses rivets. A VW gear can be altered to suit the Porsche in a pinch.

A worn gear or broken teeth signal their appearance by a growling or thumping sound at half engine speed intervals. To replace the defective part is a remove-refit and pretty good tear-down job. In addition the new gear must be heated before being joined to the shaft. There are tolerances between the gear pairs (crankshaft and camshaft) regulated by the sizes of the gears themselves. The grades are marked on each cam gear (facing the cam) 0,+1,+2,−1 and −2 and the new gear must be of the same grade as the old one. "0" is standard, the others represent .01mm over or undersize radius in gradients.

With the engine out of the car, the three-piece case proves to be a relatively simple customer because the timing cover can be removed which shortens the task. Follow the disassembly outlined in this book if you intend to do the job yourself, pull the cam gear with a gear puller and replace it with the pre-heated one. (180° in oil for an hour, is the recommendation, 350° in an oven for 30 minutes works too.) Put everything back in order, being sure to clean out any debris that may have been deposited in the oil from chewed teeth.

0 on cam gear mates with punch marks on crank shaft gear for proper valve timing

FOLLOWERS

Tappets, placed between cam and pushrods, do not cause the trouble often associated with their equivalents in domestic engines unless a reground or billet **hard-faced** cam has been substituted for the stock item. Pre 1955 Porsches are especially vulnerable, however, since a softer material was then used. For this reason, in the section on increasing performance, we do not advise changing to anything but a Porsche or reground Porsche cam. Should your car be of the earlier type, the new replacement units you will get from your dealer will have a different appearance signifying an improved alloy or process for hardening.

Running low on oil and at excessive temperature is probably the most destructive usage that this part can be subjected to. Symtoms of wear are an inordinate amount of "valve" noise. Acceptable clearance between tappet and its guide should be .0004" to .0008" . . . this is a loose drop fit when oiled. (In other words the tappet should slide by gravity but not rock excessively.)

Crankshafts, Pulleys and Crankcases

The multiple heading over this section reflects the changes that are instituted from time to time by the factory which modify the basic engine yet keep its proven design intact.

When the company decided to go racing back in 1953, they called on the Hirth works to provide a roller bearing crankshaft suitable for high rpms and sustained high speed. Porsche's association with Hirth goes back even farther, of course to the GP Cisitalia and other designs, and, until 1957 when the units were dropped in favor of plain metal bearing cranks, all Supers were fitted with these shafts. 1600 S engine 81200 was the last assembled with the Hirth

For several years, then, the hazard of a broken roller bearing crank was something to be feared . . . and still is, except for the fact that the replacement is now made with a plain shaft, unless,

Hirth roller bearing crank as fitted to Supers

Plain metal bearing crank is now used in all

of course you happen on some dealer who has been hoarding one of the built-up jobs, and that is unlikely. The factory has issued a bulletin to the effect that they are no longer rebuilding shafts and Hirth does not provide this service either.

This is really no great tragedy inasmuch as one of the most successful Supers on the West Coast raced most of its career with a Normal crank substituted for the Hirth which gave up the ghost in one of its first outings.

Should your Super have committed internal hari-kiri, you can make the replacement with a plain crank, rods and mains. This will call for a balancing job, too, since the original flywheel and Hirth crank were balanced as a unit.

Also, beginning with engine #41001 to the end of the 1500 series and engines (1600) 80001 to 81101, it is necessary to replace the camshaft with the new smaller Super type cam to avoid interference with connecting rods. The Hirth rods, of course, were solid and the big ends were actually of a smaller overall diameter.

Pulley sometimes requires puller for removal

The pulley, although retaining the same character over the years, seems to cause a great deal of grief when the amateur mechanic removes and refits it. This is generally because the pulley nut, which makes up into tapered threads, has been leaned on at some time in the past with an eight foot extension or some such. Such application of muscle is not necessary but it often occurs. The nut loosens counter clockwise, of course. The real rotation preventer, naturally, is the woodruff key, not the nut. A puller (P43 or VW 203b) is also specified by the workshop manual but at least a couple of these jobs were handled at home without this tool by gently (?) prying and tapping with the plastic-headed hammer. You may be equally lucky.

① belt pulley

② oil return thread

③ Woodruff key

④ pulley locking bolt

⑤ washer

⑥ crankshaft oil deflector

⑦ pulley cover plate

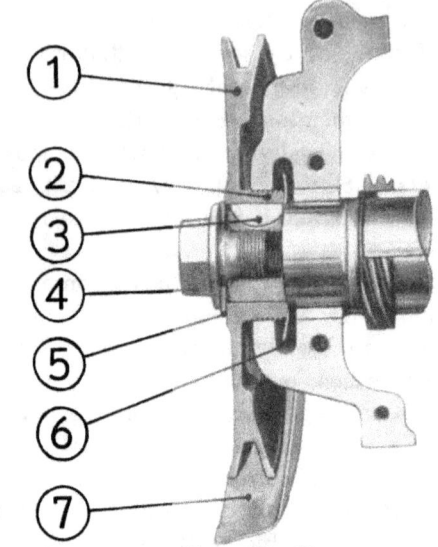

Cutaway of crank pulley shows (1) pulley, (2) oil return threads, (3) woodruff key, (4) locking bolt, (5) washer, (6) crankshaft oil deflector, (7) cover

If the pulley is a source of oil leaks, it should be replaced with a new part with larger oil slinger threads (see diagram). At least clean the threads before replacing. Check that someone hasn't left out the oil-deflector on the crankshaft if excess oil at this end of the engine has been a problem. The concave side of the washer faces the pulley.

Under instruction #25 in engine dis-assembly steps you will find "disassemble crankcase" and under #9 in reassembly, the simple notation "re-assemble crankcase". Under these heading might be included the following points to be observed.

The right side comes off first. Or comes off, if you prefer. Not easily, usually. It takes some tapping and cajoling to make the separation. Don't pry the sections apart with a screwdriver blade or other sharp instrument. Repeated blows with a rubber mallet are the answer.

Before putting the thing back together, scrape away all old gasket material and gunk the unit thoroughly. Rinse the oil lines and blow out passages with compressed air. Be sure that timing marks on crank and cam gears are properly aligned. Don't use too much permatex. Use a torque wrench to tighten all bolts. Cap screws (acorn nuts) require 22 lb./ft. of pressure, the 8mm nuts at the pulley end (#4 bearing) require 15 lb./ft. and the remainder 22 lb./ft. To be sure the mains are not cinched down too tightly, the shaft should rotate easily by the flywheel.

Which brings us to installing the crank and rods.

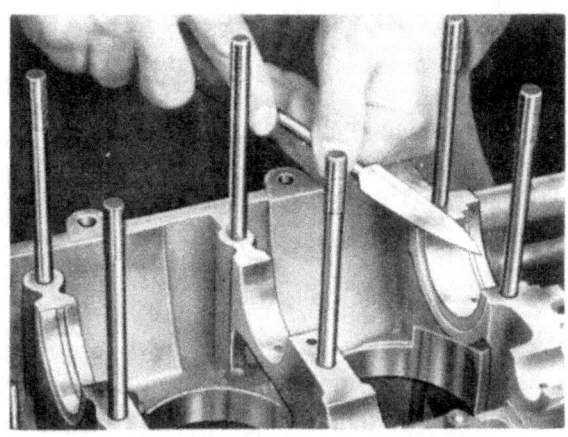

When replacing rod and main inserts, take care that there are no sharp edges on the new bearings, "Break" the edges, so that there is a slight chamfer or radius, with a knife blade or other edged tool.
1. Put insert #2 into crankcase first.
2. Put halves into left half of case, matching oil holes.
3. Mount bearing #1 on crank so that offset hole (for locater pin) faces flywheel.
4. Place #4 bearing on shaft so that oil hole in housing aligns with hole in bearing and hole for locater pin is properly aligned.
5. When mounting crank, begin at bearing #1 being sure that locater pins fit properly.

Removal and refit of crankshaft requires care

DIMENSIONS

Here are the dimensions of bearings used in conjunction with each of the crankshafts:

64mm stroke crank: Rod journals 50mm (1 31/32")
74mm stroke crank: Rod journals 53mm (2 3/32")
Main bearing journals: #1, #2, #3-50mm, #4-40mm (1 37/64")

END PLAY

End play of crankshaft on all models is given by the factory as .1 to .14mm (.004" to .0055") and maximum permissible wear as .20mm (.008"). End play is adjusted at the flywheel end before the crank is installed in the engine. With Bearing #1 in place on the crank, lay on the proper shim, tighten flywheel hollow bolt to 270 lb./ft. and check end play with feeler gage. Shims are available in .05mm increments beginning with .80mm-gasket.

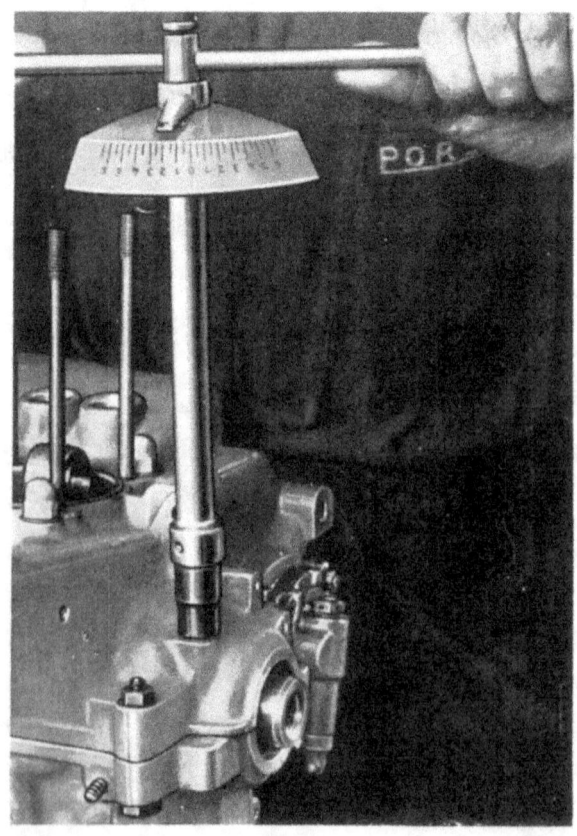

Torque wrench is important in assembly process

CONNECTING RODS

Rods are color keyed by weight. Permissible variation in weight according to the factory manual is 5g. This seems a trifle liberal to an old hotrodder but Porsche engines seem to be pretty satisfactory. Any enthusiast who disassembles his engine and does not have it balanced out to the smallest unit before re-assembly does not deserve the name enthusiast anyway. .5 gram, not 5 grams is more like it, if you are interested in quality.

Rod cap screws should be tightened to 36 lb./ft. pressure. Oil the bearings before assembly and pound on the cap from time to time (lightly, of course) while tightening. The rod should "fall" around the shaft when you are done.

Cylinders and Pistons

Cylinders are of aluminum alloy with hard chromed inner surfaces. They are not suitable for re-boring and should be replaced completely with accompanying piston if damaged or excessively worn. The selective assembly method of mass production is used at Porsche where components are categorized by variations in tolerance and mated accordingly. Never will random matings occur that might pair an outsize cylinder with a minimum size piston. For which, much thanks.

Accompanying photos or drawings show how piston types vary in different engines. Both piston and cylinder are marked with a letter to designate its size group. A mates with A, B with B and so on. Cylinder marking will be found on the top fin, piston designation is stamped into the crown. If a piston is damaged and the cylinder remains whole, the replacement should bear the same letter as the part being discarded.

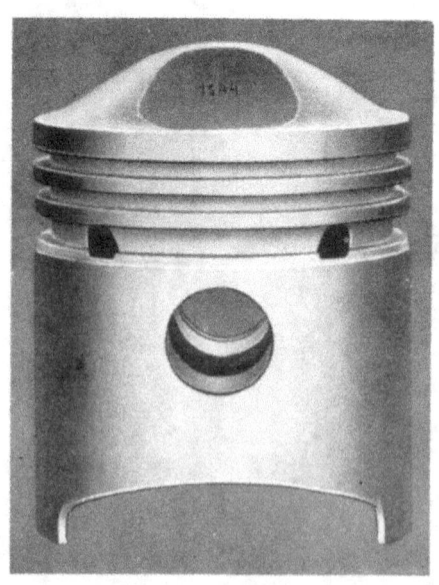

1100 Piston, 73.5mm dia.

1300 Piston, 80mm dia.

1300 Super Piston, 74.5mm dia.

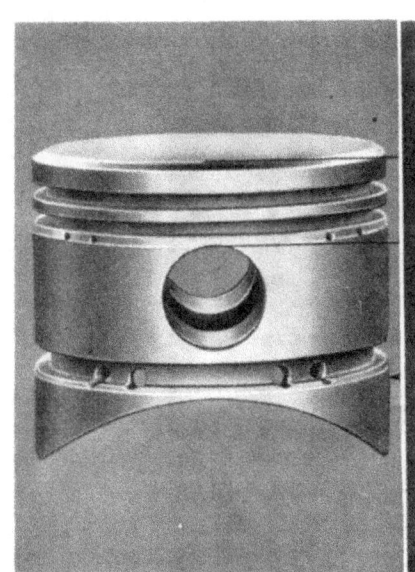
1500 Piston, 80mm dia.

1500 Super Piston, 80mm dia.

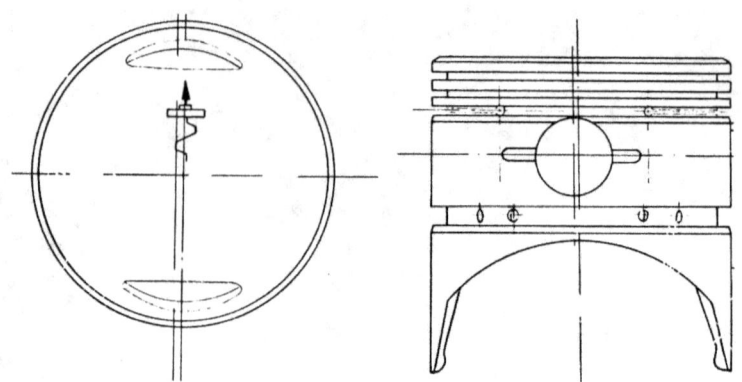

1600 Piston, 82.5mm dia.

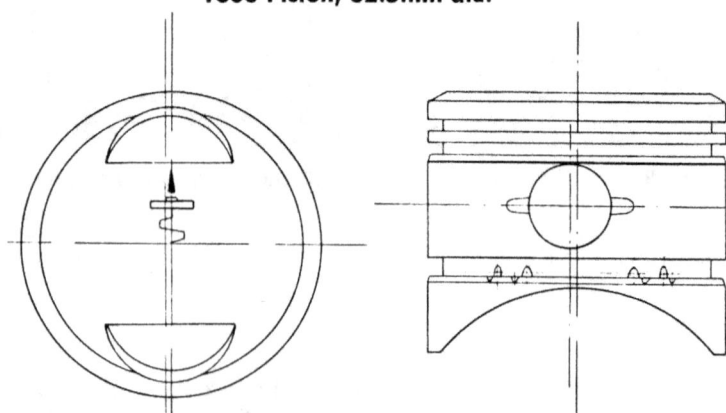

1600 Super Piston, 82.5mm dia.

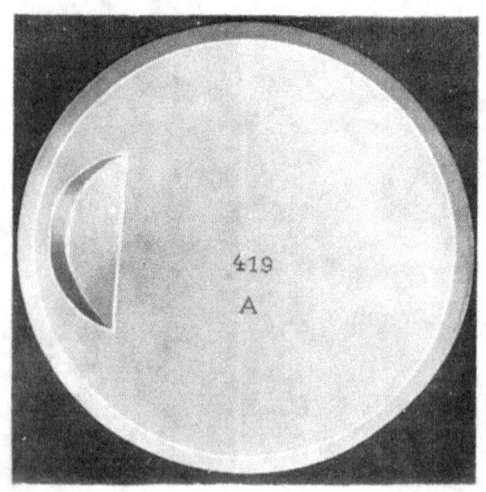

Carrera Engine

When it was announced that the highly successful "Spyder" engine would be made available in a series production car, there was considerable rejoicing among Porsche owners. The prospect of having this powerplant of advanced design in an already proven Gran Turismo envelope was exciting to contemplate. The fact that the Carrera has since not proven to be a fantastically popular sports car in this country cannot be traced to any basic fault in the car, surely, but rather to the necessarily conservative road techniques that we must adhere to inorder not to run afoul of the law. In short, it is rather certain that the Carrera will not be driven to its fullest potential on our city streets and highways. In racing, of course, they continue to finish well up among cars of greater displacement and to dominate their classes.

Although he may not be able to exert the Carrera's muscle consistently, the non-racing driver still has a great amount of pleasure in store through the use of his car. Being careful to maintain it in accordance with factory recommendations and to follow the tips presented here can add to that pleasure by keeping service problems to a minimum.

Our technical advisor on this chapter is Vasek Polak who has maintained the fastest and most consistent Carreras and Spyders on the West Coast since 1956. Jack McAffee '58 West Coast Champion, Ken Miles, Jean Pierre Kunstle have driven Polak-prepared cars to an inordinate number of wins and he was selected by the Porsche factory to care for Jean Behra's entry in the Riverside Grand Prix when that fine driver visited this country. His Carreras go well and stay together. As a consequence, his shop at 356 S. Sepulveda in Manhattan Beach, Calif., is well stacked with customers at all times.

Polak's opinion is that the Carrera is a "really good car but the owner usually doesn't find out enough about treating it like it should be used." Cardinal sins, in his experience are (1) too short warmup period, (2) warming up at too slow RPM, (3) not changing oil regularly, (4) "lugging" the engine. Commonest complaints that come to his shop are poor performance traceable to improper float level in carburetors, wrong plugs and improper ignition timing.

Since all of these come under the heading of minor tune up, it is apparent that most owners really don't understand just what the Carrera should have in the way of adjustments and they may also be committing the sins listed above for the same reason.

Let's look at the engine:

Introduced into competition in 1954, the double overhead cam 547 produced 125 SAE horsepower as it went into the first Spyders and could be twisted to 7,500 RPM maximum. By the time this design had been planted in the 356 chassis the racing engine had been tweaked up to about 140. The Carrera was slightly de-tuned by lowering the compression ratio and was rated at 115 SAE horses. By 1960 the power output of the competition engine had been raised to somewhere in the vicinity of 175 SAE, RPMS to 8,500-9,000 and the 125 hp of the first model is on tap in the production Carrera.

Using the same opposed-4 cylinder ("Boxer") layout as the pushrod engine the Carrera differs largely in that it employs two camshafts to operate the valves in each head. The heads, cylinders and case are light alloy aluminum with the cylinder bores chrome plated and knurled. Prior to 1959 and the 1600cc engine, Hirth roller bearing crankshafts of the assembled type were used, now the same drop-forged plain bearing cranks as used in pushrod engines are employed. The engine is a dry sump type using two parallel

ENGINE - SECTIONAL VIEW

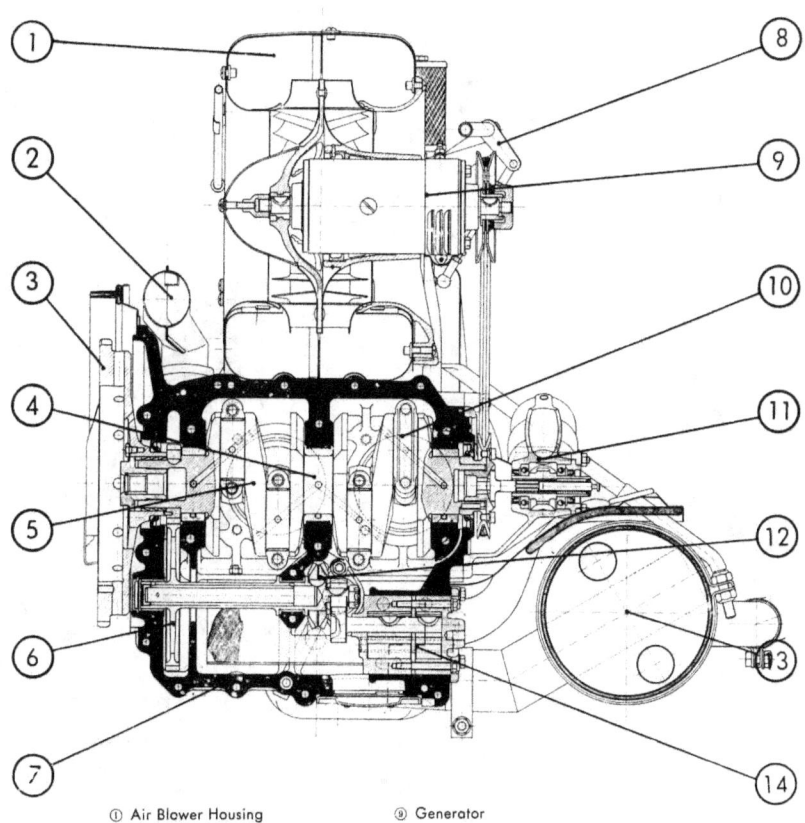

① Air Blower Housing
② Crankcase Breather
③ Flywheel
④ Crankshaft Main Bearing
⑤ Crankshaft
⑥ Drive Shaft for Interm. Gear
⑦ Crankcase
⑧ Accelerator Linkage
⑨ Generator
⑩ Connecting Rod
⑪ Drive Case for Ign. Distr.
⑫ Bevel Gear Drive for Camshaft with Drive for Oil Pump
⑬ Silencer
⑭ Oil Pump

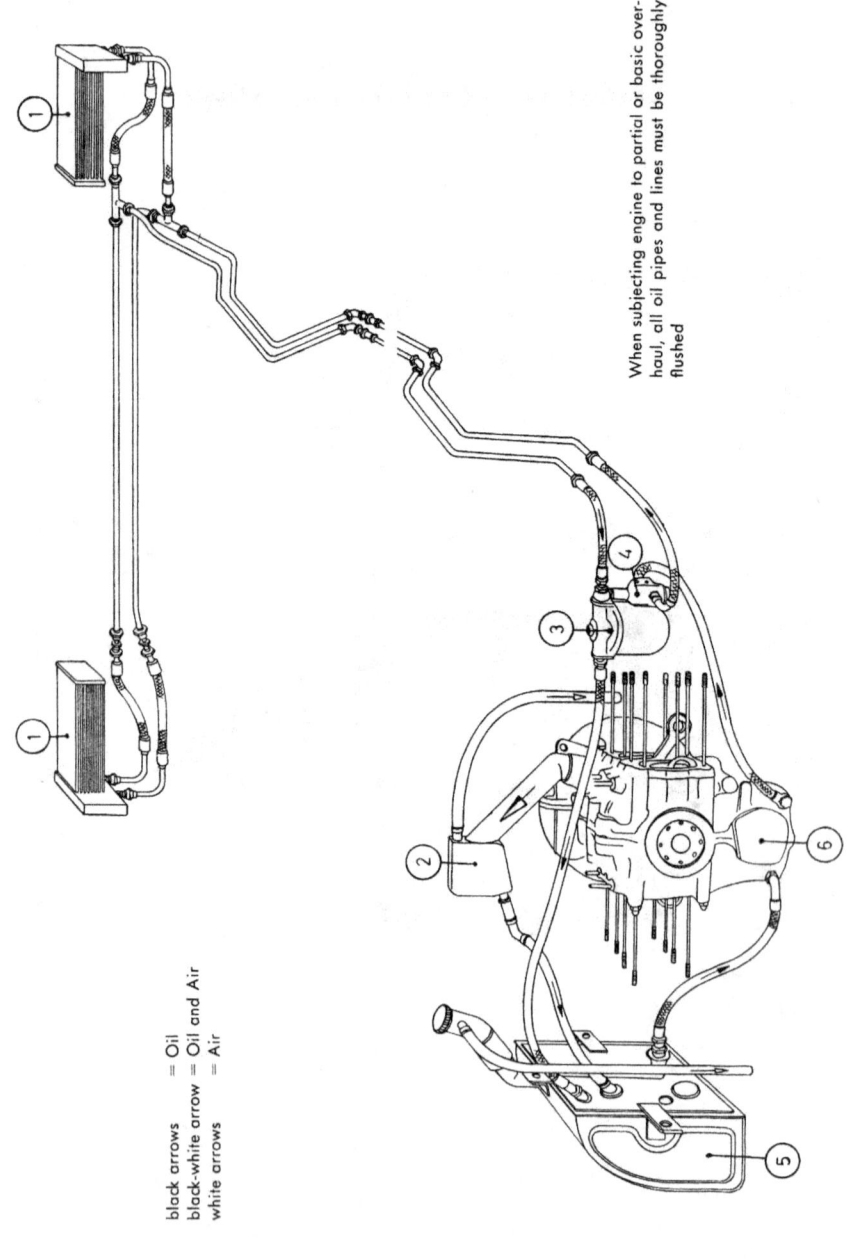

Skeleton Sketch of Valve Train

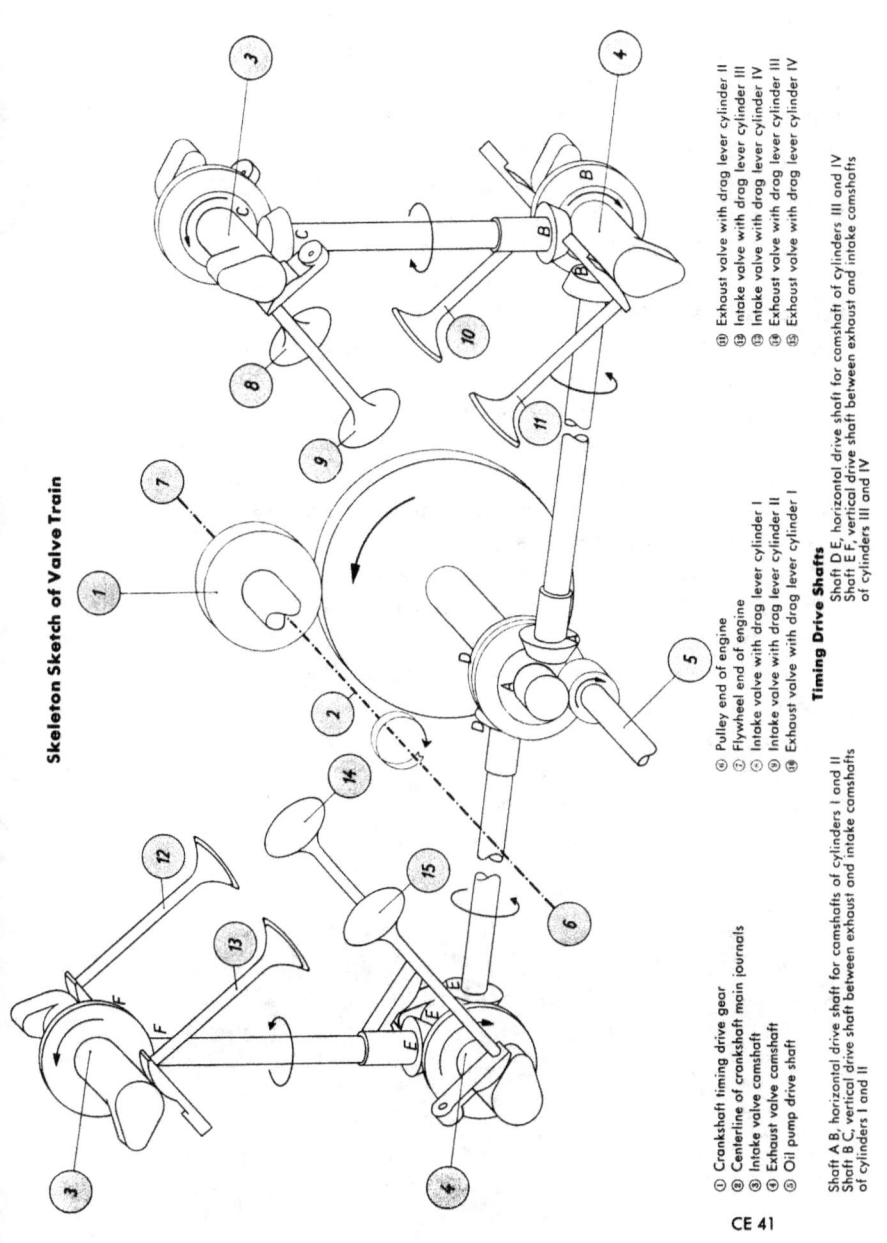

① Crankshaft timing drive gear
② Centerline of crankshaft main journals
③ Intake valve camshaft
④ Exhaust valve camshaft
⑤ Oil pump drive shaft

⑥ Pulley end of engine
⑦ Flywheel end of engine
⑧ Intake valve with drag lever cylinder I
⑨ Intake valve with drag lever cylinder II
⑩ Exhaust valve with drag lever cylinder I

⑪ Exhaust valve with drag lever cylinder II
⑫ Intake valve with drag lever cylinder III
⑬ Intake valve with drag lever cylinder IV
⑭ Exhaust valve with drag lever cylinder III
⑮ Exhaust valve with drag lever cylinder IV

Timing Drive Shafts

Shaft A B, horizontal drive shaft for camshafts of cylinders I and II
Shaft B C, vertical drive shaft between exhaust and intake camshafts of cylinders I and II
Shaft D E, horizontal drive shaft for camshaft of cylinders III and IV
Shaft E F, vertical drive shaft between exhaust and intake camshafts of cylinders III and IV

CE 41

oil coolers, thermostatically controlled, for cooling. Ignition by two spark plugs per cylinder is the conventional battery-coil-distributor layout with distributors in early models driven off the ends of the camshafts and now motivated by a V drive from the crank. Two coils are used. An electric fuel pump raises fuel from the tank to a pressure reducer and thence to the two double choke carburetors either Solex 40PII, PJJ or Weber 40 DCM. Cooling is by a double inlet fan driven at crankshaft speed by a V belt.

The operation of the cam gear is fascinating to most mechanics and the Fuhrmann-Porsche design with its contra-rotating shafts "fingers" and assembled camshafts is indeed interesting. Two lateral drive shafts take the motion from the crank and transmit it to vertical cross-shafts through bevel gears. The same type of gears are used to rotate the upper and lower camshafts (intake and exhaust) which bear on drag levers interposed between the cam and the valve stem. All this "monkey motion" poses a lubrication problem in cold starts and requires quite a bit of torque to overcome the resistance of springs and surface drag. For this reason it is important that firing up the car and warming it to operating temperature be caried out as recommended.

The 8 quart oil reserve naturally takes quite a bit longer to become thoroughly warm than the 2.5 to 5 quart amounts generally carried by most sports cars and it is a good idea to let the needle of the oil temp gage come fully off the peg before engaging in any strenuous activities.

On the other hand warming up the engine at the normal idle is to be avoided. The same hazards that appear under the condition of excess load/low speed that we call "lugging" are in evidence here too. At slow speeds the crankshaft bearings (in the Hirth crank)

do not rotate and the same individual bearing receives the thrust of the power explosion on each revolution with resultant flattening. In the plain crank this is not so marked but "lugging," i.e.: putting the engine under an overload at low speed, will cause the same type of damage nonetheless.

Most drivers, Vasek Polak opines, do not keep their engines revved up high enough. They will use 4th gear, for instance, simply because the car will run in that cog, instead of downshifting to 3rd. Keeping the tachometer needle in the 4,000 & up range will not hurt the engine but dropping consistently into the 2,000 area surely will.

The average Carrera, right off the boat, is not tuned properly for the type of fuel in common use in this country according to more than one specialist. The Carrera is an extremely sensitive engine to fuel/air ratio and to float level. Part of Polak's secret of success in running racing engines is that when they leave the shop he follows them. Every race week end he is at the track to lend assistance to the owners of cars he has set up. The reason is that a change in weather (humidity, temperature) calls for a change in jets. The owner who merely intends to drive his Carrera on the street does not have to be quite so critical, but selection of the proper jets for altitude and overall weather conditions is vital.

As mentioned in conjunction with the pushrod engine, German fuel is not the same density as the gasoline we use in the United States and, consequently, supports the float at a different height plus providing a different air/fuel ratio through a given jet.

To specify a set of jets for each area of the country is absurd, naturally, but anyone who has access to a chassis dynamometer (or to a good Porsche specialist who **knows** Carreras and Spyders) can get an idea of his requirements quickly. Sparkplug examination is a clue, the condition of the tailpipe, surging, backfiring, "hunting" at the idle are telltale signs of a poor mixture.

Champion N 5 plugs should present a tan center insulator with no carbon on the electrodes and a light gray rim. The tailpipe should be on the black side of gray. The engine should hold 6,500 or better on free revs with no surging or backfiring and should accelerate from the idle with no hesitation.

If the car is to be run consistently in traffic or under high temperature conditions, the float levels in the carburetors should be set lower than what otherwise is satisfactory. (Fuel expands and pretty soon you have spewing, flooding and attendant poor performance.)

Actually each car should be tuned to the individual habits of its owner. If one is accustomed to accelerating away from each stop sign and to taking the fast way on back roads, his car can use a different tune from the one required by the man who drives only to the office through traffic morning and night.

Oil changing should take place every 1,500 to 2,000 miles when using HD of a good brand. Castrol R will get you 2,500 to 3,000 miles between changes. 30 wt. is specified for normal use, 40 for racing, lighter for cold weather. How much lighter depends on low temperature expected.

Sparkplugs, although tricky to change, (it takes a good man about 5 minutes per plug under normal conditions) are seldom a problem if the right heat range is selected in the first place. Champion N 5's (gapped at .016") for non-competitive activities and N-4's for racing get the nod. "Most plug problems are carburetion problems," says Polak about plug fouling.

A great deal has been written about the hazards of valve timing and, in a sense, the operation is more critical than on less complex engines. The method, perhaps, rather than the end result is what causes alarm, but exact valve timing and clearances are easily attained by careful procedure. However, sloppy or hasty work here can result in a discouraging loss of power.

Ignition timing, too, is critical and the factory admonition to not exceed 27° advance should be heeded. A dyno check using your local grade of gasoline is a good idea although the Carrera's 9.5 to 1 compression ratio should not cause detonation on premium fuel.

Having generalized about the commonest Carrera complaints, let us be specific in a couple of areas where the owner can well do his own maintenance and certainly should know the specifications.

Get a Specialist: Advice to Carrera owners to employ only factory-trained mechanics on major problems is well to heed. Typical Carrera expert, **Vasek Polak (r.)** whose shop in Southern California is mecca for performance-minded drivers, served as advisor on this chapter.

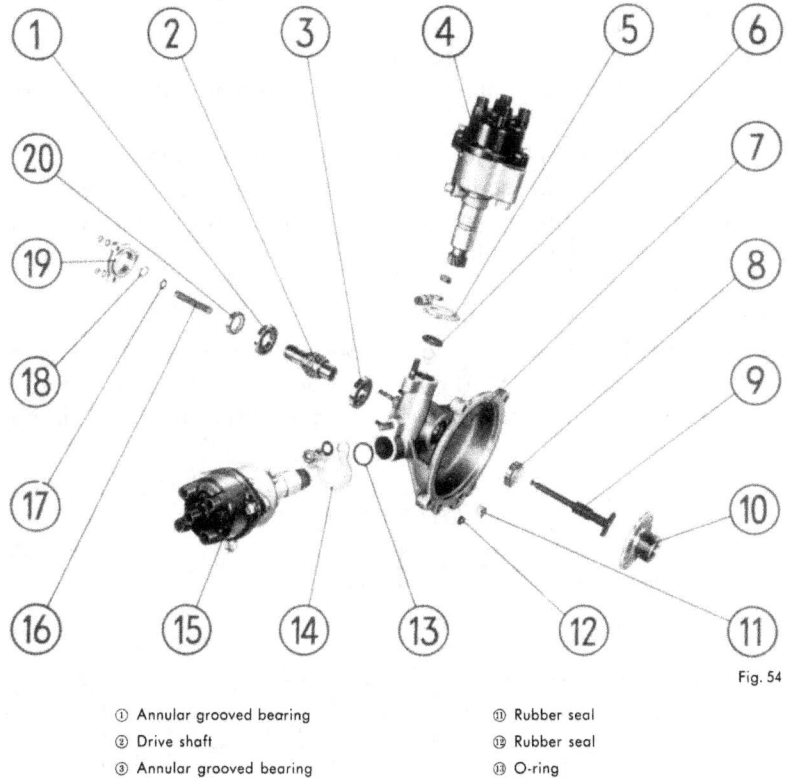

Fig. 54

① Annular grooved bearing
② Drive shaft
③ Annular grooved bearing
④ Ignition distributor
⑤ Clamping ring
⑥ O-ring
⑦ Distributor drive housing
⑧ Radial seal
⑨ Coupling part
⑩ Bolt for V-belt pulley (follower)
⑪ Rubber seal
⑫ Rubber seal
⑬ O-ring
⑭ Clamping ring
⑮ Ignition distributor
⑯ Pressure spring
⑰ Washer
⑱ Circlip
⑲ Bearing cover
⑳ Radial seal

IGNITION TIMING

Before adjusting ignition timing, check the point gap. A .014" feeler gage should be a drag fit. Rough points should be dressed with a point file (never use emery cloth). Crank the engine until points are fully open, loosen set screw and adjust points, retighten set screw.

This is the procedure for adjusting timing using a test lamp:
1. Set ignition timing mark on crank pulley to coincide with crankcase spit.
2. Remove distributor caps.

3. Connect test lamp to ground and terminal 1 on one distributor.
4. Switch on ignition.
5. Loosen clamping screw of distributor.
6. Advance centrifugal mechanism by turning rotor clockwise to stop.
7. Turn distributor body clockwise until breaker points close.
8. Turn distributor body anti-clockwise until points open and lamp lights up. Keep rotor in position with fingers so that centrifugal advance is fully held.
9. Tighten clamping screw.
10. Repeat on second distributor.

In setting ignition advance using a stroboscopic timing light, engine speed must be 6,000 RPM. The marking on the crank pulley should be made plainer with a small brush and black paint before a strobe check.

Compression Diagram for Engine Type 1600 GS

ε = Compression ratio
Vh = Cubic capacity of one cylinder in c.c.
Vc = Capacity of one compression chamber in c.c., spark plug bore filled, minus 2 c.c.

$$\varepsilon = \frac{Vh + Vc}{Vc}$$

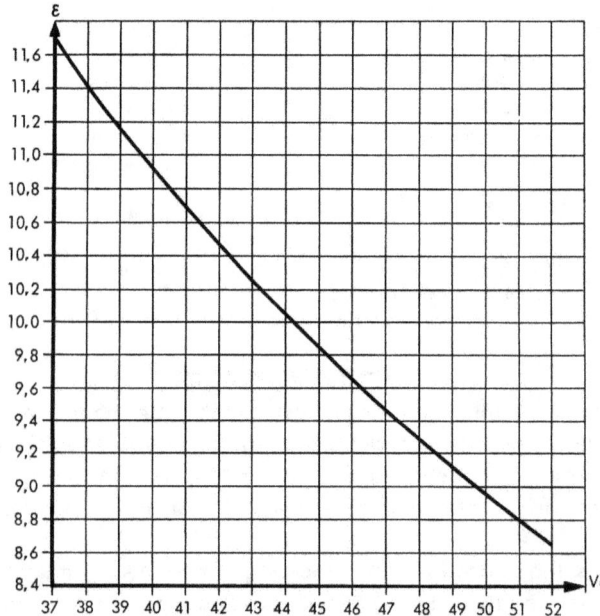

This compression diagram exclusively serves the purpose to check the specified compression ratio. A compression ratio higher than the one specified by the factory will lead to premature engine wear and is therefore not permitted

CARBURETION

The dual downdraft Solexes fitted to Carreras are adequate carburetion for any non-racing activities. Webers are selected for competition because they are handier for quick adjustments and are a bit more polished. There is no doubt that the Weber has achieved an enviable reputation and, next to fuel injection, offers the best performance to be had. The following idling adjustment procedure can be followed for both Webers and Solexes, essential differences in the two carburetors can be determined from accompanying diagrams.

IDLING ADJUSTMENT

1. Remove air filter and determine that all throttle valves close evenly. Make sure that linkage does not jam or bind at any point. Closure should be smooth and even in pressure. Clean filter in gasoline, oil lightly and re-install later.
2. Run engine until warm, loosen idling adjusting screw on both carburetors.
3. Turn idling adjusting screw in on one carburetor until approximately 1,000 RPM is reached.
4. Turn in idling adjusting screw on the other carburetor until RPM increases slightly, then back off to even setting.
5. Turn mixture regulating screw until engine reaches maximum rpm.
6. Repeat step 5 on other carburetor.
7. Re-adjust idling speed with the idling adjusting screws to 850-900 RPM.

A Unisyn or Porsche tool P-75 can be used to balance carburetors more accurately. (See Carburetion data in Pushrod Engine section.)

ACCELERATION PUMP INJECTION

Using a Porsche tool P-25 (or the measuring glass described in the carburetion section of Pushrod Engine chapters) check the acceleration pump injection quantity. **.4 to .5 cc per two strokes** of the pump for each nozzle is correct. Adjustment is made on the Solex at (15) pump operating rod. On the Weber as shown by arrow in photo. Both rods have locking nuts and care must be taken that the adjusting nut is not moved as the locking nut is set tight. Clockwise adjustment of nuts increases quanity of injection, counter clockwise reduces quantity.

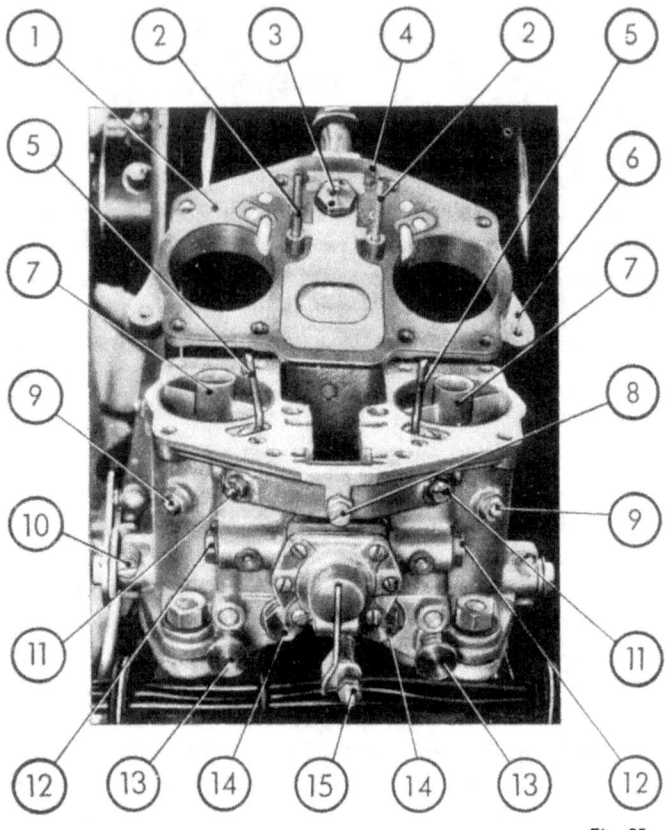

Fig. 55

① Gasket
② Mixture tube
③ Float needle valve
④ Coil spring for float bearing
⑤ Injection tube
⑥ Carburetor cover
⑦ Dual venturi
⑧ Level adjusting screw
⑨ Retaining screw for main venturi
⑩ Idling adjusting screw (stop screw)
⑪ Idling fuel jet
⑫ Pump jet
⑬ Idling mixture regulating screw
⑭ Main jet holder
⑮ Connection rod to diaphragm pump

SOLEX FLOAT LEVEL

Check the float level by removing plug screw as shown in photo. With car on level ground the fuel should not flow out. With the engine running turn adjusting screw (8) out or in to raise or lower float in the chamber. Turning the screw **in** causes the float level to **drop, out** causes it to **rise**. At first, if you lower the float level fuel will run out the screw plug opening but after the engine has run for a few seconds the proper level will be reached. The proper level is just below the opening.

Dual Downdraft Carburetor Weber 40 DCM 1

Fig. 59

① Annular adaptor for fuel supply
② Dual venturi
③ Idling jet
④ Main jet with air correction jet
⑤ Dual venturi
⑥ Accelerator linkage
⑦ Screw for float valve
⑧ Hollow bolt for injection tube
⑨ Idling jet
⑩ Float chamber breather
⑪ Main jet with air correction jet
⑫ Bearing bracket for accelerator linkage

VALVE CLEARANCE

Valve clearance is measured between the cam lobes and the "fingers" or drag levers. Measured with the engine cold a .006 feeler gage is a light push fit. (The drag lever spring exerts a certain amount of pressure.)

With the engine on the car, this procedure can be followed:
1. Remove cam cover.
2. Set cylinder to be adjusted at OT on firing stroke.
3. Check valve clearance with broad feeler gage.
4. Loosen retainer nut by approximately 4 turns to permit retainer to disengage locking nut.
5. Turn locking stud for adjusting screw in or out as required to create correct tolerance.
6. Re-tighten nut of retainer. Be careful that retainer is not twisted when tightening nut and re-engages locking nut.
7. Repeat on other valve of same cylinder.

Correct cylinder sequence of adjustment is 1-2-3-4.

Valve timing requires tools found ordinarily only in shops specializing in Carrera or Spyder service and the process requires careful study of the shop manual.

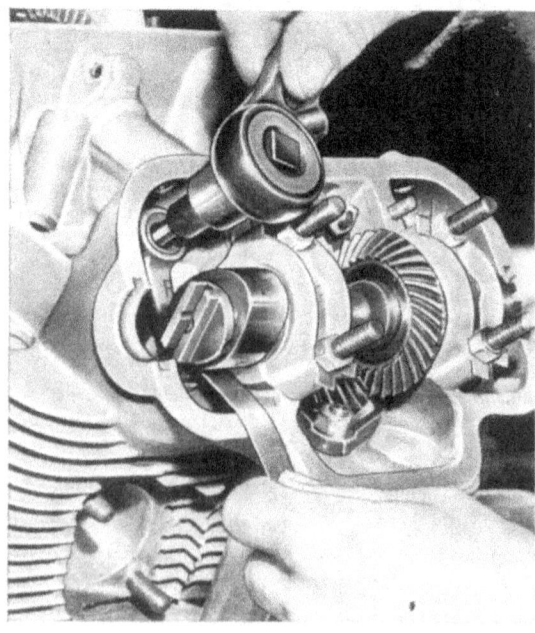

The Clutch

Commonest clutch problems center around adjustment inasmuch as both clutch wear and cable stretch can play a part. The clutch cable must be installed in such a way that 2mm to 2.5mm of clearance exists between the throwout bearing and the plate when clutch is engaged. There are two places that adjustment can take place: at clutch lever on the cross shaft or the nut on the clutch pedal.

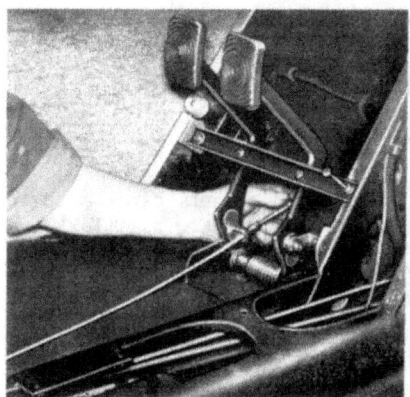 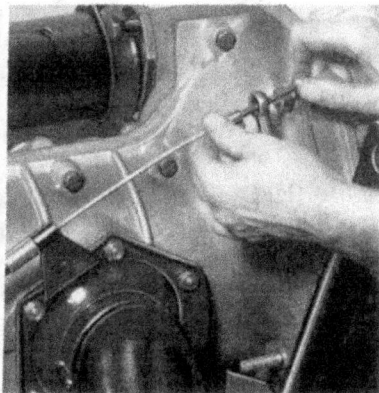

ADJUSTING: Note: Be sure that cable sleeve has no play between conduit piece and angle bracket.
1. Jack up car and remove left rear wheel.
2. Loosen adjusting nut and safety nut on cable end piece.
3. Tighten or loosen adjusting nut until there is a play of 20 to 25mm (25/32" to 1") at the foot pedal. Check for consistency by repeating the test several times, depressing the foot pedal fully and releasing it between measurements.
4. Tighten safety nut against adjusting nut. Note: Put a dab of grease on the threads, between adjusting nut and lever.

If the adjustment is completely consumed at the transmission end of the cable, adjust at pedal in this manner:
1. Remove seats or slide fully to rear of track.
2. Remove floor boards.
3. Loosen safety nut and adjusting nut.
4. Adjust nut until pedal play is as described above, re-tighten safety nut.

REPLACING CLUTCH CABLE

Cable breakage is not seemingly as common in the Porsche as in the VW and other cars, possibly because it is shorter—what usually goes is the threaded rod at the lever end. However, it gen-

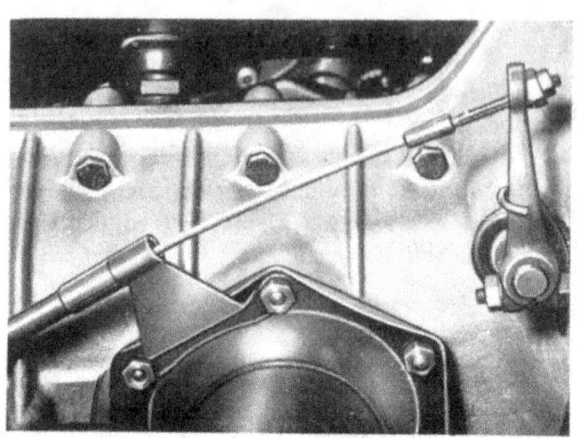

Adjusting rod is common breaking point

erally happens without warning and many owners carry a spare cable in the tool box just as they do a fan belt and sparkplugs. It doesn't take much room and having one can keep you from being stalled in some out-of-the-way place.

Remove the old cable by jacking up the car and taking out floorboards to gain access to both ends, as described above. Install the new cable by following this process:

1. Lubricate cable sleeve at grease nipple with grease gun until grease is pressed out the other end.
2. Pull cable back and forth several times in sleeve.
3. Attach grease nipple to adjusting sleeve at end of chassis and lubricate well.
4. Turn back adjusting sleeve at chassis as far as possible and lock with safety nut.
5. When inserting cable, grease nipple of cable sleeve must rest against adjusting sleeve.
6. Push conduit piece of cable sleeve through angle bracket and end of cable through eye of clutch lever.
7. Screw on adjusting nut (beveled face toward eye) and safety nut.
8. Pull cable through driver's compartment and through eye of foot pedal.
9. Screw adjusting nut and safety nut on cable end.
10. Adjust play as described above.

Other clutch difficulties seem to arise from myriad causes, not the least of which is improper shifting. Slipping, keeping the pedal depressed for overlong periods and the same hazards that ruin the clutches in any other car will have a similar effect on the Porsche.

Slipping the clutch repeatedly, especially when new, will overheat it and glaze the lining. Keeping the pedal depressed while waiting for the light to change is a bad habit. This keeps the throwout bearing engaged against the plate and friction plays its well-known role. Not bringing the engine up to the appropriate rpm to match the gear during down shifts throws an added load on the clutch as well as the synchro rings. Starting the car from a dead stop in other than competition circumstances should be accomplished by putting it into first gear engaging the clutch gently enough to get the car off the mark, engaging it fully **then** applying throttle, not by putting it in second and slipping the clutch. This may seem absurdly elementary but it is astounding how many otherwise intelligent drivers seem to be trying to save first for a rainy day. Revving up the engine and dropping the clutch is sometimes necessary but clutches are expendable under these circumstances.

What may seem to be clutch chatter is often motor mount play. In models prior to the 1600, the front mount in shear (a rubber block bonded to two metal plates) suffers from deterioration and the U or strap hanger mount can work loose. Later types have an improved mount (the "doughnut" style) which lessens this hazard.

New pressure plate assemblies are often "whippy" merely from being under tension since assembly. The perfectionist will have his surface-ground before installation. This is a must if drag racing or track racing is contemplated.

The most frequent troubles are presented in tabular form, taking the factory hints as a guide. Another problem, and one perhaps not too common by this time, is that early 1500s used a soft steel release plate (that bears on the throwout bearing) which permitted excessive wear on the finger side. Later models have a harder plate. Another feature common to later models is a vented bell housing. Cutting these vents in older boxes is mentioned under "More Push" in this book.

A less desirable feature on the 1600, but one that had to come in conjunction with the new transmission, is the clutch return spring that requires an engine remove-refit to replace. It is anchored internally to the cross shaft. This is another VW piece, by the way, if your Porsche dealer isn't aware of it. Still another interchange and you might keep this in mind if you blow up way out where the Stuttgart product is a rarity, is that the pressure plate assembly from the VW Microbus or Van fits late 1500's and the Stock VW fits the early models.

Incidentally, a number of issues of PORSCHE PANORAMA the Porsche Club of America publication, have carried good, detailed articles on clutch problems and are well worth studying.

Clutch Troubles, Causes and Remedies

1. NOISY CLUTCH

a) Worn bushing in hollow bolt of flywheel
b) Worn throwout bearing
c) Clutch disc interferes with pressure plate
d) Weakened springs or unequal tension
e) Damper spring in clutch disc loose or damaged

a) Replace bushing and fill with graphite grease (approx 2ccm)
b) Replace bearing. Note correct adjustment
c) Replace or straighten clutch release plate
d) Replace springs
e) Replace clutch disc

2. GRABBING CLUTCH

a) Transmission loose in suspension
b) Clutch greasy
c) Pressure plate worn
d) Clutch release plate whips
e) Clutch springs have unequal tension
f) Cable sleeve without tension
g) Inadequate setting of clutch disc

a) Tighten screws and nuts
b) Replace leaky oil seal on crank or transmission. Replace disc, clean pressure plate and flywheel
c) Replace or reface pressure plate
d) Re-align release plate. (max. deviation: 0.3mm or .012")
e) Replace clutch springs
f) Adjust tension at conduit piece
g) Renew disc

3. CLUTCH FAILS TO RELEASE

a) Excessive clutch play
b) Clutch disc or driveshaft whips
c) Cracked lining
d) Insufficient radial play between hollow bolt and main drive shaft
e) Clutch release lever in release plate damaged

a) Adjust play to 20mm-25mm (25/32" to 1") at pedal
b) Align or replace shaft or disc
c) Replace
d) Correct radial play
e) Renew clutch release

4. CLUTCH SLIPS

a) Not enough clutch play, decreases as linings wear
b) Greasy lining

a) Adjust as above
b) Renew disc, replace oil seal at engine or transmission. Clean pressure plate and flywheel

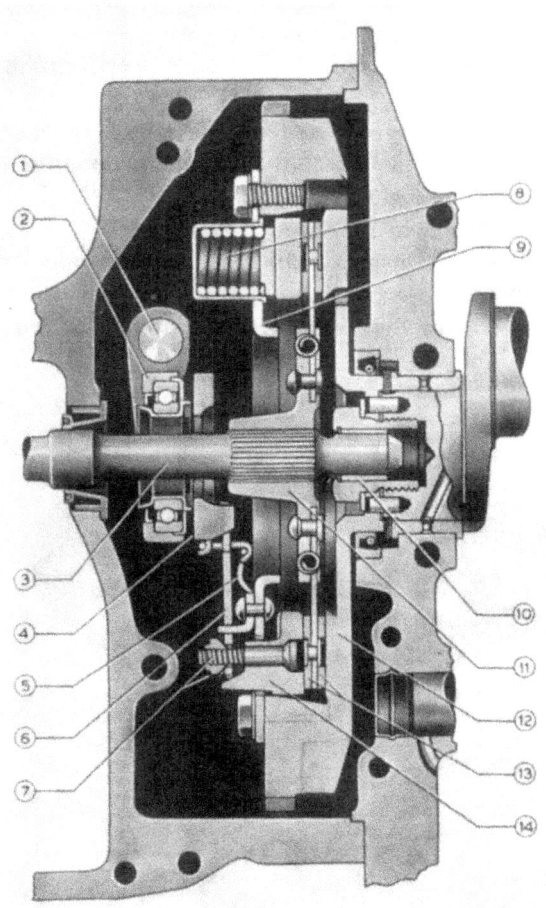

1. Cross shaft
2. Clutch pressure bearing
3. Drive shaft
4. Clutch release plate
5. Return spring f. clutch release lever
6. Clutch release lever
7. Bolt and special nut
8. Clutch thrust springs
9. Clutch cover
10. Bush for hollow bolt
11. Clutch plate
12. Flywheel
13. Clutch plate lining
14. Clutch pressure plate

If you plan to replace the clutch disc or pressure assembly this is the step-by-step method recommended by the factory:

(With the engine removed from the car.)
1. Mark the flywheel and clutch cover clearly to facilitate reassembly.
2. Loosen the hex screws holding the clutch cover to the flywheel uniformly a few turns at a time, opposite screws alternately (to prevent warping).
3. Remove cover, take out plate.

With the clutch out, inspect it for wear and damage, overheating (tarnished or purple appearance) and alignment. If in doubt, replace everything. In Europe they rebuild these units, but we exchange them.

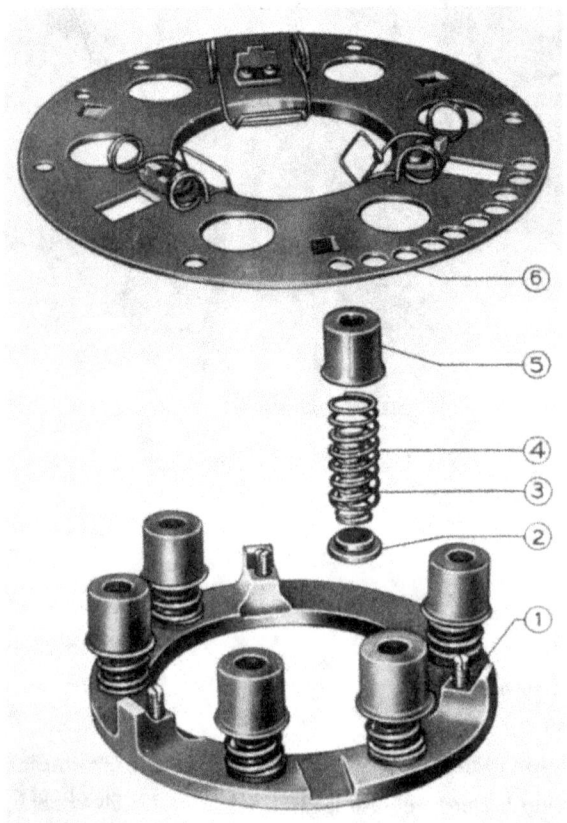

Clutch assembly showing (1) pressure plate, (2) spring seat, (3) inner thrust spring, (4) outer thrust spring, (5) spring housing, (6) cover

Common faults to look for are broken or weak springs, scored pressure plate, warped pressure plate, worn disc, warped disc, greasy disc or scored flywheel.

In re-installing be sure to match the marks placed on cover and flywheel before dismantling. It is a good idea to have this assembly balanced if a complete teardown is in progress.

Clutch plate surface should be true within .02"

LATE MODEL CLUTCH

The new clutch with its single plate-spring instead of the many coil springs is an interesting and progressive design. As can be seen from accompanying illustrations, the clutch consists of a (1) cover, (2) snapring, (3) plate spring, (4)-(5) a face plate with tension springs and a (6) pressure plate. The pressure plate is cast iron in 1600 N & S engines, steel in Carreras. Numbers on the plate spring (616 for pushrod engines and 692 for Carreras) indicate their applications. Since specialized tools are required to dissemble this piece, en-toto replacement is advised with such reworking left to an adequately equipped service garage.

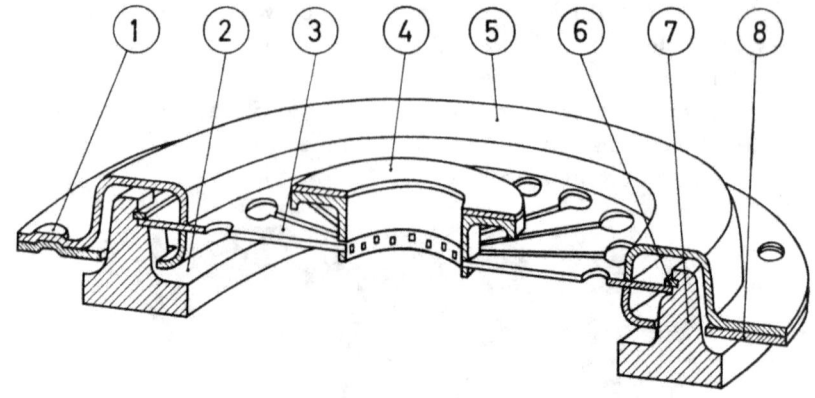

① Cup-shaped impression
② Pressure plate
③ Plate spring
④ Clutch release plate
⑤ Cover
⑥ Snap ring
⑦ Undercut for snapring
⑧ Spring face plate

Clutch pedal stop on late model.

FINAL REMINDER

The factory is most explicit in warning that an improperly adjusted clutch can cause transmission troubles . . . and with the price of labor and parts at their present level, this is a situation not to be courted. Insufficient play and a dragging clutch cause rapid wear on the synchronizing elements. So, don't wait till something happens, check the travel frequently.

Transmission-Differential

The "Trans-axle" as it is currently being called by the name coiners, is almost a Porsche trademark, being a pet package of the late Dr. Porsche. As a research and development firm, Porsche has designed and caused to be made some of the world's finest transmissions, large and small. The units installed in the cars that bear the firm's name are no exception. Given average care and attention, they remain smooth, efficient and a joy to manipulate. The "rear end" and axles are one of the most trouble-free units in existence. A blown-up rear end or ring-and-pinion casualty, fairly common to more conventional units (particularly in racing) is almost unheard of in Porsches. Transmissions, yes. Synchro rings, yes, but differentials, no. Rigidity, the absence of a long propeller shaft to build up "whip" and sound design are the reasons.

A gearbox will always remain a mystery to some and to others, who don't care how it works as long as it functions, the following explanation of the Porsche box can be skipped over. To the reader who is encountering a description of it for the first time or for the enthusiast who may be preparing to have one on the bench shortly, this brief rundown might be worth while.

Gear changing is accomplished by a hand lever mounted on the floor and operating remotely by rod and linkage through the central tunnel of the car. As the years have passed, Porsche has shortened and "firmed up" the shift lever and introduced a refined transmission but the elements remain pretty constant. 1st, 2nd, 3rd and 4th gears are synchronized, reverse is not. The main (or driving) shaft and the motion (or driven) shaft—which also ends in the pinion gear—are carried in ball and roller bearings. The case is in three pieces, split vertically along the centerline and having a separate rear (or end) cover housing reverse gears. (Type 518 & 519—Type 644 is one piece.)

The synchronizing elements consist of an operating sleeve, a shift guide, a synchro ring and the "clutch shoulder" of each gear. The shift guide is splined to the driven shaft and in constant engagement with the operating sleeve. The sleeve is held in neutral position by the selector fork clamped to the operating rod. The outer edge of the synchro ring is tapered to match the inner edge of the sleeve and the ring itself is held in position on the "clutch shoulder" of the gear by a snap ring. (A perusal of the accompanying schematic drawing will make the terminology clearer.) The outer diameter of the synchro ring in normal tension is greater than the inner diameter of the operating sleeve.

In making a downshift, for example, from 4th to 3rd, the selector fork moves the operating sleeve along the prongs of the shift guide until it encounters the 3rd gear synchro ring. The ring is compressed by the ID of the sleeve and attains a friction grip on the clutch shoulder of 3rd gear quickly bringing it up to the same speed as the sleeve. Moving farther, the sleeve forces the engagement of 3rd and locks it "in gear".

(Type 519-644)

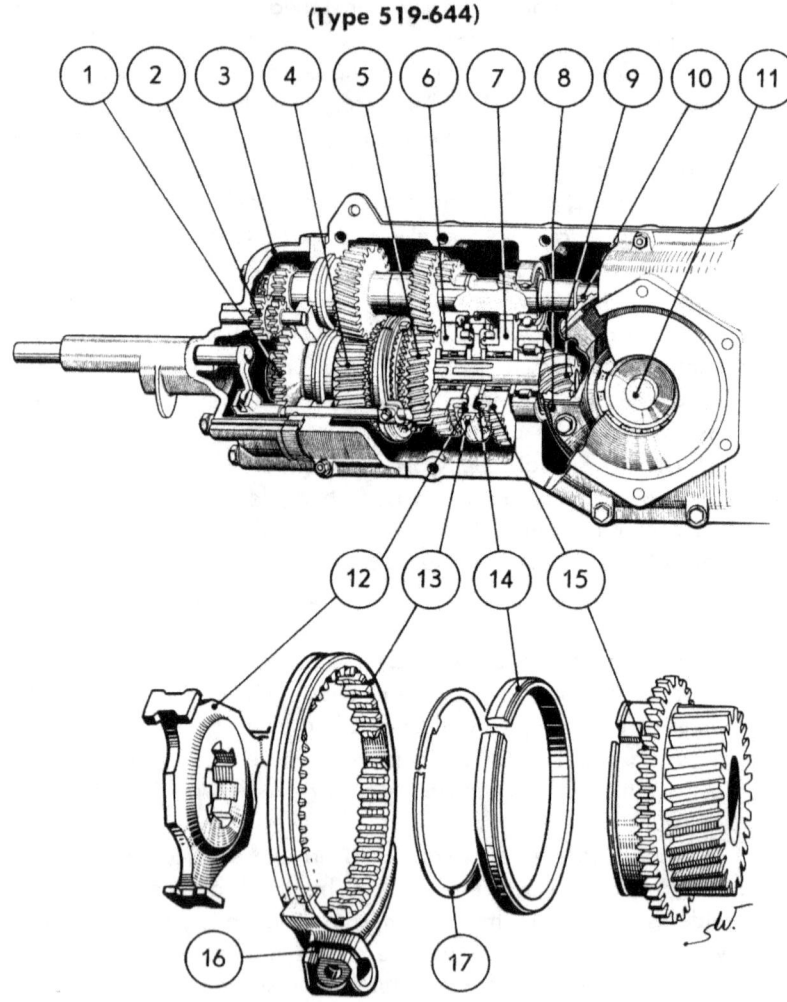

Porsche-Synchromesh-Transmission-Rear-Axle Cutaway

① gear 2 for reverse gear
② gear 3 for reverse gear
③ transmission housing end cover
④ gear 2 for 4th gear
⑤ gear 2 for 3rd gear
⑥ gear 2 for 2nd gear
⑦ gear 2 for 1st gear
⑧ housing for differential with crown gear
⑨ bevel pinion
⑩ main shaft
⑪ rear axle shaft
⑫ three-pronged shift guide
⑬ operating sleeve
⑭ synchronizing ring
⑮ gear 2 and synchronizing clutch shoulder
⑯ selector fork
⑰ safety ring

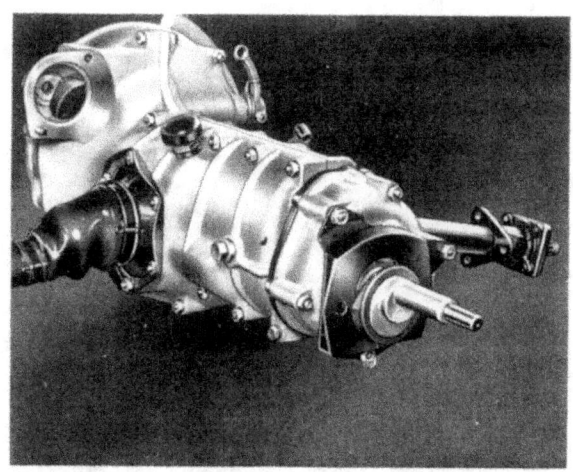

Older transmission had separate reverse cluster

Oil capacity of the combined housing is 2.5 litres (5.3 pints), but a **refill is only 2.3 litres (4.8 pints)**. SAE 90 Hypoid is recommended for both Winter and Summer, but most owners in colder climates go to 80, or even 70, if severe weather is expected and the car is not to be driven steadily. A drain and refill is advised every 6,000 miles at which time the magnetic trap plug should be removed and cleaned. A bit of Permatex (the always-soft variety) to caulk the plug is advisable and be sure that about ⅜" of the threads project, else the plug can foul the selector fork.

Transmission troubles usually arise from the same type of thoughtless operation that spells quick death for clutches. Many drivers, under the impression that the transmission is made to assist the brakes under all conditions, use the gear box to reduce speed constantly. This habit stems from the good old days when square cut gears were stronger and better engineered than brakes. In a long race, the odds that you would finish by putting a little less pressure on the binders and more on the transmission were pretty good. Nowadays, however, particularly with the superb brakes attached to Porsche wheels, this is not true and to "gear down" for every casual corner, letting the box take the brunt of deceleration, is absurd. Use the brakes as they are intended. Bring the engine RPM up to meet the new gear, double de-clutch when down-shifting and don't speed-shift going up.

At least 90% of all transmission "failures" are broken synchro rings or bent selector forks, stemming from over-stresses described above, consistently "beating" the synchro action, improperly adjusted shift lever linkage or carelessly resting the hand on the shift lever.

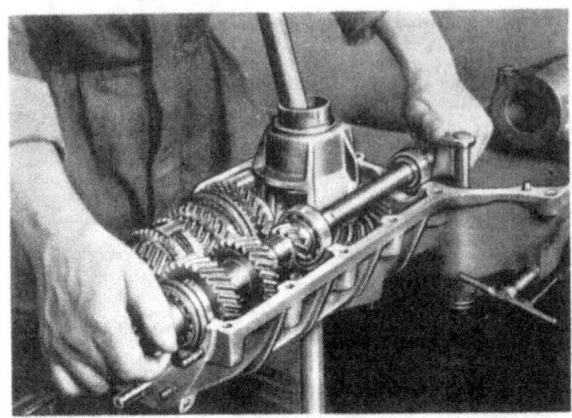

Removal of driving shaft in early (split case) transmission. Correct assembly is critical

To take up the latter first; after making a shift, release the pressure on the gear, operating sleeve and fork by moving the shift lever slightly back from the lock position. Just a fraction of an inch is all that is required. This good habit will pay off in a full life for the box. On the other hand, draping an arm over the lever while it rides in 4th, as so many MG and Healey owners find it convenient to do, will give you headaches.

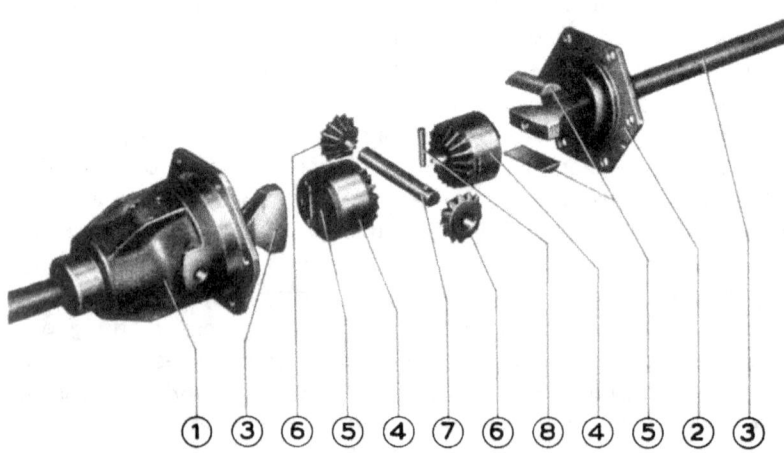

① Housing
② Cover
③ Rear Axle Shaft
④ Differential Side Gear
⑤ Fulcrum Plates
⑥ Differential Pinion
⑦ Differential Pinion Shaft
⑧ Dowel Pin

Exploded view of differential unit

One more tip, if you don't already practice it; be sure the gear is fully engaged before releasing the clutch . . . particularly in first and third which call for a thrust that is slightly farther away from you than one expects. Having the lever "pop out" of first is not only hard on the transmission, it can get you a bashed posterior when the car behind you at the stop light climbs up the rear deck.

Symptoms of a bad synchro ring, and somehow, 3rd gear is the one that ordinarily goes out first, are difficult engagement, popping out under load and "noises" . . . (The "noises" can be varied, but you'll know they are not normal.) Proper adjustment of shift linkage will prevent most of the failures in this department. You, or your mechanic, can set the external linkage without too much trouble, the internal connections, of course call for a dis-assembly.

LINKAGE ADJUSTMENT

There are two places where adjustment can occur and both are easily accessible. The semi-spherical plate in the back of the driver's compartment on the floor, between the back seats (you man have wondered what this inspection plate covered), provides access to the adjustment that controls gear lever play in 1st and 2nd. The plate immediately below the shift lever itself controls play in 3rd and 4th.

If there is more free play from engagement of 1st back to engagement of 2nd than there is from 3rd back to 4th, take up the slack at the front plate . . . and vice versa. The throw should be equal, in other words. Check the ball and socket assembly between the shift rod and the hinged shift link to be sure the spaces on either side of the ball are equal when the lever is in neutral. Also, when in neutral the lower part of the shift lever should be vertical.

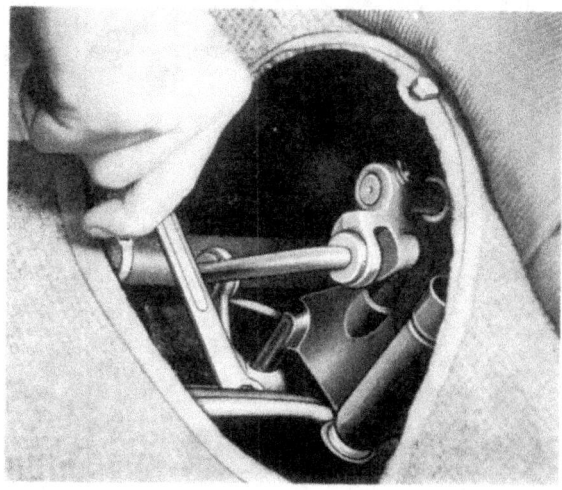

Type 716 Gearbox

The late transmission, designated Type 716, differs from the 644 only in the method used to make it fully syncro-mesh. The new system incorporates an internal expanding "brake" which utilizes the rotational energy of the unit to bring the synchronizing effect to a quicker conclusion — in essence a "servo" mechanism. Consequently the long "whippy" gear change lever could be exchanged for a shorter, stiffer shaft which has often been longed for by Porsche owners. A comparison of the exploded diagrams of the two boxes will reveal the new parts now incorporated in the transmission. A discussion of gearbox repairs is purposely avoided here because it is not a unit that should be opened by an untrained mechanic.

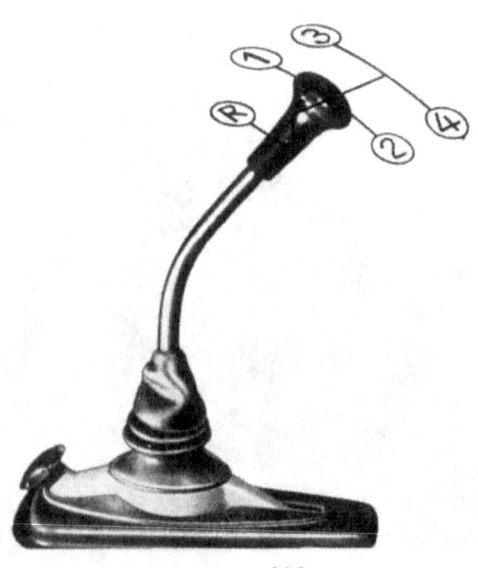

GEAR RATIOS

Unless you happened to be interested in racing, you might never take the trouble to investigate gearing possibilities inherent in the Porsche transmission/differential. The factory has always made available three ratios for each of the four forward gears and, until recently, a choice of ring and pinion ratios as well. The various ratios are designated by letter A, B and C, with the highest numerical difference (the "lowest" gear ratio as we mis-call it) as A, the next B and the "highest" ratio as C. Here is a table of those ratios:

	Driving gear,	Driven gear,	
First Gear set:	# of teeth	# of teeth	Ratio
A	11	35	3.18 to 1
B	11	34	3.09 to 1
C	13	33	2.54 to 1
Second Gear set:			
A	16	31	1.94 to 1
B	17	30	1.76 to 1
C	18	29	1.61 to 1
Third Gear set:			
A	22	27	1.23 to 1
B	23	26	1.13 to 1
C	24	25	1.04 to 1
Fourth Gear set:			
A	25	24	.960 to 1
B	26	23	.885 to 1
C	27	22	.815 to 1

(A recent addition is the "E" 3rd gear ratio. This 20 to 27 set gives a ratio of 1.35 to 1 and is being installed in Carrera GT's for short-track racing with a "C" 3rd in place of 4th.)

The following ring and pinion ratios have been used in different types through the years: 8:35 (4.37 to 1), 7:31 (4.42 to 1), 7:34 (4.85 to 1) and 6:31 (5.18 to 1). At the present time only the 7:31 and 6:31 (Carrera) ratios are available on order from the factory.

Any combination of transmission gears can be had by ordering plenty far in advance, or they can be changed locally by anyone who understands the principles involved in fitting up the Porsche box.

Porsche back axle and synchromesh gearbox unit Type 716

(sectioned drawing)

① Radial sealing ring

② Gearbox front cover

③ Intermediate plate

④ Shock absorber mounting flange with arm on axle tube

⑤ Input shaft

⑥ Output shaft with bevel pinion

⑦ Bleeder screw

⑧ Planet gear

⑨ Crown wheel

⑩ Starter flange

⑪ Axle shaft pinion

⑫ Axle shaft

⑬ Radial clutch bearing

⑭ Coupling lever shaft

⑮ Spider

⑯ Sliding sleeve

⑰ Selector fork

⑱ Locking ring

⑲ Stop

⑳ Brake band segment

㉑ Synchronising ring

㉒ Gear II for 3rd gear with toothed synchromesh drive ring

㉓ Slider

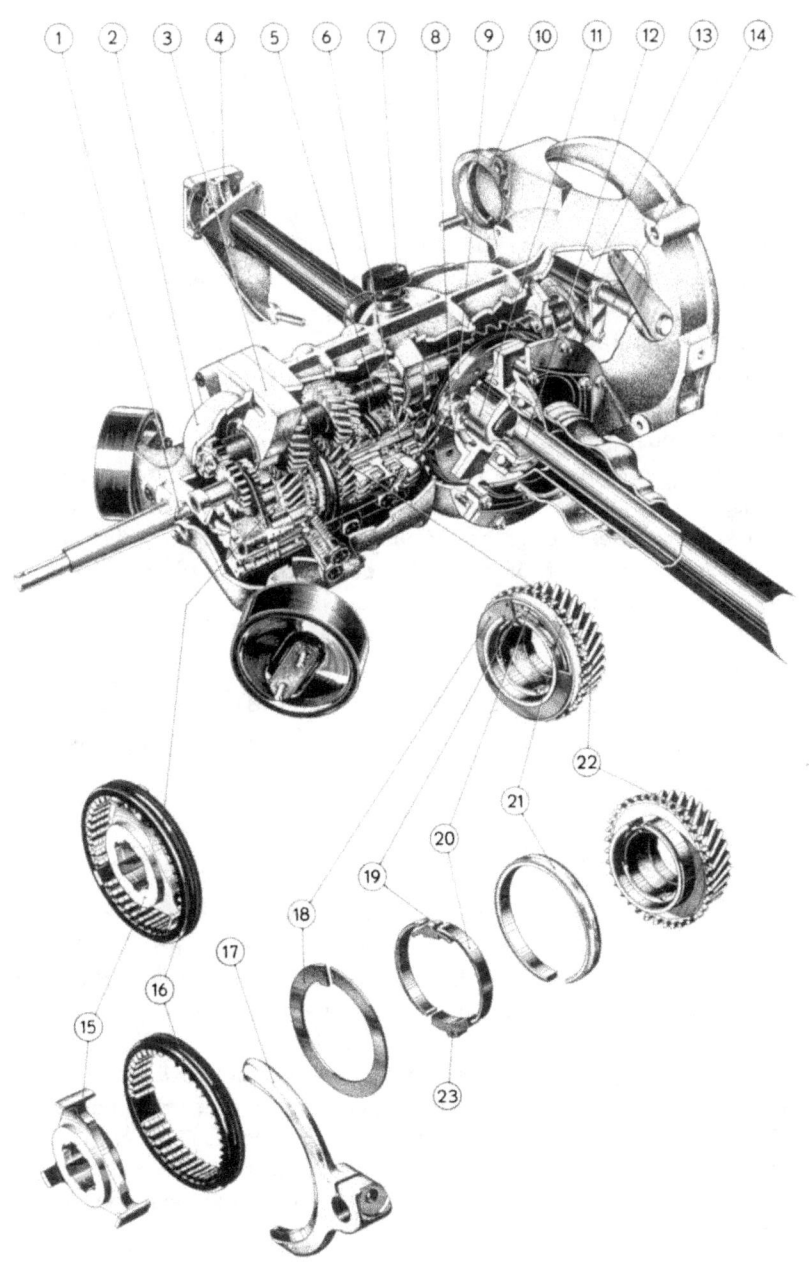

In this case, it is our recommendation that only the factory shop manual, well studied, be used as a guide to any repairs or alterations. For the best selection of ratios, and the reasons for their choice, refer to "More Push" in this book.

How do you know which gears are currently in your car? Generally, coupes and convertibles come with B, B, B, C ratios, Speedsters B, B, A, B (going from first up to fourth). You will find the original factory installation recorded on the left side of the transmission case split in type 519 by stamped letters. The cast letters and numbers are parts numbers. (Of course the gears may have been changed by a previous owner if yours is a used vehicle.) In Type 644, single piece housing, the gearing is stamped on the plate that separates the housing and the rear cover. The numbers refer to month and year of manufacture.

Which ring and pinion depends on the year and type. If you are really curious, jack up one wheel and turn the engine over on the starter with the transmission in 4th (or, after pulling the spark plugs, by hand with the fan nut wrench). Count the revolutions at the pulley needed to accomplish one revolution of the wheel. Here are the number of turns for each possible 4th gear, ring & pinion combination:

Fourth Gear

	Set 8:35	Set 7:31	Set 7:34
Set A: Pulley turns:	4 1/5	4 1/4	4.6
Set B Pulley turns:	3.8	3.9	4 1/4
Set C Pulley turns:	3.53	3.58	3.9

As can easily be seen, there is ample opportunity to mistake a B/7:34 and an A/7:31, or for that matter, the 8:35 and 7:31 almost all the way down the line. If you want to experiment farther, the differences in ratio show up more markedly in the lower gears . . . but most people get tired of cranking.

One revolution of the wheel with only a slight difference at the engine may make the discussion of gearing seem of only theoretical interest. Such is not the case. The choice between a 7:31 and a 7:34 can mean much to the outcome of a race or the owner's personal satisfaction with performance . . . hence a rather extended discussion in another chapter.

Brake Troubles Causes and Remedies

1. **PEDAL TRAVEL TOO GREAT**
   - a) Worn linings
   - b) Worn drums

   - a) Adjust brakes, exchange brake shoes
   - b) Install oversize brake shoes, replace brake drums

2. **SPONGY PEDAL ACTION**
   - a) Air in the system
   - b) Low fluid level

   - a) Bleed brakes
   - b) Refill and bleed

3. **PEDAL FALLS THROUGH WITHOUT ACTION** (after adjustment)
   - a) Fluid leak
   - b) Bad cups in master cylinder or brake cylinders

   - a) Check for leaks
   - b) Replace cups

4. **PEDAL FALLS THROUGH WITHOUT BRAKE ACTION**
   (although system has been bled and adjusted)
   - a) Bad check valve in master cylinder
   - b) Check valve seat dirty

   - a) Replace check valve
   - b) Clean check valve

5. **BRAKE ACTION OBTAINED ONLY AFTER PUMPING PEDAL**
   - a) Air in the system
   - b) Weak piston return spring

   - a) Bleed
   - b) Replace piston return spring

6. **OVERHEATING**
   - a) By-pass port in master cylinder clogged
   - b) Too little clearance between pushrod and master cylinder piston
   - c) Return spring broken
   - d) Rubber parts expanded

   - a) Clean master cylinder, ream port with .7mm wire
   - b) Adjust pedal play so that by-pass port is cleared
   - c) Install new spring
   - d) Drain fluid, remove all rubber parts, flush system install new rubber parts. Check valve and valve seat

7. **POOR BRAKE ACTION**
   - a) Oil or grease on linings
   - b) Worn linings

   - a) Clean brakes with carbon tetrachloride (never gas or solvent)
   - b) Replace shoes

8. **BRAKES ACTIVATE THEMSELVES**
   - a) and b) of Item 6
   - c) Use of improper brake fluid

   - a) and b) or Item 6
   - c) Flush and refill with fluids recommended for Porsche

9. **BRAKES PULL UNEVENLY OR GRAB**
   - a) Drums out of round
   - b) Diameter of drums unequal
   - c) Damaged tires or low pressure

   - a) Have drums trued
   - b) Make sure drums on opposite wheels are equal
   - c) Replace or inflate to correct pressure

10. **BRAKES CHATTER OR LOCK**
    - a) Linings not beveled on ends
    - b) Worn linings
    - c) Drums out of round

    - a) Fit only Porsche factory shoes
    - b) Replace
    - c) True drums

Brakes

The Porsche system is of the conventional hydraulic type with a cable-operated mechanical handbrake linked to the rear wheels. Porsche brakes have a good reputation for efficacy and long life. This is due in part to the generous lining area, 132 sq. in. per ton of car weight (Corvette : 109) and to the bi-metallic drums which dissipate heat readily. Much of the swift action of the brakes can be traced to the effect of weight transfer during deceleration which makes full use of both rear and front brakes. The front wheel cylinders differ from those used at the rear in that there are two single-acting units per wheel. A single double-acting cylinder serves each rear brake.

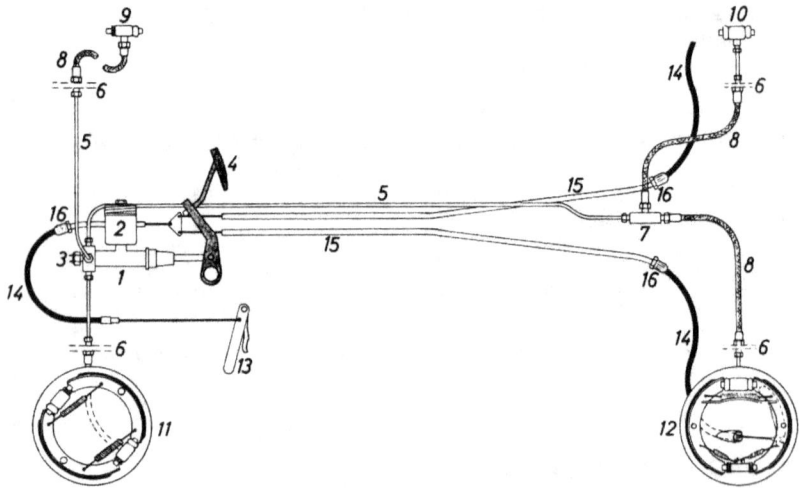

Schematic drawing of brake system

All metal lines are secured to the "frame" or axles and, in general, the possibilities of damage or failure are slight. Most maintenance consists of adjusting brake shoe clearance, topping up fluid and inspecting for leaks. In older cars, of course, repair and replacements will be necessary and for the owner who may be interested in such pastimes, we will give a rather complete run down on brakes.

As can be seen from the accompanying "Trouble Chart" there are one or two critical points in the system that might otherwise escape attention: the master cylinder check valve and the amount of play between the piston and pushrod. So, let us take up the master cylinder first:

To remove this member, take out the spare tire and clear the luggage compartment.

1. Remove inspection plate.
2. Jack up front of car.
3. Unfasten stop light wires from master cylinder.
4. Detach brake lines.
5. Take out floor boards.
6. Loosen pushrod and remove pedal block.
7. Remove pushrod.
8. Remove master cylinder flange nuts and take out cylinder.

Replacement of the unit is a reversal of the steps but always bear in mind that brakes must be bled after any disconnection of lines.

① Cover
② Gasket
③ Vent disc
④ Gasket
⑤ Gland nut and strainer
⑥ Fluid reservoir
⑦ Gasket
⑧ Master cylinder body
⑨ Stop light switch
⑩ Piston stop plate
⑪ Locking ring
⑫ Boot
⑬ Check valve seat
⑭ Check valve
⑮ Piston return spring
⑯ Main piston cup
⑰ Piston washer
⑱ Piston
⑲ Secondary piston cup
⑳ Push rod

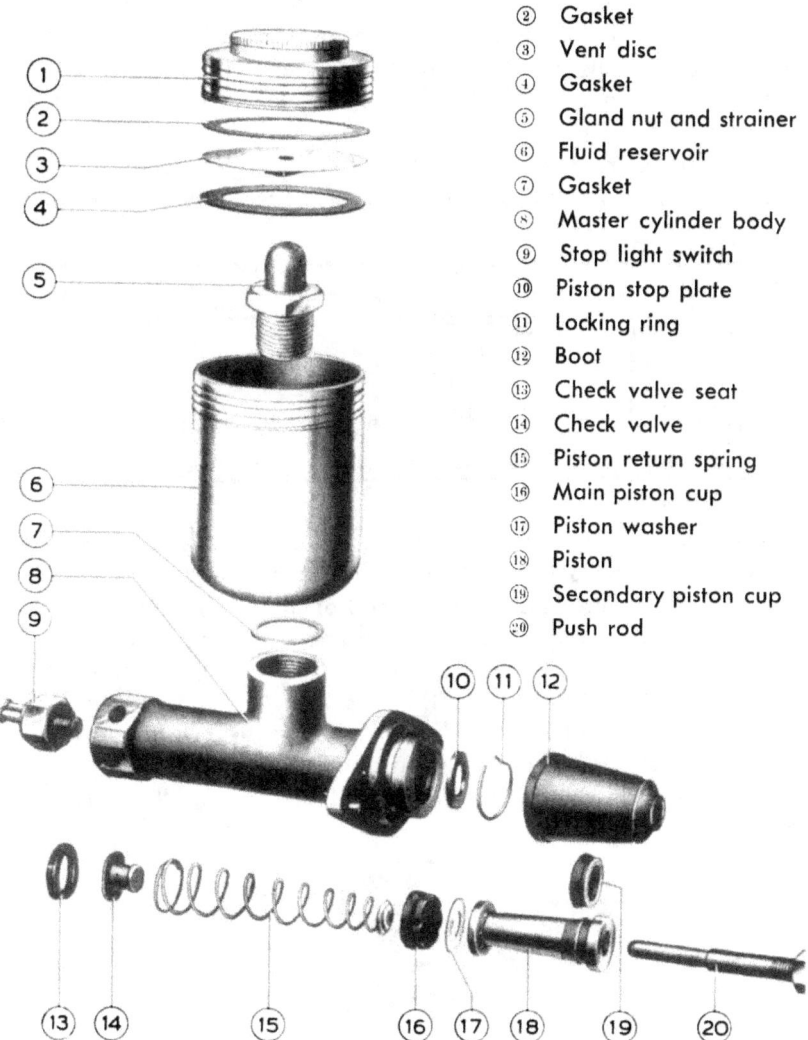

CHECK VALVE

With the cylinder in our hands, let us examine it (scanning the exploded view will serve the purpose). The unit is dis-assembled from the "boot" end. The rubber dust cover comes off if you apply a twisting, pulling force, don't take recourse to the screwdriver here. The snap ring revealed here can be pried out with the screwdriver, however. The pressure of the return spring will cause the parts to come out in sequence. The washer, secondary cup, piston, piston washer, main cup, spring and check valve with seat.

The use of cheap brake fluid, mixing fluids and general deterioration can cause these items to fail to perform correctly. It is a good idea to wash the parts in a high grade of fluid (Lockheed Ate is recommended by the factory, but if unavailable, EIS Super S, Wagner Super Heavy Duty 21 B or Puritan HD can be substituted) using a soft brush if necessary. **Never use gasoline or any petroleum solvent.**

Pay particular notice to the check valve and its seat. The insert should be firm and whole, the seat clean. (Its action is explained in the sketch.)

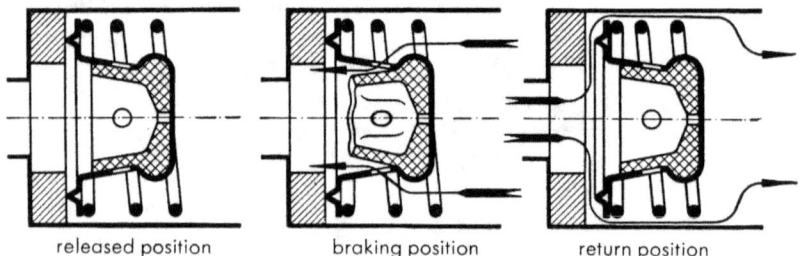

released position   braking position   return position

The reservoir should be cleaned and its gland nut and strainer blown out with compressed air. Removal of the stoplight switch and a check of the passage in the end of the master cylinder is advised if there is any rubber deterioration in cups.

Note: The clearance between pushrod end and master cylinder piston should be 1mm (.04"). This is set by loosening the lock nut on the pushrod and measuring the travel at the nut (pedal at rest against the stop). If there is insufficient clearance the by-pass port will be obstructed, pressure will build up causing the brakes to drag.

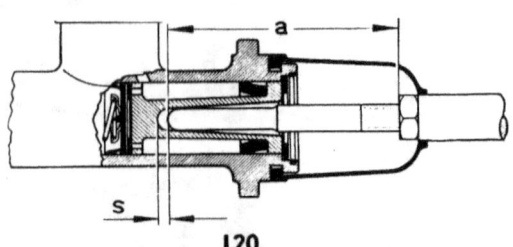

Adjustment for pushrod and lock nut on pedal

BRAKE CYLINDERS

The single-acting front wheel cylinders have one piston and an adjustment screw. The rear wheel cylinders have two pistons and no adjusting screw. Adjustment is made at two adjusting nuts at the bottom of the drum. All cylinders are provided with a bleeder valve protected by a rubber dust cap.

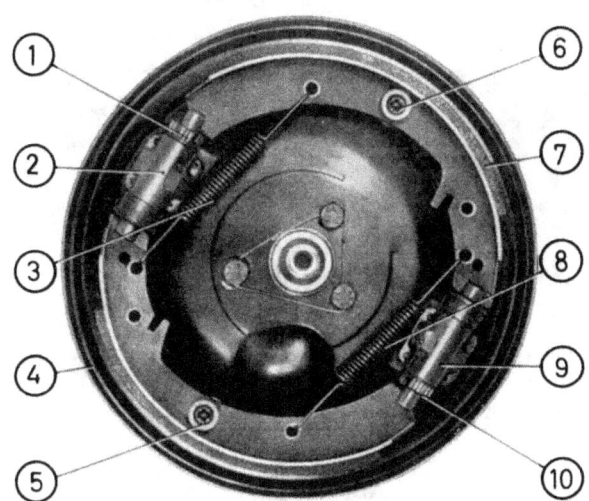

① Brake back plate
② Pressure spring with collar
③ Return spring
④ Lower brake cylinder
⑤ Lower adjusting nut
⑥ Upper adjusting nut
⑦ Upper brake cylinder
⑧ Return spring
⑨ Brake shoe
⑩ Pressure spring with collar

Rear Wheel Brake

- ① Pivot bolt for hand brake activating lever
- ② Brake back plate
- ③ Secondary brake shoe
- ④ Pressure spring with collar
- ⑤ Hand brake cable
- ⑥ Return spring
- ⑦ Adjusting nut
- ⑧ Brake cylinder
- ⑨ Return spring
- ⑩ Pressure rod
- ⑪ Primary brake shoe
- ⑫ Pressure spring with collar
- ⑬ Return spring
- ⑭ Adjusting nut

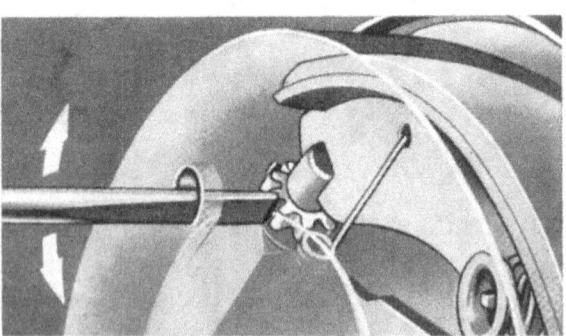

Screwdriver is used to adjust brakes

ADJUSTING

With car jacked up, or on hoist and handbrake loosened:
1. Depress brake pedal several times to seat brake shoes.
2. Rotate wheel until hole in drum is opposite adjusting nut desired. (11 O'clock and 5 O'clock in front wheels, either side of 6 O'clock at rear wheels.)

3. Insert blade of screwdriver and tighten until wheel will not rotate under firm pressure.
4. Back off nut three clicks.
5. Repeat on each wheel with each adjusting nut.

Note: since all nuts are right hand thread, this chart may help avoid confusion. To tighten:

WHEEL	NUT	ROTATE
Right rear	rear	downward
	front	upward
Left rear	rear	upward
	front	downward
Right front	top	downward
	bottom	upward
Left front	top	upward
	bottom	downward

After correct adjustment the wheels should rotate freely, there should be no pull or grabbing. If there is, suspect incorrect adjustment, greasy lining or bad brake shoe.

BLEEDING THE SYSTEM

Air induced into the braking system can cause partial or complete failure of the brakes. To insure that only hydraulic fluid is present in the lines, cylinders and reservoir, air bubbles are forced out by also forcing out sufficient fluid to eliminate them.

Two persons are required, as the factory manual says, to perform this operation; one to depress the brake pedal and the other to open and close the bleeder valves at the wheel cylinders. A short length of rubber tubing to slip over the valve and conduct the fluid to a container is advisable. The container should have a few inches of fluid in the bottom into which the tube can be inserted. When the valve is opened and the pedal depressed the presence of air will be signaled by bubbles rising to the surface of the fluid.

In an emergency, of course, these niceties can be dispensed with and the lines bled until pedal action is firm again. It is important that the reservoir be full (to within ½" or ¾" of the top) and that the vent in the reservoir cap be unobstructed.

Bleeding should commence at the valve farthest from the master cylinder. Follow this sequence: 1) right rear, 2) left rear, 3) right front top, 4) right front bottom, 5) left front top, 6) left front bottom.

Master cylinder is located in front compartment

Brake lines must be bled after disconnecting

BRAKE SHOES AND DRUMS

Porsche linings wear surprisingly well, even under severe abuse as in racing. We refer to the **Frendo** shoes which have been fitted for several years. A recent switch by the factory to another brand indicates, we hope, that still superior product has been discovered. The shoes are not ordinarily re-lineable (to coin a word) and exchange is the rule. Actually there are firms in this country that do this sort of bonding and if you have your heart set on a special lining or grade, it can be had. For all practical purposes, however, the **Frendo** is adequate.

If you pull the wheels and drums to discover that uneven wear, because of maladjustment, has taken place, the shoes can be switched from right to left and turned upside down in order to get some more wear from them.

As a reminder; The castellated nuts on the rear axles should be tightened to 253/267 lb./ft. when replacing wheels and drums.

ADJUSTING HANDBRAKE

After usage the handbrake will often take the full stroke of its ratchet to set the rear shoes sufficiently tight against the drums to prevent movement of the car. To gain some reserve, adjust the brake in this manner. With the rear end of the car jacked up:
1. Remove spare tire and steering gear inspection plate.
2. Screw cable adjusting sleeve until it drags, then back off three turns.
3. Screw out both rear brake cable adjusting sleeves until rear wheel brakes drag.
4. Pull up on hand brake until rear wheels will not turn.
5. Check each wheel for equal resistance and adjust at rear sleeve if necessary.
6. Screw in front adjusting sleeve until wheels are free to turn.

7. Check handbrake. Three teeth on ratchet is average travel required to make wheels immobile, if lever must be pulled farther, adjust at front sleeve.

Inner nut controls adjustment, outer is lock

Front End

The unique Porsche front suspension is derived directly from Dr. Porsche's first "torsion bar" experiments. The torsion bar is not a Porsche invention, but the laminated type, multi-leaf torsion bar is. In Porsche and VW the laminated bars are carried in parallel transverse tubes that form the "axles" proper. Each of the bars is secured in the center while the outer ends are free to twist. Attached to the outer ends and supported by the tubes are trailing

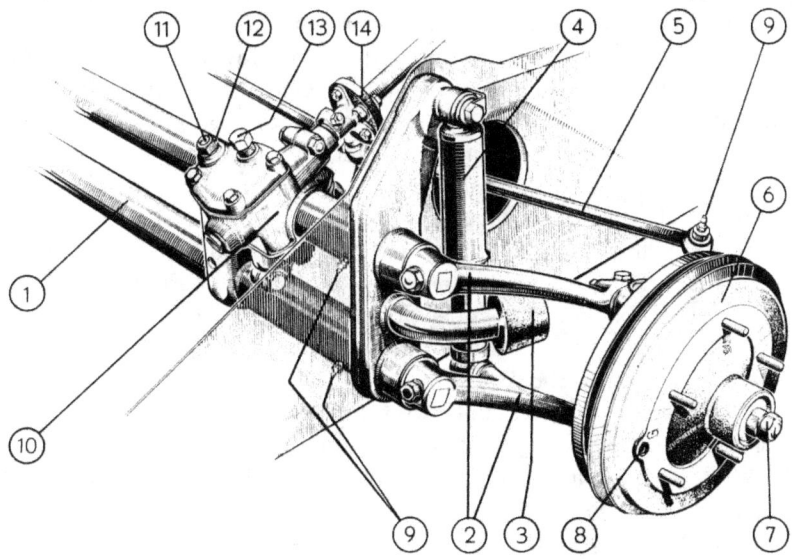

① front axle tubes
② torsion arm
③ rubber buffer
④ telescope shock absorbers
⑤ tie rod
⑥ brake drum
⑦ adjusting nuts for front wheel bearing
⑧ opening for brake adjusting
⑨ grease nipple
⑩ steering gear
⑪ adjusting screw for sector shaft
⑫ hexagon nut for adjusting screw
⑬ screw plug for oil filling port
⑭ coupling disc
⑮ torsion arm link pin
⑯ stub axle (steering knuckle)
⑰ steering arm at stub axle
⑱ suspension arm link for stub axle

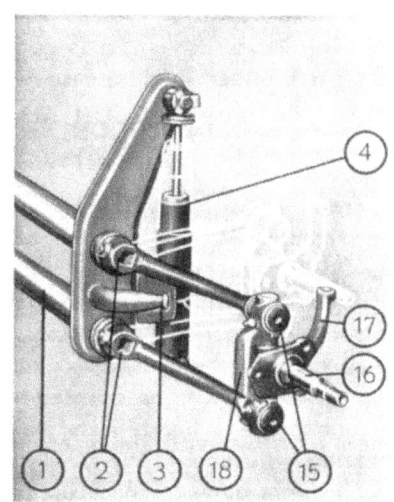

arms, a total of four per car. The upper and lower torsion arms are joined by a "link" which supports a conventional kingpin and stub axle (steering knuckle). A washer fitted between the top end of the stub axle and the link takes the thrust. Vertical hydraulic telescoping shock absorbers damp road shocks and a sturdy rubber-tipped "stop" prevents excessive travel.

As the accompanying drawing shows, there are a number of lubrication points in this unit and complete, regular lubrication is necessary to its operation. Most commonly overlooked nipples are those just inboard the frame members. Regular lubrication should take place every 3,000 miles (after break-in) but if the car is either subjected to excessive use, competition or travel on rough roads or is not driven an average amount (say less than 500 miles per month) it might be a good idea to check these lube points more frequently. The factory recommends every 1250 km (800 mi.). Once a month would be probably be ideal.

The Works lists the following inspections as part of maintenance to maintain the riding qualities and safety standards of the car:
1. Inspection and adjustment of front wheel bearings.
2. Inspection and adjustment of torsion arm link pins.
3. Inspection and adjustment of toe in.
4. Inspection of shock absorbers.
5. Inspection of wheel bolts for tightness.
6. Inspection and verification of tire pressure.

We will cover the first three items here, the rest will be found under appropriate headings.

Note: When greasing the front torsion bars and linkage, it is mandatory that the car be jacked up and the wheels not in tension. In other words, a grease job on the conventional service station rack that the car is driven on is not desirable as a regular thing. With the parts under load, grease will not penetrate bearing surfaces.

INSPECTION AND ADJUSTMENT OF FRONT WHEEL BEARINGS

Front wheel bearings have been troublesome on certain models and completely trouble free on others suggesting that supplier's quality control may be at fault. Another explanation has been offered relating to the fact that the long sea voyage could play havoc with bearings if the car were lashed down to immovability. Regardless of the cause there may be some reason to replace bearings and this will be covered later. During the lifetime of a car in one owner's hands it is almost certain to require front wheel bearing adjustment. The yearly inspection and re-packing offers a good opportunity to check up on bearing wear. Here are the steps:
1. Take off grease cap and remove all grease.

2. Check bearing play by rocking the drum with both hands.
3. Insert a screwdriver between the outer bearing thrust washer and the hub. It should be free enough to move easily.

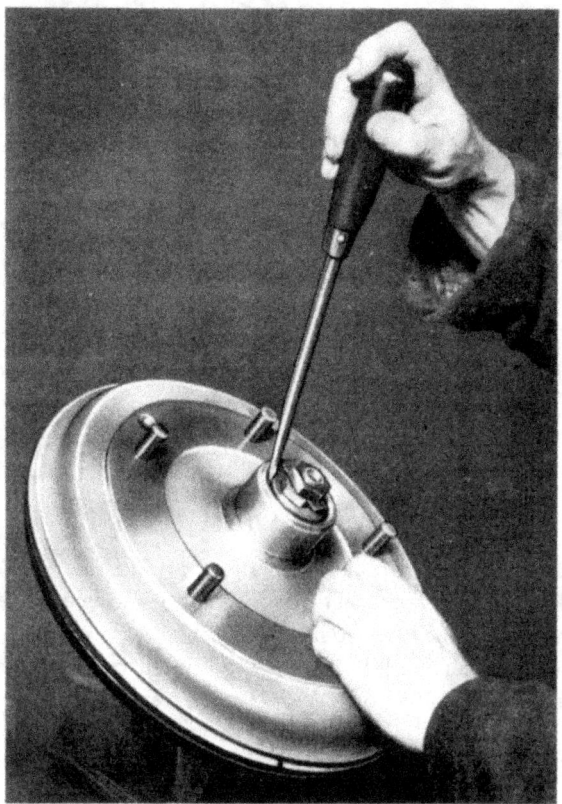

If there is any play when the drum is rocked take it out in this fashion:
1. Break noses of lock plate on stub axle nuts.
2. Loosen nuts with two end wrenches.
3. Replace lock plate.
4. Tighten inner nut until thrust washer can just be moved with the screwdriver and no play can be felt when rocking the drum. Tighten outer nut carefully so that inner nut is not disturbed. It is wise to tighten the outer nut as you go.
5. Bend noses on lock plate.
6. Fill grease cap, replace dust seal.

When your car is jacked up for a brake adjustment or for any other reason, spin the front wheels and listen carefully for any scraping or dragging noises that might be attributed to wheel bearing wear or dryness. Until recently Porsches used ball bearings but

in 1959 they began coming through with roller bearings. The ball bearings are directly replacable with roller type and the following procedure can be applied to their installation.

> Caution: **Always replace bearings in sets and use new seals, lock rings, etc.**

REPLACING FRONT WHEEL BEARINGS

1. Remove wheel & brake drum (take off dust cap, grease cap, break noses on lock plates, loosen & remove stub axle nuts. A wheel puller is not usually needed).
2. Pull off spacer and inner race of inner bearing (use screwdriver to tap lightly or VW 202 puller and adaptor) from stub axle. (The outer bearing and inner race usually stay with the hub, but . . . watch for them and do not let them fall should they be loose.)
3. Remove the bearing grease seal from the hub by pushing from the underside with a piece of wood or screwdriver handle. This frees the big bearing.
4. Tap the outer bearing out by repeated **gentle** blows on the handle of a big screwdriver as you move the blade around the outer perimeter. If it is too firm, take it to a VW garage that has the proper press.

Inspect the bearings for wear, dryness or other imperfections to determine the cause of failure.

Replacing is done as a reversal of the above process being careful to press the bearings into the hub in a flat plane and avoid wedging. Tapping them gently into place is a substitute for the VW press mentioned above. In fact it may be better since VW mechanics are used to more of a "force fit". A Porsche specialist may or may not have the press. VW 244 (sleeve) is the proper tool to drive the bearing with.

Bearing adjustment is finalized as outlined under "Adjustment". If it is desired to replace ball bearings with the longer-lived roller type, VW part numbers are: Outer bearing (19.9 mm ID) 111-405-647, Inner bearing (25 mm ID) 111-405-627. An extractor ring VW 111-504-649, is used with roller bearings. It fits between the drum grease seal and the inner roller bearing.

Seating A for inner bearing 25 h 6 —
0.9842 ins. diam. (25.000 mm dia.)
0.9837 ins. diam. (24.987 mm dia.)

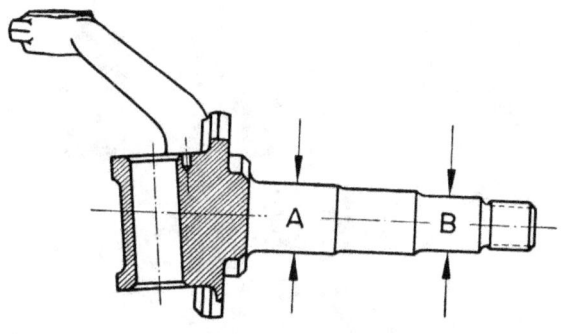

Seating B for outer bearing 20 g 5 =
0.7871 ins. diam. (19.993 mm dia.)
0.7868 ins. diam. (19.984 mm dia.)

Note: When replacing bearings, be sure that each bearing is fully lubricated with high viscosity grease.

Should emergency repairs be necessary and no VW replacement parts at hand, Timken roller bearings can be substituted by shimming the inner bearing (Timken Cup #07204, Cone #07079) with two .317 flat washers, 1" I.D., I.S." O.D. The outer bearing is Timken Cone #17089, Cup #17244.

INSPECTION AND ADJUSTMENT OF TORSION ARM LINK PINS

The link pins should be checked every 3,000 miles according to the manual but few of us manage to do it. Certainly every 6,000 miles, or when the tires are rotated, the brakes adjusted or any other prolonged inspection period is planned, these vital points should be examined. With the car on the jack or hoist, rock the assembly by grabbing the wheels (one hand on top, one on the bottom) and wobbling them, as to check for bearing play. If bearings are tight and there is looseness in the assembly, loosen the pinch bolts at torsion arm eyes Tighten the link pins until there is no play but there is still free movement between the torsion arms and links. First tighten the pins fully, then back off ⅛ turn. Finally re-tighten until the first resistance is felt. If no correct adjustment can be made the shims are worn and need replacing. Replacing shims is an undertaking properly left to a well equipped garage accustomed to Porsche-VW service.

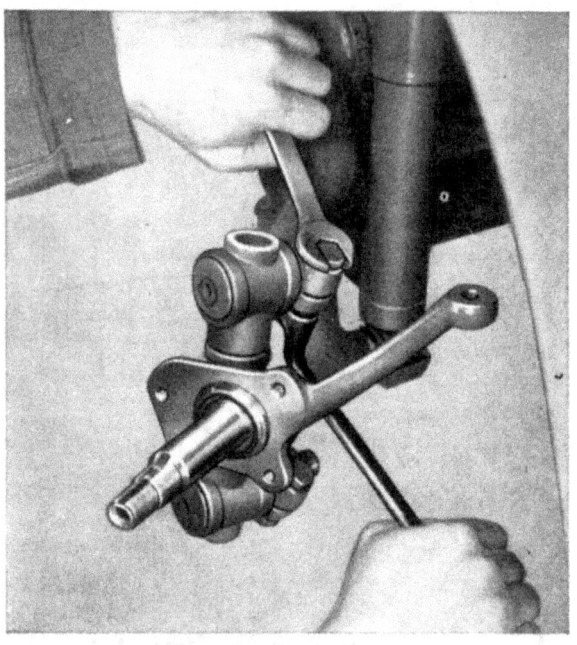

Caution: It is absolutely necessary to check toe-in after adjusting the link pins.

Replacing king pins, bushings, etc. are chores that require a number of special tools beyond the reach of the home craftsman and are well left to the expert. Toe in, on the other hand, can be measured easily, if you pay careful attention. The correct amount of toe in is 2mm to 3mm . . . this is about 1/16" in American . . . at the center of the tread. To review: The distance between the centers of the tread at the front of the tires should be 1/16" less than the distance between the centers of the tread at the back of the tires.

Steering Troubles, Causes & Remedies

1. **HARD STEERING** (Steering is equally stiff from lock to lock and wheels do not automatically resume straight ahead position after completing a turn.)
   - a) Front axle inadequately lubricated
   - b) King pins stiff or seized

   - c) Maladjusted steering gear

   - a) Jack up front end of car and thoroughly lubricate front axle
   - b) Jack up car and disconnect tie rods. Try to make king pins free by lubrication, with thin oil if necessary. If seized, replace with new parts
   - c) Check steering gear adjustment. Adjust sector shaft and worm shaft end play as prescribed. Check oil level. Replace unit if defective.

2. **HARD STEERING AND SQUEAKING**
   - a) Steering column top bushing binding steering wheel

   - b) Steering wheel hub chafing on column bushing face

   - a) Check position of steering column. If necessary, correct position of steering gear. Check toe-in. Inspect steering top bushing, lubricate or replace
   - b) Bushing projects too far from steering column tube or tube too high. Lower tube

3. **HARD STEERING, UNEQUAL RESISTANCE & CHAFING NOISE**
   - a) Steering column fouling tube
   - a) Alter position of column in tube so that it is centered. Check toe-in

4. **FRONT WHEELS DO NOT RESUME STRAIGHT AHEAD POSITION AFTER TURN ALTHOUGH THERE IS NO BINDING**
   - a) Front wheels improperly aligned
   - b) Steering knuckles bent

   - a) Check alignment—caster, camber, toe-in
   - b) Remove stub axles (knuckles) and check for straightness

5. **EXCESSIVE CLEARANCE BETWEEN STEERING WHEEL & COLUMN**
   - a) Worn bushing
   - a) Replace bushing

6. **EXCESSIVE PLAY IN STEERING GEAR**
   - a) Steering gear improperly adjusted
   - b) Steering set worn

   - a) Adjust sector shaft and worm shaft end play
   - b) Replace sector, sector shaft and worm

7. **EXCESSIVE PLAY IN TIE ROD JOINTS**
   - a) Ball studs worn
   - a) Replace ball studs

8. **EXCESSIVE PLAY IN FRONT WHEEL SUSPENSION**
   - a) Worn bearing points (torsion arms, torsion arm links, axle stubs and front wheel bearings)
   - a) Check adjustments of torsion arm link pins, and front wheel bearings. Replace worn parts

Porsche Steering Gear

Most steering troubles can be traced to improper maintenance inasmuch as the older Porsche steering gearbox is one of the most thoroughly broken in and tested parts on the car. (The gears were operated by a "rotating machine" at the factory with a flowing supply of cutting oil until they became as smooth as a greased door knob.) After being installed in the car and under load, they are checked for play and adjusted. This guarantees a first rate piece of equipment. The newer (bronze) worm and sector and Ross types do not receive this break-in but a few hundred miles mates the parts adequately.

One of the common hazards is too low an oil level caused by a worn or faulty sector shaft oil seal, a loose filler plug or, rarely, a bad cover gasket. Check the oil every 3,000 miles and top up with SAE 80 Transmission oil. Fill to bottom of threaded plug hole.

Before suspecting the box itself, if hard steering is encountered and oil level has been adequate, check other elements of the front end and steering assembly. As noted on the chart, the top bushing and column clearance is a great offender. Dry kingpins and other lube points which may have escaped attention are often at fault. If adjustment is bad (and this sometimes happens when the car has been in the hands of an unknowing mechanic) this is the adjustment procedure:

STEERING ADJUSTMENT

1. Loosen locknut and sector shaft adjusting screw.
2. Loosen adjusting sleeve clamping screw and tighten adjust-

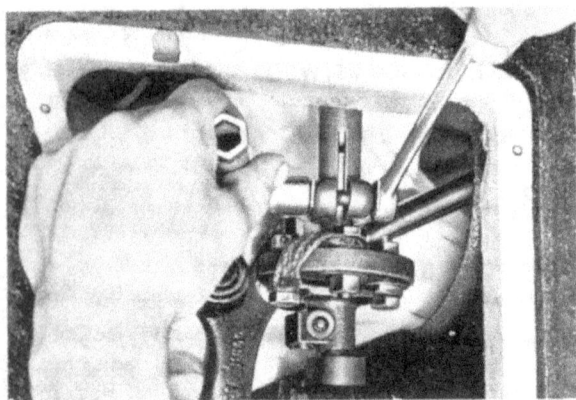

Access to steering column clamp is through inspection plate in front compartment

ing sleeve clockwise until worm shaft end play is taken up. Do not over-tighten, to do so will damage thrust bearings.
3. Tighten adjusting sleeve clamping screw.
4. Bring sector shaft arm to right angle with steering worm. Tighten adjusting screw as far as it will go. Back off ⅛ turn.
5. Hold adjusting screw and tighten locknut.

If the steering is still hard in spite of above adjustments, there is something wrong with the box and it should be dissembled and checked for wear or foreign matter.

The factory advises that steering play should be kept to a minimum (without making the steering hard) to prevent excess wear on the components. The steering should not bind at either end of the full lock position and wheels should return to a straight-ahead position after making a turn. Maximum allowable backlash between worm and sector is given as .008" which can hardly be felt at the shaft. The sector shaft adjusting screw regulates both end play of the shaft and backlash.

REMOVING STEERING BOX

If it is necessary to remove the box from the car, follow these steps:
1. Jack up car and remove left front wheel.
2. Press out ball studs at pitman arm.
3. Open front hood and loosen cover of steering box.
4. Remove clamping screw at steering column.
5. Remove spring clip at horn contact and pull out brush holder and brush.
6. Withdraw steering column from coupling.
7. Loosen screw on pitman arm after opening lock plate and remove pitman arm.
8. Remove mounting clamp.
9. Remove steering gear from front axle tubes.

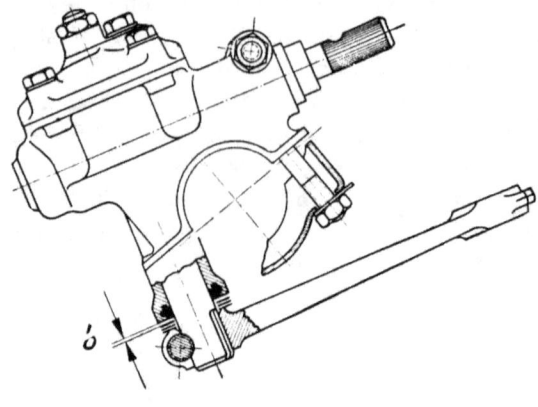

b = 0,4—1,0 mm

STEERING GEAR INSTALLATION

When replacing the steering gear, pay attention to the following points:
1. Check seating of pitman arm on the sector shaft. Clearance between the arm and the steering gear case should be within .016". Use shims if necessary to attain this clearance.
2. Install box so that the distance from the center of the filler plug to the center of the front axle tubes is 10½" (265 mm) and the steering shaft is at a steep an angle as possible. Do not let the shaft or column bind on the steering column tube.
3. Use new lockplates when re-installing.
4. Check oil level.
5. Check toe-in—The factory insists that whenever the steering gear has been removed, or its position changed toe-in must be checked. This is sound advice on any car but particularly on the Porsche where toe-in is such a function of good handling.

STEERING TOP BUSHING

To get at this piece, pop the horn button out by pushing a couple of short lengths of stiff wire or welding rod up through the two small holes in the steering wheel hub. Remove the steering wheel nut and the wheel. Maximum permissible clearance between wheel and top bushing is .03". It should be dabbed with universal grease. If a new bushing is required press it into the column so that it extends .04" from the steering column tube.

Wheel retaining nut is beneath horn button

ZF Steering Gear

The ZF "single peg" gearbox now employed on Porsche models has a different feel than older type. In straightahead (neutral) position there is no play and all adjustments are made when the wheel is at this "pressure point". On the road in a turn there is play but it is compensated for by the front wheel caster which forces the peg against the taper of the worm. Turned away from center while stationary, the steering wheel will exhibit a certain amount of play. The Gearbox should be topped up with 90 wt. SAE hypoid gear oil.

Its capacity is about ½ pint. Adjustment is made to the worm gear to compensate for end wear by fitting shims behind the end plate. It is not advisable to disassemble these boxes since factory-rebuilt replacements are rather readily available.

In case of accident damage it may be necessary to remove the steering gear, in which case this procedure may be followed:
1. Jack up car and take off left front wheel.
2. Press out track rod ends from drop arm.
3. Disconnect steering damper.
4. Open front hood and take off steering gear cover.
5. Remove spring clips, take brushes and holder out of horn contact.
6. Set front wheels to full right lock.
7. Take steering column off upper peg of flex coupling.
8. Bend back safety plates and remove nuts on mounting clamp.
9. Remove steering gearbox to the front.

Steering Gearbox

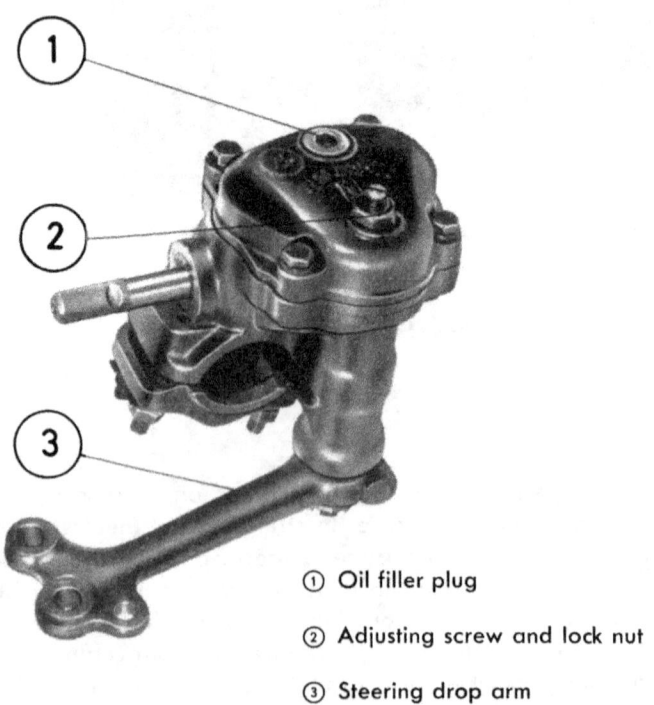

① Oil filler plug

② Adjusting screw and lock nut

③ Steering drop arm

Rear Suspension

The suspension of the independent rear axles of the Porsche is basically like that of the front except that one laminated torsion bar is used on each side and the positioning of the hubs is by a single trailing arm per side. Damping action is provided by the same type of tubular shock absorbers as used on the front.

The basic difference is that adjustments can be made (on all models) to the torsion bar trailing arm relationship to control camber. The bar is splined on both ends. The number of teeth in the splines on the chassis end of the bar indicates that they are 9° apart while the trailing arm end has enough more serrations to constitute 8°10'. Thus, by turning the inner spline upward (let us say) and the trailing arm downward, we can split a degree and get pretty close to the setting desired.

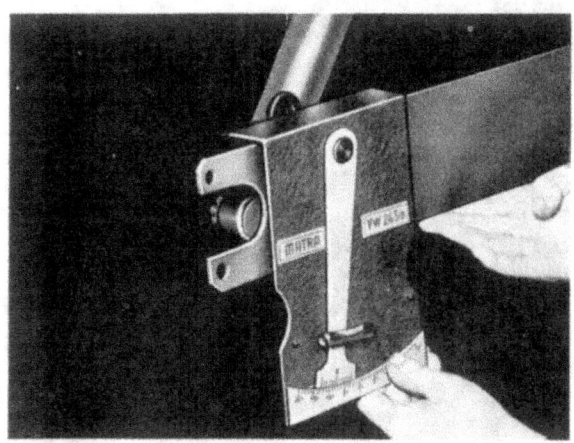

Normal setting of the torsion bars induces a 6°30' to 7° slant in the trailing arm when measured with a special tool (see illustration). You could fabricate one yourself from a good sized protractor and a carpenter's level if so inclined. However, most owners accept the fact that the normal setting is about 1°30' too high and "decamber" the rear wheels accordingly. The improvement in handling and steering which results is reward enough . . . or expense, if it is done at a Porsche or VW service agency.

The "improvement" referred to is an increased steadiness on the road at high speed and less pronounced oversteer in corners.

(Incidentally, these remarks do not apply to the new B series which have different characteristics.)

To accomplish this re-setting at the home workshop, this procedure can be followed:

1. Jack up rear end of car and set it on blocks.

2. Remove rear wheels.
3. Unbolt trailing arm from rear axle hubs.
4. Loosen brake line bracket on axles (it may be necessary to remove flex line in some instances—if so, be sure to bleed brakes later).
5. Push axles rearward to avoid interference with trailing arm.

ON THE DRIVER'S SIDE

6. Remove trailing arm hub cover.
7. Mark the relative positions of the trailing arm and torsion bar.
8. Pull the trailing arm off the torsion bar.
9. Pull the torsion bar just free from the inner splines—carefully!
10. Rotate the torsion bar two notches **counterclockwise** and replace firmly in splines.
11. Rotate the trailing arm two notches **clockwise** from the original setting.
12. Replace hub cover and refit in reverse order as above.

ON THE PASSENGER SIDE

6 through 9 above
10. Rotate the torsion bar two notches **clockwise** and replace.
11. Rotate the trailing arm two notches **counterclockwise** and replace.
12. As above.

The net effect here is of lowering the rear end 1°40'. If this is too much to suit you (and it may be marked by a slight increase in steering pressure required) try a 50' lowering by rotating each of the elements only one notch. Many drivers are so camber conscious that they split the degree to an exact 1°30' on the passenger side and 1°40' (or whatever figure they arrive at by trial) on the driver's side, when only the driver is to be in the car . . . as in racing. (To get 1°30', for instance, turn the torsion bar 8 notches up and the trailing arm 9 notches down.) If you are a heavyweight, having a little more camber on your side is advisable.

When replacing the bolts at the trailing arm-axle junction, it is a good idea to clean the contact surfaces of the trailing arm and the hub. Remove rust, paint, etc. Tighten nuts to 6 or 7 lb./ft. torque.

Another aside: some Porsches we have seen, fresh from the factory, have no grease on the torsion splines, others do. All have a coating of grease on the bar itself. The workshop manual says "grease the splines" when replacing the bar. A light coating of oil to prevent rust is certainly advisable.

Shock Absorbers

The rear shocks are identical to those in the bow . . . but, they are the most likely to fail. Really, the fact is that you are more apt to notice that they are bad first. The additional weight on the rear end and the change in camber on rebound will call defective action to your attention. A bouncy fore and aft motion on moderately rough roads, excessive bottoming and poor handling are symptoms.

Porsche shocks are of the non-fillable type and must be replaced when faulty. A standard test is to bounce the car by pushing down hard on a fender and releasing it. Do this in rhythm a couple of times to get a good stroke going then after the last hefty shove watch to see if the car does more than return to normal level. It it rises above and settles back, the shock is not performing correctly. Removing the shocks and compressing them by hand is not accurate.

Hard driving and heat combine to lessen the efficiency of shock absorbers and a shock that may be only "dubious" if you test it with the car cold in the garage will be dangerously weak after some **sturm and drang**.

Installing new units involves only jacking up the car so that tension is removed from the shocks, removing the cotter pins and nuts at the rear, the lock plates and nuts at the front. You may have to pry with a long handled screwdriver, particularly if the

car is a little old, to separate the rubber bushings from the bolts. A small amount of glycerine or rubber dressing squirted on these bushings from time to time will help prevent rubber deterioration—especially since some shocks have natural rubber grommets. Tighten the nuts firmly when replacing them to prevent rattling and excess bushing wear.

The Dutch **Koni** shocks of the adjustable type are preferred by many Porsche owners as replacements, particularly on the rear. These, too are progressive in action and are highly resistant to "fade" engendered by heat. Three settings, soft, medium and hard can be achieved in a few minutes with the shocks installed. "Soft" relates to the normal Porsche shock action.

Koni Shock Absorbers

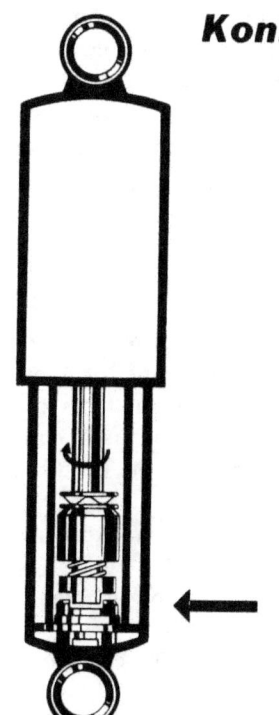

ADJUSTING KONI SHOCK ABSORBERS

The factory setting, as noted above, is at "soft". Owners of cars so equipped may want to alter the action. With the car on a hoist, remove the lower mount nuts and free the shocks from tension. Push up on the bottom segment (compressing the shock) until the plunger touches the adjusting valve notch, turn clockwise until you feel the parts engage then turn ½ turn counterclockwise for the "medium" setting. If you remove the units and perform this operation in a vise you will probably be twisting the top half of the shock. In which case the motion toward harder is **clockwise**.

Heater and Exhaust System

The transverse muffler under the Porsche's tail is subject to the same acidic disintegration and salt-on-the-highway damage that curses more conventional installations and a periodic check here is advised. In addition to normal hazards, the heater system which uses air warmed by the forward portion of the mainfolding can draw in fumes dangerous to the occupants of the car.

MUFFLER REMOVAL & REFIT

With the engine in the car:
1. Remove rear cover plate.
2. Loosen exhaust pipe clips.
3. Remove flange nuts.
4. Pull rearward, Tapping with wooden or rubber hammer.

To replace; reverse procedure above being careful to align front flanges properly. Use new gaskets if in doubt. Make sure that all joints are tight. Older models have welded junction boxes (heat exchanger) examine these welds. The rear exhaust connection can also be a source of fumes, make sure it is solid.

Porsche Special Tools

Many VW and Porsche special tools are mentioned in this volume in connection with certain shop operations. While some of these items are not necessary, American or other conventional tools can be substituted, others are peculiar to these engines or chassis components and the enthusiast may want to have them in his kit. Here are a few of the more important ones:

- P 5 15mm Hex socket for tightening cap nuts on crankcase.
- P 8 Piston ring compressor.
- P 23 Special 12mm end wrench for carburetor/manifold flange nuts.
- P 24 Special 14mm end wrench as above for 1600S carburetor flange nuts.
- P 42 Torque wrench.
- P 44 Special Hex socket for hollow bolt on flywheel.
- P 75 Carburetor Synchronizing Unit (Unisyn).
- P 76 5mm offset wrench for adjusting pump linkage (32 NDIX).
- P 77 Fuel Level Measuring Glass for checking float level with carburetor cover in place.

What To Do Till The Doctor Comes

Doing this chapter was one of those things that was put off until the last possible minute because it involves so much conjecture and going over the same malfunctions time and again. There are only so many things that can happen to an engine to keep it from operating properly and it is easy to take for granted the fact that the person of average mechanical ability knows how to check the basics. On the other hand there are bound to be readers with just as much intelligence that simply don't know where to begin. Frankly, writing this section was about like that. Where do you begin and how do you present the material? Then, behold we were saved! Through the kindness of Charles Beidler, editor of **Porsche Panorama**, we received a set of back issues of the magazine. This fine publication has always been stuffed with good things for the Porsche owner and the greatest, as far as we are concerned (with the above topic staring us in the face) is to be found on pages 10-11 of the March, 1959 issue under the heading "The Differential Diagnosis of Engine Complaints."

With due thanks, then, and an added reminder to each reader-owner that he should be a member of the PCA, we list the Symptoms and the possible Troubles as compiled by "Old Doc".

SYMPTOM	TROUBLE #
Hard to start, cold	1, 2, 3, 4, 5, 6, 7, 8, 9, 10, 11, 12, 16
Hard to start, hot	Same as above, add 19
Idles roughly	1, 4, 5, 6, 10, 12, 13, 15, 20, 21, 39
Stalls easily	1, 2, 3, 5, 10, 15, 17, 19, 39
Loss of power, acceleration	Same as above
Engine rough on deceleration	13, 15
Misfiring at high speed or on acceleration	1, 2, 3, 4, 5, 10, 12
Overheating	6, 17, 20, 21, 25, 38, 43, 47
Backfiring on acceleration	6, 13, 14, 17, 22
Backfiring on deceleration	6, 17, 41
Rapid, incessant clicking especially at mid range	22, 23, 24, 26, 27, 28
Metallic pinging, detonation under load, especially when hot	5, 6, 22, 25, 46
Heavy thumping at low speed especially when under load	29, 36
Knocking as car picks up speed	30

SYMPTOM	TROUBLE #
Double knock at idling	31
Hollow knocking when engine is cold	32
Whining sound heard when revving up	37
Rhythmic chugging or clicking during acceleration	41
Hissing	40
Excessive smoke from oil filler tube and valve covers	33
Excessive wet oil on top and under crankcase	18, 34, 35
Oil pressure low	9, 29, 42, 44, 45
Oil pressure high	43

TROUBLE

1. Burned, dirty or pitted ignition points.
2. Faulty, leaking condenser.
3. Weak or broken coil.
4. Broken, shorted wiring or loose connections.
5. Fouled spark plugs, broken insulator.
6. Ignition timing improperly adjusted.
7. Weak or dead battery.
8. Faulty generator, regulator, relay sticking.
9. Faulty or wrongly registering green light.
10. Faulty fuel pump.
11. Dirt or water in fuel lines.
12. Dirty carburetor, clogged fuel and air passages.
13. Improperly adjusted carburetor, wrong jets.
14. Faulty carburetor accelerator pump.
15. Improper float level.
16. Choke sticking open or closed.
17. Improper fuel mixture.
18. Loose fittings, leaky connections.
19. Vapor lock, fuel in pump, lines or carbs vaporizing from heat.
20. Low compression.
21. Improper valve timing.
22. Burned, pitted or sticking valves.
23. Worn valve stems and/or guides.
24. Excessive valve clearance.
25. Excessive carbon formation in cylinder heads.
26. Worn cam followers.

27. Worn camshaft lobes.
28. Worn rocker arms.
29. Worn main bearings, excessive clearance.
30. Worn rod bearings.
31. Loose wrist pins.
32. Piston slap: worn cylinder walls/pistons.
33. Blow by: worn piston rings/cylinders.
34. Leaky oil cooler or gaskets.
35. Worn rear bearings or leaky seal.
36. Loose flywheel.
37. Worn generator brushes.
38. Malfunctioning fanbelt or fan.
39. Leaky intake manifolds.
40. Leaky rubber sleeve on carburetor balance tube.
41. Leaky exhaust manifold.
42. Low oil level.
43. Sticky oil pressure relief piston.
44. Diluted oil, improper grade of oil.
45. Faulty fuel pump.
46. Fuel octane rating too low.
47. Malfunctioning oil cooler, circulation impaired.

Porsche Club of America

The PCA was founded in 1955 by a small group of enthusiasts in the Washington D.C. area and has grown to a national membership of more than 1500 in 46 states. Local clubs conduct rallies, gymkhanas and other events plus social gatherings. The national club publication **Porsche Panorama** keeps members informed on activities as well as dispensing technical information and hints. Each year the club has a four-day gathering which features visits by factory personnel to discuss the car. Club members are also elegible for a special annual European trip to the factory when a mass delivery of new cars is made.

Any owner, or co-owner (over 18 years old), of a Porsche can become a member of the PCA. Annual dues are $12.00. Contact: Porsche Club of America, 1542 Mt. Eagle Place, Alexandria, Virginia.

Maintenance Plan

Breaking in period			Maintenance	Every
300 m. 500 km	1500 m. 2500 km	3000 m. 5000 km		
░			Clean air filter	
			Check fan belt tension	
	░		Clean fuel system, check carburetor adjustment	
			Check contact breaker points and ignition timing	
			Check valve clearance	
			Check compression	3000 miles (5000 km)
			Check spark plugs	
			Check battery	
			Check generator, cables and connections of electrical system	
			Check front wheel bearings, torsion arm link pin, steering, and toe-in	
			Check tire pressure, check wheel nuts for proper fit	
			Check foot and parking brake, check all tube- and hose connections for leaks, check brake oil level	
			Check shock absorbers for proper fit and effectiveness	
			Check clutch clearance	
		░	Check rear axle and engine for leaks	
			Exhaust, intake manifold, carburetor, fuel pump, engine, transmission front and rear axle, steering } check screws and nuts for tightness	6000 miles (10000 km)
			Remove brake drums and inspect brake linings	

148

Maintenance

This section will be devoted to general maintenance hints as passed along from a wide assortment of Porsche owners in all parts of the country. It is not particularly segregated since most of us can benefit from perusing the whole chapter.

PROPER V BELT TENSION. This is important not only for belt life but because generator bearing life also depends on it. Fierce acceleration and down shifting tend to induce slippage with consequent overheating and wear if the belt is too loose, bearing damage and belt breakage results if it is too tight. Proper tension is being employed if the belt can be deflected ¾" (2cm) by pressing with the thumb at a point halfway between the two pulleys.

ADJUSTING THE V BELT. New belts tend to stretch after a short period of use. Between 50 and 100 miles after first driving the car, check tension and adjust. Check at 1,000 mile intervals thereafter. To change tension: Remove outer pulley half (at generator) using a screwdriver and 1⅜" wrench as described in Engine Dissassembly section (BLOWER HOUSING). Remove spacers as needed to increase tension, replacing them between the outer pulley half and the nut. There are two thicknesses of spacers. Two 1mm (3/64") and eight 2mm (5/64") and various combinations will assure correct tension. Take care that the belt does not ride on the spacers but on the pulley flanges. If removal of all but one of the spacers is necessary to restore tension, the belt has stretched too much and should

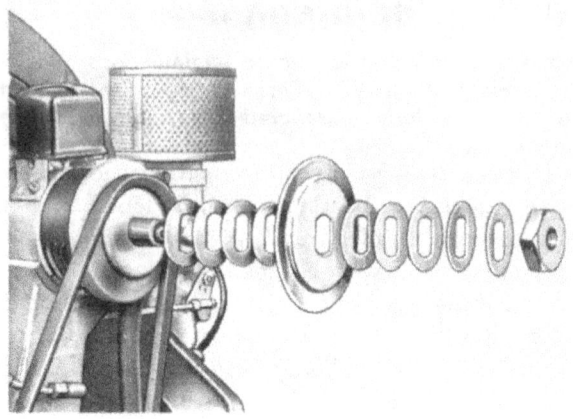

be replaced. Under no circumstances should the belt be forced over the outer rim of the pulley by screwdriver or other means. Tighten shaft nut carefully to 72 lb./ft. with a torque wrench.

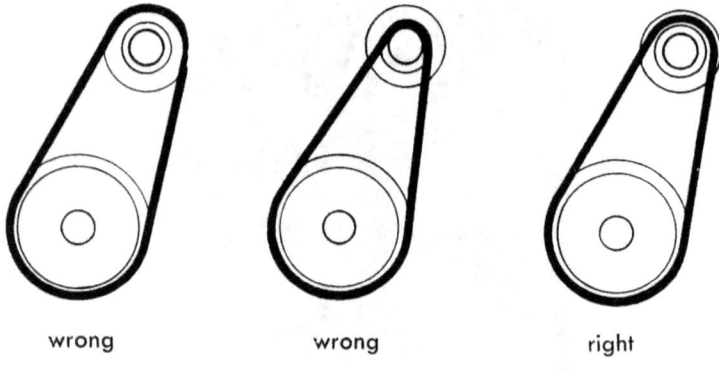

wrong   wrong   right

OIL STRAINER. This trap should be periodically (about every 5,000 miles) washed in cleaning fluid to insure its effectiveness and a full flow of oil into the pickup. It is to be found in the bottom of the crankcase adjacent to the drain plug. The cover is retained by six hex nuts and, with oil drained, the cover can be removed. With it will come the mesh strainer and two gaskets. The gasket between strainer and crankcase may adhere to the case and have to be scraped clean. Wash the strainer and the magnetic unit in the cover, replace the gaskets and renew them if necessary. Note: This cover, carelessly replaced, can be a source of oil leaks. Use new gaskets if in doubt and always tighten nuts firmly but not severely. Be sure the oil pickup tube fits snugly into the strainer.

CARBURETOR AIR CLEANERS. The manual advises that these units be cleaned every time the oil is changed. Few of us take the trouble, but it is a good idea because better mileage can be the reward . . . especially if you habitually drive over unpaved roads. Remove the cleaners from the carburetors dip them in cleaning solvent or white gas and rinse throughly. Use a stiff brush if this hasn't been done in some time. Shake dry and squirt a few drops of engine oil at various places on the screen. Replace, making sure the screw is tight.

It is interesting to note that there are domestic cleaners with paper cartridges that serve as replacements in case yours gets battered or unsightly. Fram makes a filter that fits the 2⅝" barrel Zenith 32DIX and the little "hot rod" air cleaners for Strombergs fit also.

FUEL STRAINERS. The Porsche is one of the best-protected of all cars as far as clean fuel delivery to the engine is concerned. A

Three-way valve in bottom of tank incorporates water trap

strainer in the tank, a water and sediment trap in the shut-off valve and a conventional filter bowl at the fuel pump give three-way assurance that no foreign matter will enter the carburetors. The fact that these safeguards are present often makes us careless and they fail to receive proper attention. The factory recommendation that the fuel system be cleaned every 3,000 miles is over cautious in the United States where gasoline is handled so swiftly and turnover is so quick. Every 5,000 miles will suffice. If you have an older car, one with more than 50,000 miles on the odometer, it is not a bad idea to remove the fuel tank and give it a thorough cleaning, making sure that the tank screen and reserve pickup are intact and clear. Small flakes of rust and sediment can collect here with bad results. For procedure see the general heading FUEL in this book.

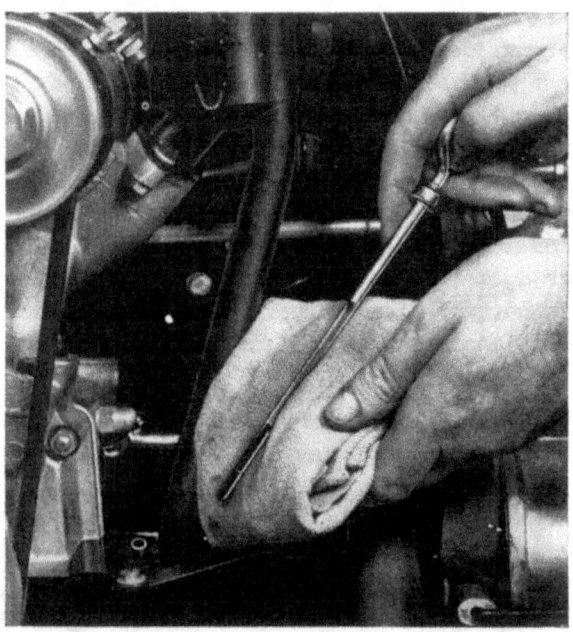

OIL. The opinions as to brand, character and viscosity of oils best suited to the Porsche vary directly as the number of individual owners polled. In the early days we were warned specifically by the factory that only a high grade unadulterated mineral oil was acceptable. This was later changed to "high grade commercial oils" and still later an announcement was made that HD or detergent lubricants were satisfactory but that multiple-grade (10-30) types were not advised followed by an ok. In the midst of all this, the owner is understandably either confused or non-concerned.

The factory still breaks the cars in on non-detergent oil (Shell

"Rotella") as do many manufacturers and lots of owners stick with this type throughout the life of the vehicle, using Oilzum, Castrol or Kendall—to name only a few brands. These people either keep a close check on the color and condition of the oil and change it in accordance with evidence (rather than every so many miles) or change the oil after a relatively short run as a matter of principle.

With a detergent oil, which discolors rapidly, there is no way to maintain a visual check—until it becomes obscenely dirty—it is advisable to change the fluid at stated intervals. These intervals can vary according to the type of use the car is subjected to. Competition, for instance, calls for an oil change before every race. Short distance driving as a regular habit with few long (100 miles or more) trips requires a change every 1,000 miles. Very cold weather operation when the engine seldom attains a good temperature or where the only use the car gets is an occasional run to the office is the most deleterious and might require monthly or 500 mile changes. If you drive your car quite a distance to work daily over open roads or freeways or you use it consistently between cities a normal change period would probably occur every 2,000 miles.

What makes the difference? Principally dilution from condensation and fuel. When the cold engine is brought up to only a moderate temperature, moisture condenses within it and combines with by-products of combustion to form acids. Choking, prolonged idling in traffic, short runs, extremes of temperature, increase this hazard. On the other hand longer operating periods, "blowing the engine out" in high speed travel and so on lessen this formation. Perhaps you have noticed that the oil level will drop sharply after only a short highway jaunt. You may jump to the conclusion that your engine is using oil. Not so, it has burned up some of the contaminating fluids that had mixed with the oil.

Why HD? Compounded and additive oils contain emulsifying agents (detergent-soap) and anti-acid chemicals to keep carbon, dirt etc. in suspension and to counteract acids which combine with the oil to cause "sludge".

If this is the case, most people ask, why not use detergent oils to the exclusion of anything else? The only thing wrong with these oils (and every good thing has a weakness somewhere) is that they keep foreign matter in suspension and it is circulated and re-circulated through the system. "Sludge", as it is formed by non-detergent oils settles out. You have seen this in old cars when the crankcase is removed. A sticky, gummy black deposit covers the bottom of the oil pan. The HD oil does not exhibit this tendency and there is a hazard that smaller passages can clog, although the claim of the oil **companies** is that detergent oils help keep rings, lifters and so on free. Nonetheless we still have sticky lifters (in the modern V8) and have to buy GumOut or some such additive.

Other oil considerations, aside from cleaning properties, include proper viscosity ratings for the driving conditions encountered. Factory recommendation of 30 SAE Summer and 20 SAE Winter can be followed in moderate climates. Under severe cold a 10W might be indicated. (The W suffix indicates that the viscosity rating is made at Zero, other viscosities are at 210°—both Fahrenheit). The **viscosity index** is a measure of the change in viscosity due to temperature change. The 10/30 type has a high viscosity index, for example.

Why is the grade and quality of the oil so important? Simply because oil is the buffer between the engine and unlimited wear. Proper attention to oil can reduce the need for overhaul and replacement of parts and prolong engine life. In our system of planned obsolescence where the family transportation is to be traded in every two years, who cares? The engine is bound to last 25,000 miles if we keep oil in it at all. With the enthusiast, especially the Porsche owner who can reasonably expect to attain he best depreciation/resale point somewhere between three and four years, there is reason for selecting the proper lubricant and maintaining it correctly.

Pick a good brand of oil, stay with it, change it as required, keep the level up, change the filter and you will be doing the best you can for the engine.

FILTER: Factory recommendation to change the oil filter cartridge every 6,000 miles is valid. This can be shortened to 4,000 miles if much driving is done under dusty conditions, over dirt roads, etc. In the winter, in the northern part of the country under city driving, the filter can get pretty sludgy in 2,000 miles. Take the top off occasionally and look at it.

FILTER CARTRIDGES: The Fram Co. advises that there are these equivalents for the C-3 cartridge used in the Porsche bucket.

AC P-203X
Allstate 4559
Atlas (Standard) M42
Baldwin C40-F
Briggs BR 42
Cyclone P-3 XN-3
Engine Life FC-3
Purolator P-70
Rol-Pak F3
Wix PC-10, CW-10

In addition, many Porsche/VW dealerships and service garages carry **Royze** filters, a good element at a reasonable price.

OIL PURIFIERS: While doing research for this book we came across a rather unusual young man in Los Angeles and consider that it was a lucky meeting. He is unusual in that he likes to work on Porsches and maintain them for his friends but that he resists taking money for advice, help or out-and-out repairs. His name will be kept confidential to prevent his being bothered, but this man has as much know-how on both pushrod engines and Carreras as anyone engaged in professional repair work that we have ever met. One of the acts that set him apart, as far as a certain Porsche dealership is concerned, was that when he took delivery on a new Carrera he insisted on draining out the new oil and replacing it with the oil from his Super Coupe he was trading in!

The oil in the coupe had not been changed in 80,000 miles.

This called for an investigation, and his experience is detailed here. If you want to utilize the same principle, you will be joining a number of truck lines, the Greyhound Bus Co. The U.S. Navy and the Air Corps. There is understandable opposition from oil companies and auto manufacturers for the simple reason that (in addition to the resultant drop in oil sales) the average service station attendant' or car owner hasn't the inclination to do anything more than change the oil after a stated number of miles, regardless of condition. Therefore the oil purifier or clarifier will never be a world beater.

The 80,000 mile oil (plus subsequent mileage in the Carrera) was 10 Wt. SAE Kendall Black Label which had been replenished at necessary intervals. In place of the conventional FRAM filter, a Briggs G-300 Clarifier was put into the system. This is a "Fuller's Earth" or Diatomaceous Earth filter that removes not only rocks, gravel, sand and particles too fine to be trapped in regular filters but also traps water, acid, tar, gum, varnish and sludge. In addition to the Briggs, there are other trade names, Luberfiner, etc. that operate in the same manner. Operators of Industrial engines, trucks, and boats and the customers of these firms and you won't find the products on sale in the average parts house. The replaceable element was changed every 1500 miles on an average, more frequently when the oil revealed by its brown tinge that varnish was building up and that the element was saturated.

Our acquaintance demonstrated that the interior of an engine equipped with one of these devices was just as clean on the inside as on the outside when dissassembled: No varnish, no sludge, very little carbon, rings free, valves clean and generally immaculate.

The oil used is a non detergent high viscosity index 10 SAE. The reason for a non-D type is that the HD will destroy the property of the filter, 10 weight because it affords the best cold-starting lubrication and better cooling. Experiments by a leading oil company revealed that the greatest amount of wear occurs during the first few revolutions when starting an engine. A lighter oil, especially 10 weight, tends to "explode" when the engine cranks over, offers less resistance to small passages and lubricates more areas quicker.

Although subjected to the toughest conditions of summer heat on the desert, the Coupe under discussion never suffered low oil pressure or failure of any type. The car was broken in on 10 weight and never changed, as a matter of fact, winter or summer.

To begin such a routine with an older car with greater clearances might be chancy, but after an overhaul with everything fresh it would be quite satisfactory. One benefit from the lighter oil, (even 20 Wt. will show this effect) in an increase in gas mileage and top end revs.

OIL TEMPERATURE

There is no "Normal" oil temperature and the needle on the oil temp. gage will not hang at one spot such as the 180° we are accustomed to seeing on water temperature indicators. Depending on ambient air temperature and operating conditions, the gage may indicate almost anything and the engine will not be suffering. There is a limit, of course, the maximum for sustained operation is 250°F (120°C) and the engine should never be "raced" or driven hard after first starting until the needle has swung up from the peg. The Porsche has a built-in safety factor in that the oil temp. reading is taken at the hottest point. The fact that the cooler lowers the temperature by 50° or so after this reading is taken gives some consolation.

A "warmed up" engine, such as specified for making adjustments and so on, should have an oil temperature indicated of 160°F (70°) or slightly above.

OIL CONSUMPTION

Just as there is no 'normal' oil temperature in the conventional sense, so is there no normal oil consumption. This, too, is a function of usage. One Porsche owner often boasts to another that his 1500 has never used a drop of oil between changes in the 20,000 miles he's had it, or some such figure. And, it can well be true. If he drives casually around town, starting and running the car only a couple of times a day, dilution is keeping the oil level up. Another pusher may complain that he never abuses his car yet the level is always down. This one ignores the spotted garage floor and the tiny puddles that form on the street after a run.

A high performance engine with proper clearances and driven smartly will use oil. The bigger the engine, the bigger the clearances, the harder the usage, the more oil will be consumed. Experience with the Porsche indicates that any consumption of more than a quart per 1,000 miles under "average" conditions should be cause for investigation. Figure it by comparison with gasoline economy, if you like. If you, as a driver, habitually get good gas mileage, you will also expect good oil mileage from a normal engine. Spot checks for leaks are easy to make, and should be routine. A clean engine is usually an economical engine.

Maintenance pays off. 1952 Coupe now owned by E. Forbes Robinson Jr. has been driven nearly 150,000 miles, is still in good condition. Car was first sold by Glockler, has had three owners.

Tires

Tires are the subject of nearly as much individual opinion as oil, fuel and sparkplugs or thoroughbreds and women. Without going into a discussion of brands and tread patterns, it may be well to point out a couple of basic items. Number one is that tire grades (and therefore prices) are based on the amount of abuse, high speed or strain that the unit will withstand. This is especially true in European tires whose manufacturers do the buyer a service by specifying the highest sustained speed the tire is capable of. There is no point, then, in buying Englebert Competition 'P' designed for 180 mph use and fitting it to a car capable of 100 mph tops. This common sense in selecting a grade can save you a lot of money. Don't go the other route and buy the cheapest grade then go racing, either. Pick a tire that suits your driving conditions and weather or climate. Snow tires give so much added security that having a set and switching to them when winter comes is a good investment. In case you live in the South or Southwest and you do a lot of high speed driving in the summer, indulge in a slightly higher grade of tire than your top speed calls for.

Number two is so basic that it hardly bears mention except that so few owners bother: **Check the pressures frequently.** Neglect has ruined more tires than abuse ever did.

Here are the symptoms and hazards of **underinflation:**

Wear occurs at the outside of the tread. Overheating causes deterioration of the fabric and separation of the cords. Symptoms are the appearance of parallel lines inside the tire running at an angle across the sidewall. Carried far enough, the cords will break and rupture of the tire will result. Real underinflation, driving the car with little or no pressure will cause the tube valve to pull out, or, in the case of tubeless tires, the tire to leave the rim.

Overinflation shows up as rapid wear on the center of the tread.

Overloading the car. This is not an ordinary hazard but on a long trip or move across country an owner might invite this trouble. Symptoms are a wavelike unevenness of wear across the tead. Cord damage can also result and you run the risk of a blowout.

Improper alignment of the front wheels is revealed by uneven tire wear. Too much toe-in results in wear on the outer edge of the tread, excessive toe-out causes the same situation on the inner edge.

Unbalanced wheels will be noticed in the steering and riding qualities of the car long before damage shows up at the tread, wheels and tires should be both statically and dynamically balanced and tires "skimmed" to assure perfect roundness before the critical driver is satisfied. Static unbalance shows up as bouncing or pounding vertically. Dynamic unbalance is caused by an uneven distribution of weight around the tire centerline and wobbling is the symptom. An out of round tire reveals itself when correction of the above defects does not produce smoothness.

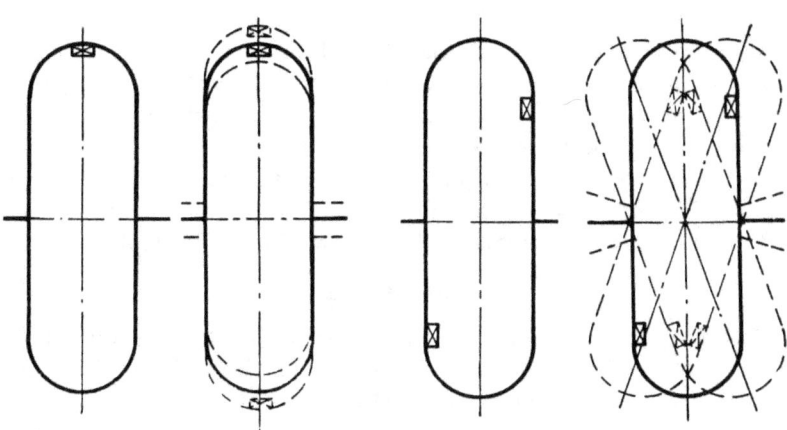

It would be nice if we could originate or pass along a tire pressure chart that would encompass all conditions, tires and driving styles, not to mention age, and previous servitude of any car. With this number of variables, however, such recommendations as it is possible to make are purely in the nature of idle chatter. Follow the factory settings (20 front 26 rear) until you find another combination that suits you better. Porsche fits an assortment of tires, as do all European factories, proportioned according to a cartel agreement. All are equal in standards. If you want to move up to another grade the factory pressure notes will probably not apply. Seeing that the factory was running its competition coupe on Continentals a few years ago probably accounted for this writer's switch to that brand and it took a little experimenting to determine that 30/30 suited that tire, car and driver combination best.

In addition to Contis, a number of Porsche drivers like the action of Englebert **Stabimax** skins. This is especially true of those who race on a budget and don't want to buy special racing tires that are too quick-wearing for regular street use. The **Stabimax** (guaranteed for 125 mph) is also a good rally tire inasmuch as it is stressed circumferentialyl for minimal "growth" or expansion at speed or temperature. It is a shoulderless type of tire, where the tread continues around the sides, that doesn't "fight" the swing axle and drifts under side load.

A word here regarding certain types of tires that boast excessive sidewall strength. This construction is not, in the opinion of many, compatible with the Porsche "Wischen" rear end action. Under side load the tread of these tires compresses, the wheel breaks loose and "hops" slightly. While in the air the tread expands, compresses again under the side thrust as it comes back in contact with the surface and hops again. This "scuffing" action is, naturally, productive of extreme tire wear.

Checking the pressures at the 20 lb. level is a little easier if you learn to transpose and get one of those atmosphere dial gages (assuming the one that was supposed to come in the tool kit went the way of all flesh between Hamburg and you).

Lug nuts should be torqued to 92 lb./ft. according to factory advice. Few of us will observe this, but it might be an idea to get a torque wrench sometime and see how 92 lb./ft. feels.

Driving

This may be a curious topic to include in maintenance but I have a personal feeling that most Porsches are "babied" to their ultimate harm. I have noticed that Factory personnel are usually about a gear lower than most drivers under the same set of circumstances.

In other words they rev the engines up at all times and they use the brakes in a much more vigorous fashion than the average owner tends to do. At first I thought this type of operation was a "show-off" affair, or that the car was being checked out, but after longer association I concluded that the accepted method of driving these little cars is vigorously. Another point is that these people "warm up" the brakes before driving very far or very hard, in the same manner that the engine is warmed up. We might well consider that it is wrong to keep the car in cotton batting at all times.

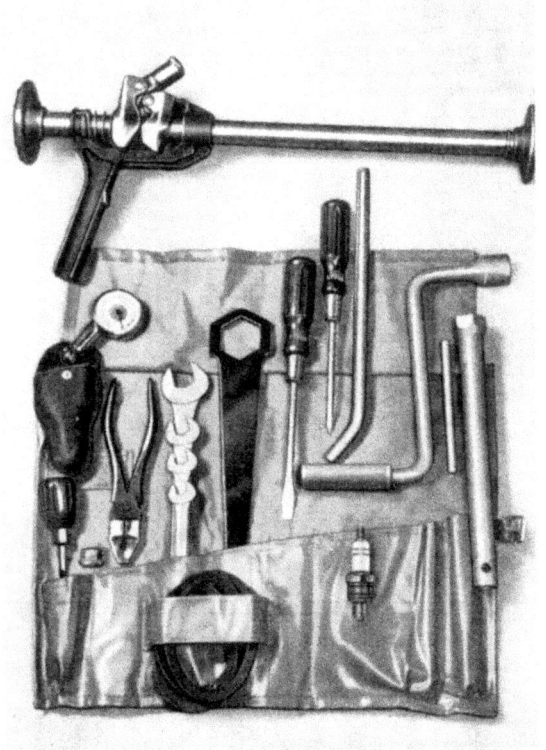

Contents of Tool Bag
(from left to right)

Short screw driver
Tire gauge in case
1 spare wheel nut
Combination pliers
4 open end wrenches
Special wrench to loosen pulley
Screw driver
Philips head screw driver

Jack lever
Wheel nut wrench
1 Spark plug
Spark plug wrench pin
Spark plug wrench
At top:– jack
At bottom:–
Coiled spare fan belt

Wiring Diagram Type 356 B

1 Headlight
2 Directional light
3 Fog light (optional)
4 Signal horn, high pitch
4a Signal horn, low pitch
5 Battery
6 Fuel gauge sending unit
7 Relay for horn
8 Relay for light signal
9 Fuse box
10 Windshield wiper motor
10a Windshield wiper motor switch
11 Interior light*

12 Door contact switch**
13 Dash socket
14 Stop light switch
15 Cigarette lighter**
16 Directional-dimmer and light signal switch
17 Blinker unit
18 Signal horn button (steering wheel)
19 Combination switch for ignition and starter
20 Light switch
21 Combination instrument (oil temperature and fuel gauge)
22 Tachometer

23 Speedometer
24 Electric clock (optional)
25 Oil pressure control switch
26 Oil temperature sending unit
27 Ignition coil
28 Back-up light switch
29 Voltage regulator
30 Generator
31 Starter
32 Distributor
33 Spark plug
34 Directional brake and tail light
35 Licence plate light
36 Back-up light

*) not supplied on Roadster, on Coupe on left and right door post, on Convertible and Hardtop on dash board
**) not on Roadster

Electrical Diagram Type 356 B

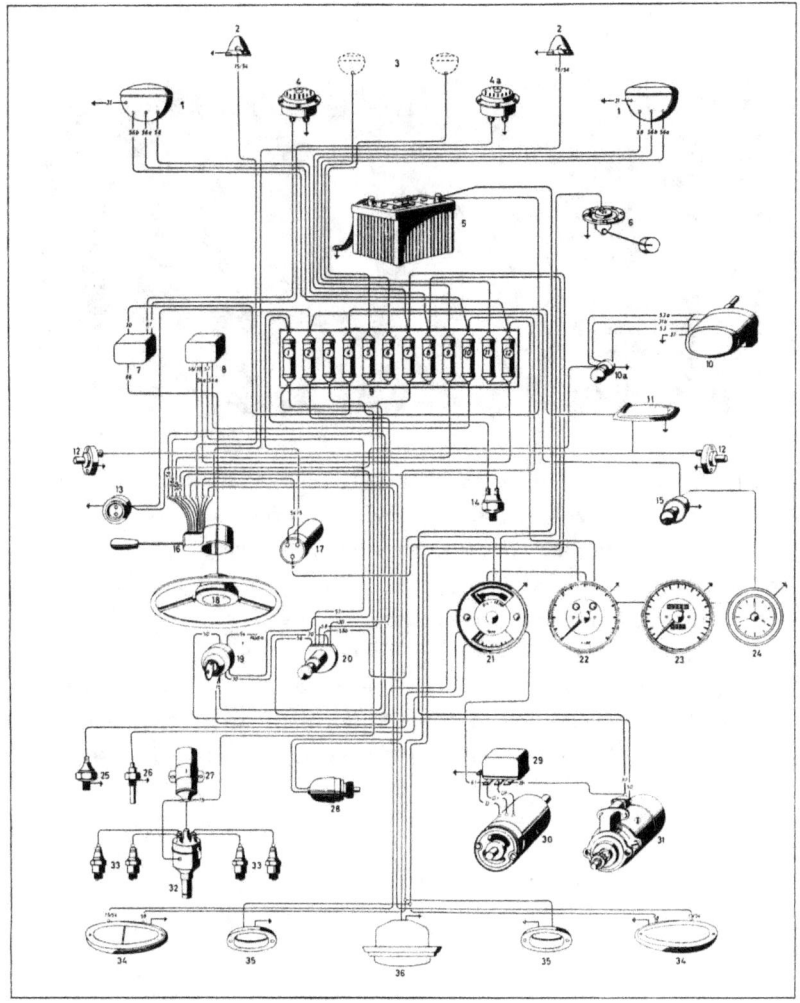

Replacing Fuses

Fuses

No.	12	11	10	9	8	7	6	5	4	3	2	1
	|	|	|	|	|	|	|	|	|	|	|	|
Amp.	25/40	25/40	25/40	25/40	8/15	8/15	8/15	8/15	25/40	25/40	8/15

The fuse box is located in the center under the dash board. The fuses can be easily removed by pressing down the spring bow holders. A plug fuse under the instrument panel is provided for the instrument panel light. The fuse can be replaced easily after removing the bayonet holder.

After a fuse has burnt out it is not sufficient merely to replace it. Always determine and remedy the cause of failure or overload.

Repairing of fuses with wire or tin foil is not recommended, since this may result in further serious damage to the electrical system. Spare fuses (8/15 Amp. and 25/40 Amp.) should always be carried in the car.

Position of Name Plate, Chassis, Engine and Transmission Numbers

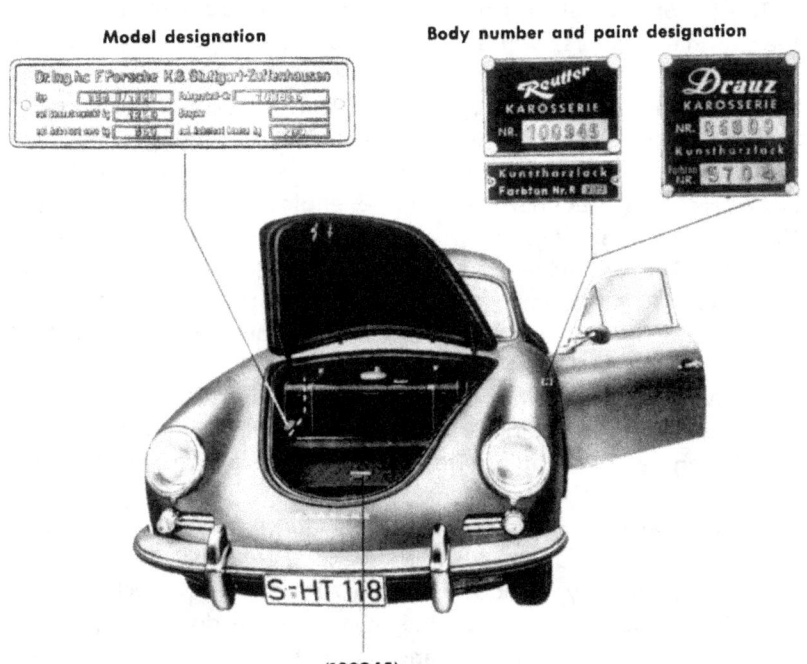

Model designation

Body number and paint designation

(108945)
Chassis number

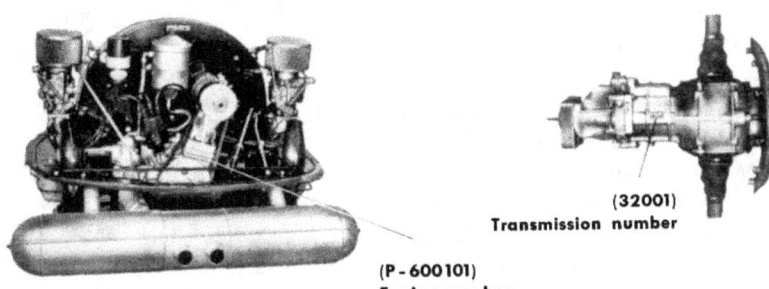

(P - 600101)
Engine number

(32001)
Transmission number

More Push

In the Porsche, the enthusiast has an automobile of exceptional abilities. Considering its displacement, even the 1300 N has outstanding acceleration and top speed. All models have fine brakes and superior handling qualities. The competition record of Porsches in weekend sports car events all over the country demonstrate that they are tops when put to the test. Yet, such is human nature that a high percentage of Porsche owners are anxious to increase the performance of their cars.

The factory has always held the idea that if you want more than the Normal delivers, you should buy a Super and if you are still not satisfied, get a Carrera. This is a logical approach, it must be admitted, but perhaps because of our "Hot Rod" background in this country a great many of us pefer to bring our Normal type up to Super specs or to hot up our Super so that it can challenge a Carrera. The fact that the Porsche engine is a simple straightforward design and easy to work on undoubtedly encourages modifications. The additional factor of its inherent strength lends impetus, too. It is extremely rare to see a pushrod engine scattered or sawed in two at the track compared to the number of failures observed in upright, water cooled types.

So. We have determined that there is a natural desire to improve the Porsche, that it is relatively simple to tinker with and offers a high degree of reliability after being stressed above normal loads. Then where do we go?

The answer to this question is another question, or series of questions: How much do you want to spend, how much time do you want to devote to your hobby and how much of a perfectionist are you? These factors will determine what you can do to the pushrod engine to enhance its performance. One thing is sure, if you are willing to perform various mechanical tasks yourself you can make a Super (or improved Super) out of your Normal for less than if you had paid the difference when new . . . A hotted up Super won't beat a Carrera GT on the track but the Cal Club "production" 1600 S speedsters race with regular Carreras and beat them. The California Sports Car Club allows certain "modifications" that are taboo in the SCCA but you can be assured that all of them put together don't cost as much as the extra tab for a GS.

We are fortunate in Southern California to have a great number of garages specializing in Porsche or VW service. Ferde Hannig in North Hollywood, Hellie Koch in Montrose, Jack McAfee in Studio City, Vlacek Polak in Manhattan Beach, to name but a few, not only have the know how to maintain the stock engine but have a lot of tricks up the sleeves of their shop coats when it comes to making modifications. The area also abounds with owners of more than amateur ability who bring hot rod or competition experience to bear on the care and feeding of these little cars. As a consequence, this part of the country has more non-stock Porsches beetling around the freeways than you can shake a crescent wrench at.

The author's 1500 coupe (rt.), leaving the starting line at dragstrip, won 1956 National Championship.

Would you like to have a 1500 that will turn 7,000 in three gears? A 100 cubic incher developing better than 1 hp per cube? A 1600 Super that beats AC Bristols? These are products of the procedures outlined in this chapter. You can use as few or as many as you desire.

Whether you own an 1100 or a 1600S, tuning the stock engine to its peak is the first step. Factory jets and normal timing are given in appropriate sections of this manual. They are adequate for going after the groceries and if your wife drives the car all the time. If you like to get on it a little more, accelerate away from a stop light now and then or drive for fun, remember two basics: **Go rich, add advance.**

It might be well to digress at this point long enough to say that if you have access to a Dynamometer equipped tune up shop the $10.00 per hour that is the usual charge is the best money you can spend to get the most out of an engine. The chassis dyno simulates road conditions to a degree and gives irrefutable evidence of power. This is so much better than relying on the seat of your pants as an accelerometer!

Even with a dyno, you have to start someplace, so try this: If you are in the habit of standing on it away from stop signs, give the idling mixture screws an extra half to ¾ turn to the left (counterclockwise) to richen the mixture after you have gotten the engine idling at its best speed as described under "Carburetion". If you have a flat spot around 1500 to 2000 RPM, (or anywhere up to 3,000) go one step richer in the idling jet. Normally your Solex had a 55, substitute a 60 or 65 even. A "flat spot" is hard to separate from a "hesitation", but the latter is pronounced on sudden application of the throttle while the flat spot occurs while passing through that range in acceleration. If your engine does not respond immediately to the throttle, recheck the accelerator pump delivery. If it is correct, but requires a full stroke to account for delivery, change the pump jet up a size.

Fuel is power, you know, so don't hesitate to go richer in jets. We discussed jets and fuel in other departments, so with a working knowledge of their functions, let us talk about ideals. The stock jets . . . assuming that you have the correct ones for climate and altitude (not to mention specific gravity of fuel) . . . are a compromise between maximum power and maximum economy. If you want to featherfoot and keep the throttle in the midrange you can go leaner and save gas. If, on the other hand, you expect the engine to put out top power and are inclined to romp on it, you have to put more fuel into the chamber. Unless your plugs now show a definite rich condition, go up one step in the main jet. Then:

(1) Put in a new set of plugs of the correct heat range (presumably you have them now) go out for a 5 mile run with the new jets, keeping the engine above 3,500 RPM as much of the time as possible. Shut it off at speed and coast in. Pull the plugs and inspect them. Unless they show definitely wet . . . or unless the engine hasn't performed as well as before, stay with the jets.

(2) Run the engine up to full throttle and hold it for a few seconds. If it surges or backfires, put in smaller air correction jets.

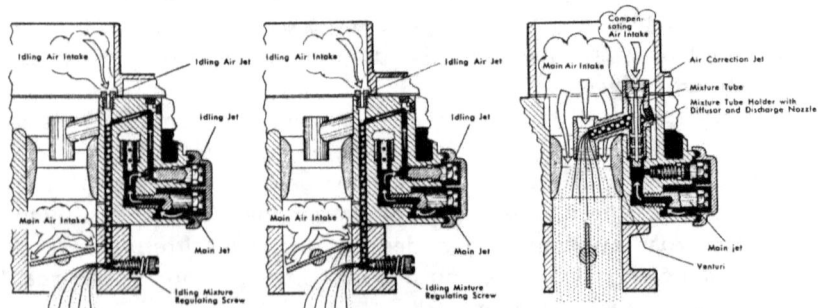

Three stages of carburetion: Idling, transition and high speed showing action of appropriate jets.

Stock ignition advance setting for the Normal engine is 5° BTDC static, 6½° for the Super. I see no reason not to use the Super timing on both engines. The mark on the pulley rim should be 13/32" to the right of the TD mark for timing purposes.

With new points (or dressed points) take a piece of cigarette paper (tear up a Pall Mall if you don't roll your own) and insert it between the closed points. Line up the timing mark with the split in the crankcase. Loosen the nut on the distributor locking plate and turn the distributor case by hand while tugging gently at the piece of cigarette paper. The points should release the paper to a slight pressure, then tighten the locking nut. This method of determining that the points are breaking at exactly the right time is quicker and easier than using a timing light and more accurate than observing the spark break. After a little practice you will be able to tell the exact moment they break.

We may have gotten the car ahead of the horsepower by not mentioning the correct point gap: .016". The gap should be set, of course, before timing.

Centrifugal Advance Curve

The measured value on the scale shall lie in the shaded area at corresponding engine r.p.m.

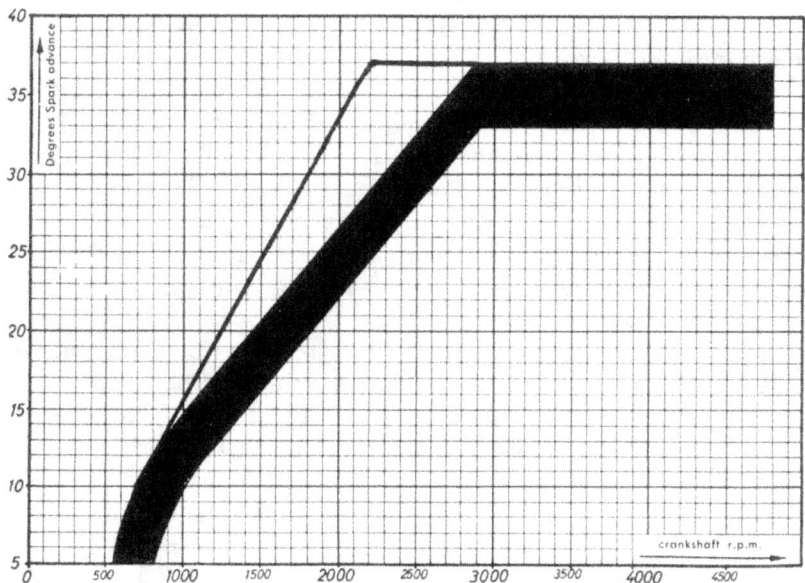

Factory recommended ignition advance curve is plotted by shaded area. Altering distributor weights to bring peak advance at 2200 rpm (line to left) has been successful variation. Job must be done by ignition shop with proper equipment.

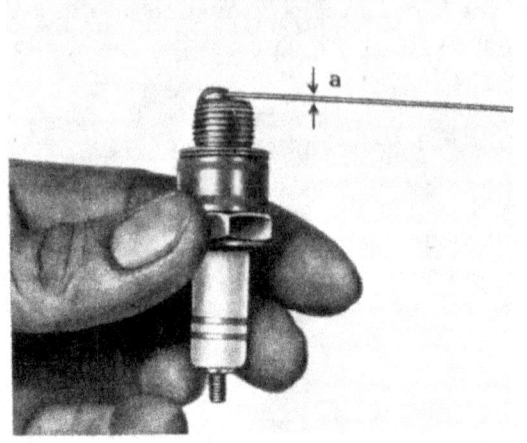

Correct Bosch plug gap is (a) .027-.028"

Changing sparkplugs won't gain you any horsepower unless your old ones were worn out or totally wrong. But keep 'em clean and do have the right heat range. After a few miles of driving the center insulator should show a tan color for correct, black is too cold, white or blistered is too hot. Sooty electrodes reveal a too rich mixture (or lots of stop-and-go driving) and burned or fried electrodes, too lean.

This writer is personally sold on Platinum tip plugs for Porsches because of the different temperatures and mixtures apt to be present in each cylinder plus the varied driving conditions most of us encounter. The wide heat range of the platinum point covers these adverse situations very well. True, they are more expensive, but experience indicates a longer life and better performance. I started buying platinum point plugs for my Porsche when the only place they were aavilable was in Motorcycle shops.

Incidentally, the Porsche owner can learn a lot from cycle people. They have been fooling with aircooled engines for a long time and have the scene pretty well in hand. Compression, for instance. The cycle boys know that an aircooled engine has such heat dissipation qualities that the rated compression is actually about 1.5 points low compared to a watercooled engine. The Porsche owner is sometimes abashed, I know, to learn that his engine is only rated at 7 to 1 compression when even a Ford is running 9.5 to 1 these days, but it would be a mistake for him to up the pressure in his flat four to 11 to 1 just to get ahead. He wouldn't have a head long.

Increasing the compression on any model is a worthwhile move, however. To raise the ratio by approximately 1 point, or a little better, depending on the bore, take .060" off the bottom landing

of the cylinder barrels . . . where they mate with the case. This can be done to any model engine, 2pc. or 3pc. case . . . unless someone has already beat you to it. If you own a used model that has been rebuilt, better check the compression ratio before getting too wild. If disassembled, you can examine the barrels for lathe marks . . . and the pistons will have been flycut under the valves.

Assuming it is virgin, take the cut from the bottom of the barrels . . . **NOT** off the top where the head mates. Remove a like amount from the pistons under the valves for clearance and clean up the burrs. This will get the pressure in a Super up about to the limit and you will have to re-jet the carburetors, go to colder plugs and change the advance to take advantage of the situation. Don't worry about the bottom end. It can take it if you run clean oil and warm up the Hirth crank at the proper speed.

While the engine is disassembled to have the barrels trimmed, a small amount of time spent in porting and polishing can pick up several HP. I have yet to see a stocker that couldn't be improved upon by mating the intake and exhaust manifolds to the head ports and by hogging out these passages to a degree. There is plenty of meat around the valve guides that can be trimmed out and the passages should be polished to a mirror smoothness. The pushrod engine will always suffer from a siamese manifold (except in the new Super 90) but cleaning it out and making the flow easier into the head will help equalize the system.

Cleanup of head ports will show gain in performance

Still on the subject of things that can be done to any engine: Lightening the valve train to gain those extra revs. Take the valves, undercut the heads and concave them. By judiciously machining these little goodies you can take off 15 grams . . . and that's a lot of unbalanced weight to save. In addition, you can bring them all to equal weights (see diagram). When this operation is concluded, "break" the radius (a) with cutting oil and a crocus cloth (with the valve chucked up in a drill press or lathe) and knock the corner off

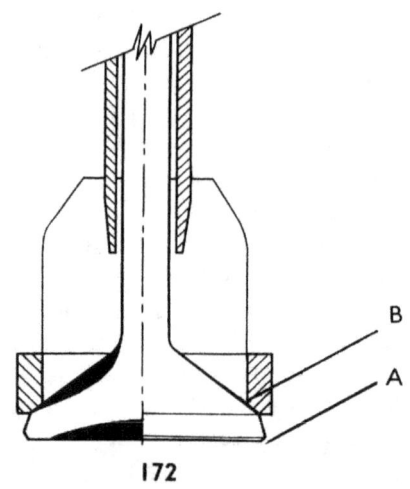

at the seat bevel (b) very lightly. This will induce better flow characteristics around the valve when closing.

Are you a perfectionist? Do you want to turn 7,000? Then grind all the unnecessary metal off the rocker arms and polish them up like mirrors. The diagram will give you a rough idea of how this is accomplished but common sense has to be applied. Then, as a final gesture grind the adjusting nut off by about 2/5. The grams saved here are reflected in more RPM and quicker revs.

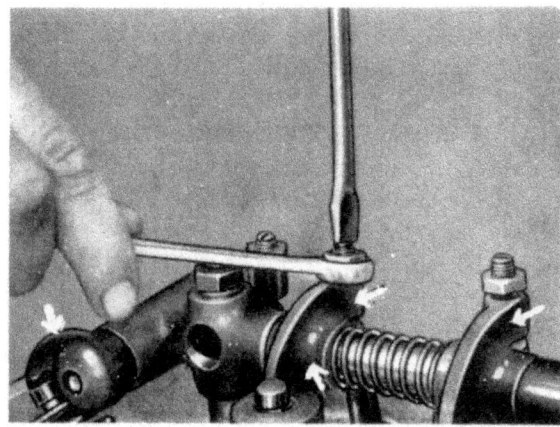

Arrows indicate where grinding and polishing of rocker arms can be accomplished. Shaded area denotes amount of metal to be removed from adjusting nuts.

Of course you are going to balance any engine intended for high performance. The factory allows 5 grams difference in connecting rod weights but we should be satisfied with nothing less than perfection in piston and con rod assemblies. .5 gram is far enough out. The flywheel and crank should be zeroed in, too. A hot rod shop generally has the balancing equipment to accomplish these tasks quickly and correctly and the charge runs around $15.00 to $20.00.

This leads naturally to the flywheel. A good 5 to 7 lbs. can be shaved off the flywheel on the outer diameter (engine side) without harm. The contact area should be surface ground to insure a perfect mating with the clutch plate. The pressure plate should be balanced, too, and the plate surface ground. These units warp from internal pressure.

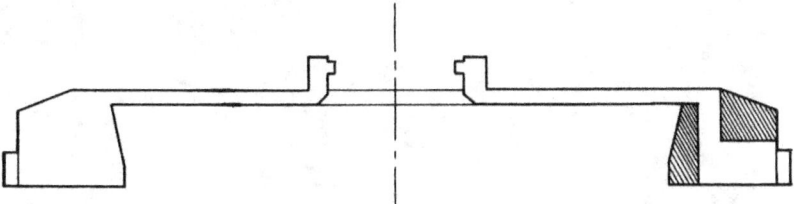

Shaded areas show where metal can be removed from flywheel to lighten it and provide for Spyder clutch use

Moving back to the clutch. A Frendo lining bonded to the Porsche disc is the choice of many as a replacement. BID, a Los Angeles clutch outfit does this sort of thing and there are others around the country. The best idea is to adapt the flywheel to take a Spyder clutch assembly. This necessitates turning out the flywheel recess to accept the 8" diameter of the RS clutch. (Stock is 7⅛".) The net gain of better than 25% in lining makes clutch problems a thing of the past.

The exhaust system is bad only in the Normal muffler with its one outlet. The least you can do is trade for a Super muffler. Even the VW has two outlets! Whether the Abarth setup adds as many horsepower as they claim is open to debate but it seems logical that it is an improvement if the flow is freer and the scavenging effect still takes place. One thing, the collector tube allowed for racing will gain 5 or more HP at the wheels by actual test. There are two or three types of these "straight pipes" in use and most owners make up their own but it is important to note that 4 direct pipes unconnected simply will not work. There has to be a crossover to allow #3 to scavenge #1 and so on. Take a good look at the photos of the racing exhausts shown here. The little "funnels" shown on Ed Barker's speedster were added to help at the low end. Before they were devised the system worked fine at high speed but it died coming out of the turns.

Now, let's consider what can be done to various models. If you have the 2pc. case, you are stuck as far as dropping the later barrels on. However, you can have the crank (plain metal) stroked to a maximum of .80" to get a little less than 1600cc. This must be done by the welded (not sprayed) metal method. The journals are built up and then turned to the first undersize .040" off center. This also automatically increases the compression and the pistons must be flycut .040". If you want to take another .020" off the barrels and a similar cut from the pistons, this is o.k.

After stroking, it will be necessary to notch the crankcase to provide clearance for the rod journals and you may have to grind the journals to clear the old Super cam.

Unfortunately the German pistons which many thought superior to the factory jobs that used to be available as replacements are no longer to be had. And now in order to get Super pistons and be sure of a fit you have to get sets with the barrels. If you want to move from a N to an S, buy the pistons and barrels outright and get a set of heads and manifolds at the same time. This is expensive, but you can sell the N stuff if it is in good shape to recoup part of the outlay.

Direct exchange of 1500 cylinder & piston (left) for 1600 (rt.) is possible with 3-pc. case engines

At this point some one is sure to say "Why not just get the whole Super engine?" The answer is that I wouldn't want a used Hirth crank as an albatross around my neck. Stick to the plain crank, it's good for 7,000 and that's all you'll ever turn a pushrod engine.

You can make do without the heads and pistons by getting up to maximum compression in the N and obtaining only the S manifolds and carburetors. The ports have to be enlarged to match and you will have to do a good porting job in the had to allow for the extra volume possible through the bigger venturis.

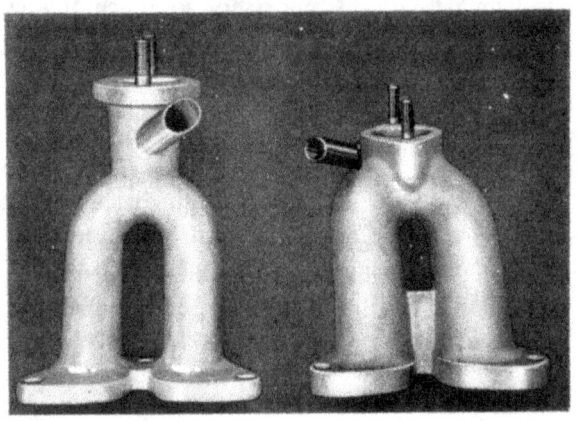

Super   Normal

Without going to the 40PBIC's, do all you can to the manifolds and substitute the 26mm venturis (if yours has the 24's now). This will help the top end considerably. The 26's come from later 32 PBI Solexes or can be turned down from 40PBIC 26mm venturis to fit the smaller carburetor. Fitting new venturis calls for new jets, naturally. Try about two complete steps richer; mains, air correction and idling, leave the pump alone if it is now satisfactory.

Now is about the time to take up cams. The S cam, can of course be substituted for the N in any engine but is not advised unless you are going to take advantage of its greater top end by enhancing the breathing in related fashion. In other words the manifolds and 40 Carbs are mandatory. As you may have observed the S mani-

olds are higher, an attempt to take some advantage of "ram" induction tuning, and are co-related with the cam dwell. Ed Iskenderian makes a street grind for Porsche & VW but it has little to offer except price. With your core, the regrind costs $35.00. The same price holds for his 2-J which corresponds pretty closely to the Super: Intake, 18°-55°, Exhaust, 53°-20°. (Super: 19°-54°, 54°-19°) and the inner springs he offers for $4.00 a set to go with this cam are a good buy.

I wouldn't put any other cam in my car without a moneyback guarantee and then you are running the risk of beating up the lifters. Either get the factory Super or Isky's 2-J grind on your cam.

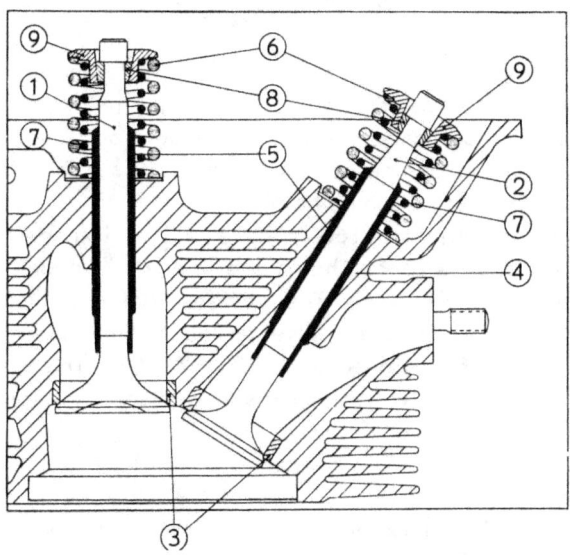

1. intake valve
2. exhaust valve
3. valve seat
4. cylinder head
5. valve guides
6. outside valve spring
7. inside valve spring
8. cotter
9. valve spring retainer

The springs mentioned here are good to use with a stock cam. They are the short **inner** springs, heat treated and shot peened. The top coil has to be chamfered on the inside before they are installed to let the retainer seat properly and not "cock". Put the valve in the seat without springs, measure from the top of the keeper notch to the recess in the head. Add enough shims in the recess to bring this measurement to exactly 36mm. Then add 3 more .20" spacers. Install springs and keepers and you will have enough tension to rev 6,500 or better if your train is lightened and polished. Refer to the diagram for this procedure.

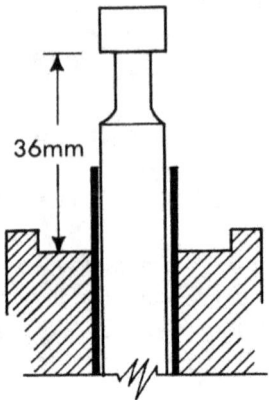

If yours is the later 3 piece case, the only difference is that you can substitute 1600cc barrels for 1500 at any time. You can make any of the other modifications listed above but you probably won't be able to wind the engine quite as tight if it is a later 1600 because the valve gear is somewhat heavier.

One advantage the late 1600's have is that Iskenderian's Full Race 105 cam can be used. This is the "flat out" model and was designed for Cal Club racing. The power curve is moved up the scale quite a bit. In fact the valve timing begins to look like a motorcycle enthusiast designed it: 33°-73°, 73°-33°. The assumption is that you will have an extractor exhaust and top compression . . . not for street, in other words.

It is safe to say that the speedsters currently operating on the Coast are getting well over 100 honest HP, closer to 110 or 115 would probably be more like it . . . and, they have not been stroked. A stroker 1600, approximately 100ci, with "super tuned" Super characteristics is a mighty potent street machine, and shouldn't take a bow to much of anything costing under $8,000.

At this juncture we might as well take up gearing. The fortunate position the Porsche owner finds himself in regarding a selection of transmission ratios also works to confuse the layman. With a choice of cogs suitable for anything from the dragstrip to the Nurburgring at hand, the uninitiated owner hardly knows what combination is really best. In the absence of any other determining factor, and with around-town driving as the norm, the so called "speedster" gears are probably the best for any car. This is the BBAB or sometimes BBBB with the 7:31. With the 7:34 ring and pinion you might use the BBBC with a stock engine. If you seek improved overall top speeds and have the torque to go with it, say a 1600 S stroker, go CBCC. The nice close jump from first to 2nd will gain you quite a bit in chance drags and you can pull the higher cogs.

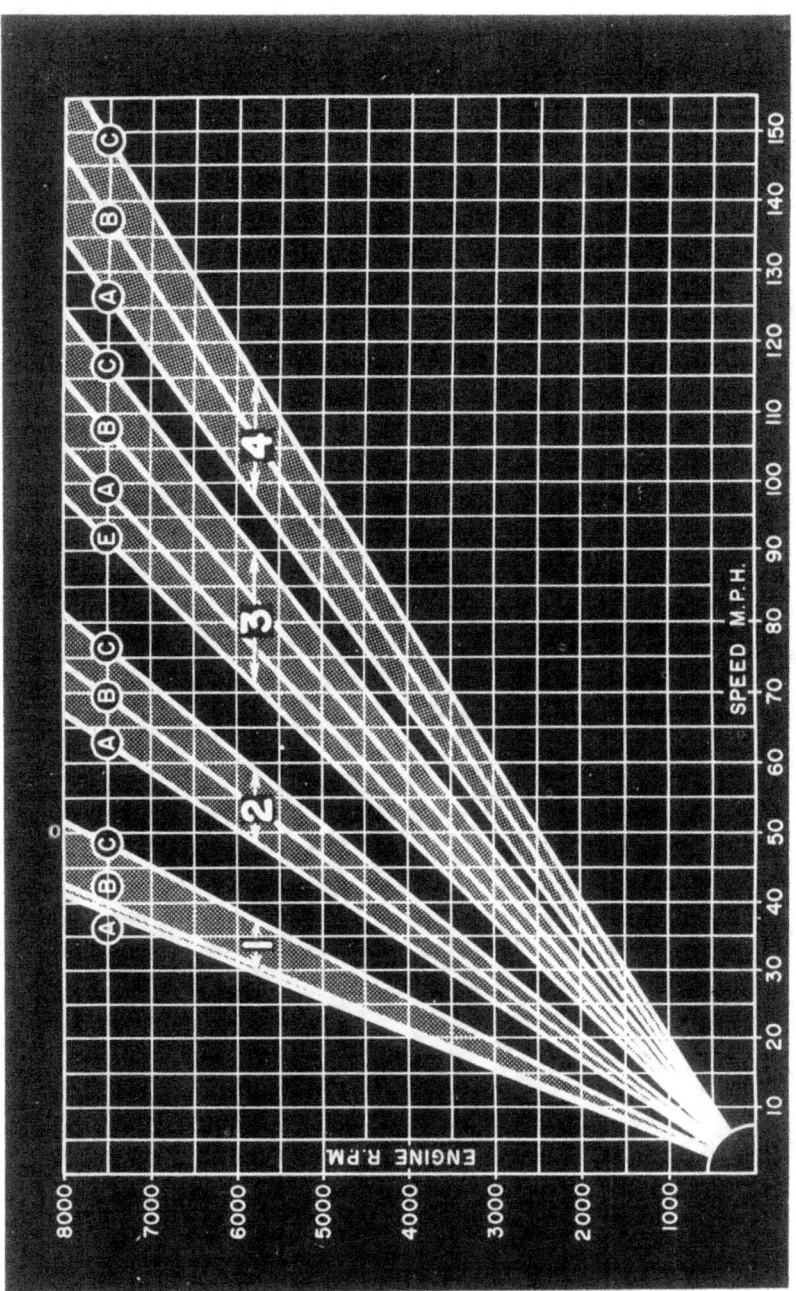

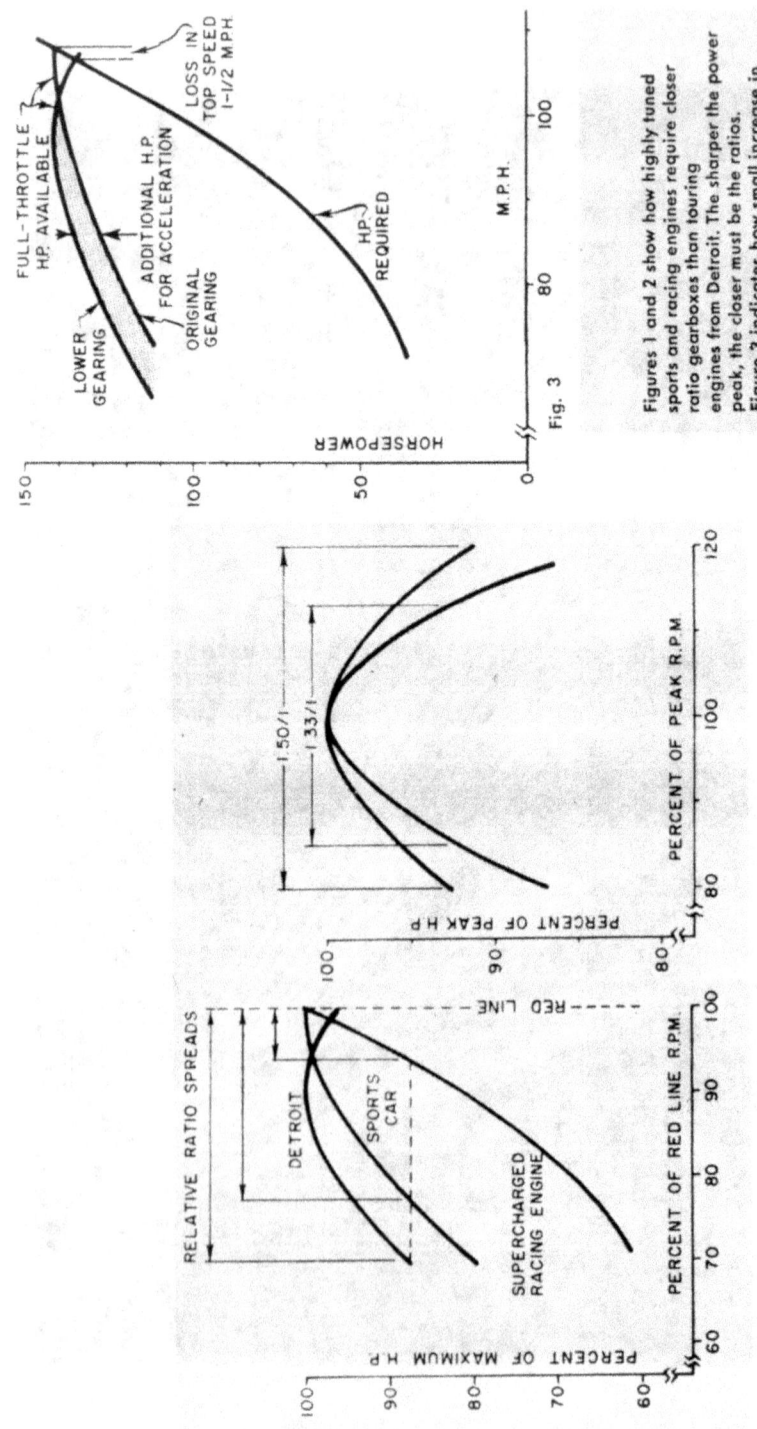

Figures 1 and 2 show how highly tuned sports and racing engines require closer ratio gearboxes than touring engines from Detroit. The sharper the power peak, the closer must be the ratios. Figure 3 indicates how small increase in final drive ratio gives only slightly lower top speed (hence term "lower gear") but sharply improved acceleration.

Around town where 3rd gear is about tops, the B series makes the most sense. It lets you use 4th occasionally without lugging the engine, too. The C is the stock overdrive .885 4th and is the best highway cruising gear, I think, and if you have an engine that can wind, dropping into third for passing at 65 is swell. Stock coupe rations are BBBC.

If acceleration is your prime joy in life stay with the BABC and try to find Carrera ring and pinion of the 6:31 ratio (5.18 to 1). Going to the A first gear does not gain enough in acceleration to warrant the change and there is no use having the low A cog in 4th because you seldom get into that gear during acceleration anyway and you may as well have some cruising speed.

You can take the chart of rations and the scale showing speeds at various RPM (with 7:31 ring and pinion) and play around with the combinations. To figure the equivalents for a 7:34, deduct 8.9% from the speed for a given RPM. If you have the torque, you can pull anything. The Carrera remember hasn't so much torque at the low end but lots of RPM so they gear it up (BBAA) you must be similarly guided by the potential of your engine. If it's a 1300 you aren't going to knock anybody dead with C gears and a 8:35 rear end.

In drag racing, or the competitive little spurts we often indulge in, the big thing to keep in mind is that you must over-rev the power peak to take advantage of the engine. (Not, mind you, over-rev the engine.) If it peaks at 4,500 wind it to 5,500 before shifting. There is a good spread of 2,000 RPM between most gears. This means you will drop back to 3,500 anyway, then you pick up the next gear. If you shift at 4,500 you'll be back to 2,500 and a glance at the HP curve on your particular engine's chart will show you how much less HP you have at that speed. Throw the 5,000 limit out the window. These engines are capable of so much more when properly tuned and will bring so much more satisfaction if driven properly that you will be amazed.

It is assumed that anyone who will spend time and money to improve his engine will also clean up the rest of the car. Under different headings in this manual there is all kinds of advice on care and maintenance of various components. To review:

Shocks: should be first rate. Either new or replacement models of added stiffness. **Brakes.** If not in top shape, take them to a specialist and have the drums and shoes trued to a common radius for 100% contact. If they are the older style, drill ¼" holes in the drums at the rim, just to clear the cast iron liners. Drill each hole at a point on a line halfway between the lugs . . . five in all. Then cut two or three ⅛" wide grooves in the lining, horizontally. Make the grooves about 1/16" deep and spaced equally on the shoe.

Camber. The rear end should have 1½° negative camber and the **Toe In** of the front wheels should be between 2mm and 3mm.

With everything in order, the Porsche owner need have no qualms about trying his car on any road in the country at any intelligent speed and from the legendary Point A to Point B he will be as quick as anyone.

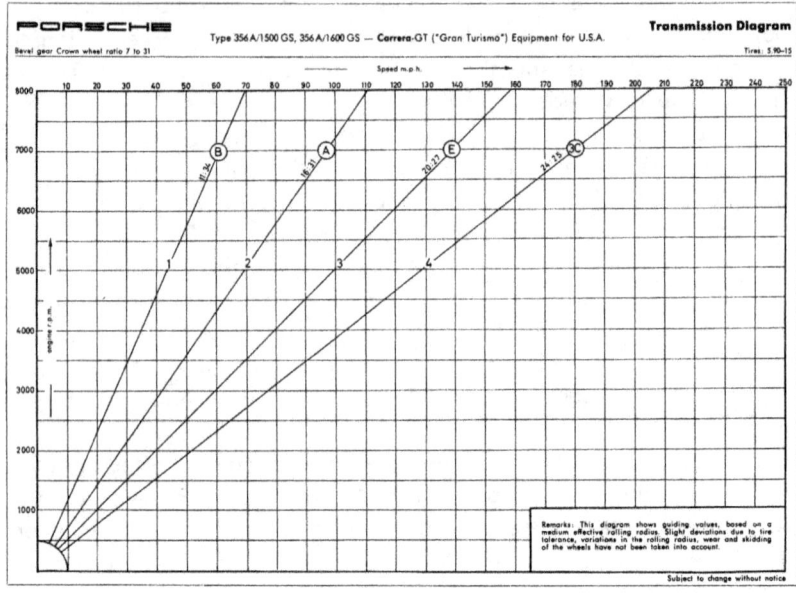

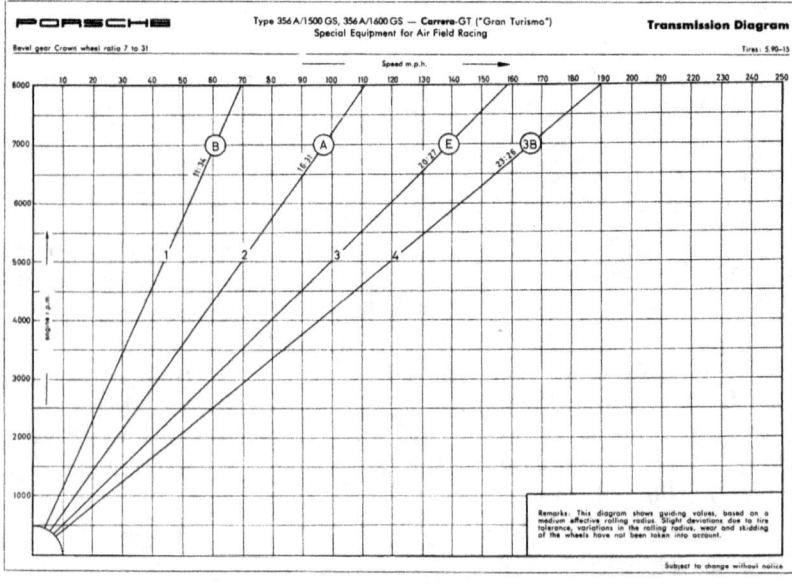

Competition

It seems to be expected in books of this type that the author will toss off a few well chosen phrases about competition driving and the technique that produces trophies. This has always seemed a bit absurd inasmuch as the owner who wants to go fast has probably already experimented with driving hard and decided he will race, that it is too expensive or he doesn't have the talent. And the only way to learn to drive is to get out on the track and drive, watching others in the same type of car and asking as many questions as you can get away with. What **can** be stated under this heading is that Porsche racing is probably as inexpensive as in any production car, and if that be encouragement, make the most of it.

The Porsche is relatively easy on tires, extremely easy on brakes and needs few serious alterations to compete in fair shape. Barring haybaling the car or totaling it, racing expenses over a season should do no more than double the car's upkeep for a year if you can tune it yourself and keep it together.

Speed tuning (as outlined under **More Push**), on the Super consists of getting away with as much as you can under the rules. In some sections of the country Technical Committees are more lenient as to what constitutes "tuning" and what is "modifying", so you will have to play this by ear. The Carrera, on the other hand, seldom arouses any protests but, of course, the amount of alterations that can be forced on this engine are limited.

D.D. ("Mich") MICHELMORE, amassed sufficient wins in Porsche 1600 Speedster and GT Carrera during 1958 season to become L.A. Region SCCA high point man overall.

There are certain safety precautions that will be required and some optional items that you will want. A modified exhaust, allowed most everywhere, is mandatory for top performance on either push-rod or overhead cam engine. A couple of specimen types as used on Southern California competition cars are shown. One, highly individual in shape, on Ed Barker's 1600 is the result of much experimentation. The cone shaped tips were added to correct a low-speed flat spot and worked out perfectly. Different methods of protecting the front end paint from rock scars are also shown; simple and elaborate, "Nerf bars" replacing stock bumpers are rather popular in this section of the country. The neat headrest, tonneau cover on Jay Hill's car is an attractive adjunct that is also functional. A simple but substantial roll bar mounting that could well be copied by other Porsches is illustrated as well.

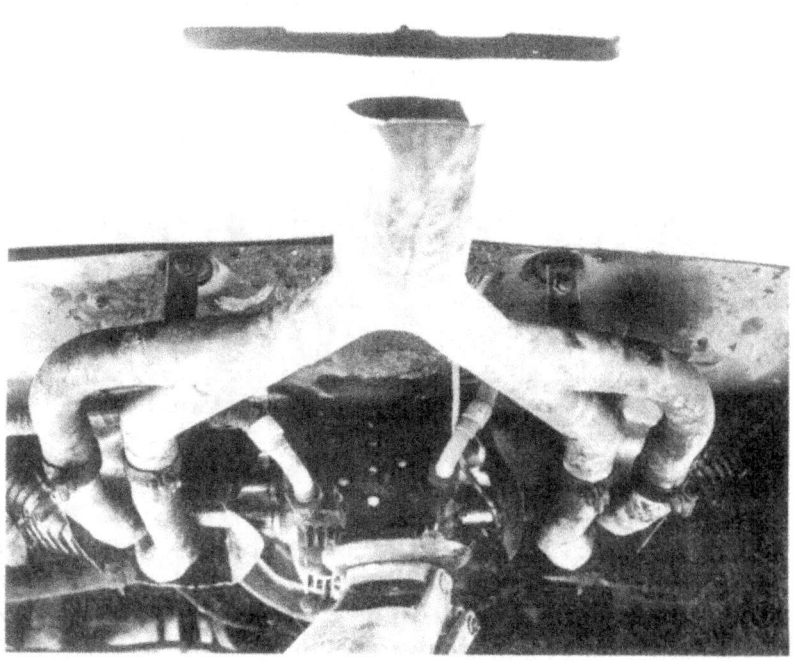

A word in passing to the owners of "Normal" Porsches: Don't be bashful about getting into competition. Quite a few of the "stockers" appear on the Coast circuits and frequently do amazingly well. Ed Tomerlin, a couple of years ago, raced a Normal Speedster with exceptional ability and, on one occasion at Palm Springs, finished second to the hottest MGA in the area beating a flock of Supers and the rest of the MGA contingent. In any event, a well-tuned Normal can often use its short spurt acceleration to give the faster Super a real tussle. Anyway, if you are a beginner, starting in the Normal will be good training before going up to something with more steam.

Driving a Porsche in competition is just like driving any other car: You go as fast as you can wherever you can. In today's races you will be surrounded by Porsches anyway, so do whatever they do. If you can drive fast on the highway you know how to handle the car itself. Racing merely calls for an extension of all that technique to a new plateau. If you can't handle the car on the road to your satisfaction either you should get a Ford or ask some other Porsche owner to show you how to drive. A book the size of this one solely about driving can't make a good driver out of a dub.

Most Porsche owners, fortunately, are interested enough in getting the most from the car to work at improving their control of the automobile under all circumstances. This is what makes driving a pleasure instead of a chore and keeps the Porsche factory behind schedule in producing cars for discriminating people.

THE END

E. FORBES-ROBINSON, one of the West Coast's top MGA drivers stepped into Porsche competition for part of a season and compiled a smart record: Five starts, four firsts, one second (to a Carrera by 20 ft. at the finish line). The Erhardt-maintained 1600S owned by Morley Kasler was a top performer at all times.

The following appreciation of the Porsche by famed motoring journalist Denis Jenkinson, although written several years ago, is such a fine critique that it bears reading today. We have obtained permission of the British magazine MOTOR SPORT to reprint it here.

PORSCHE MOTORING

Some Reflections After 30,000 Miles With a "Damen"

BEFORE becoming too deeply involved in the question of driving a Porsche it might be as well to pay a quick visit to the factory and find out something about the cars. Situated on the north-west edge of Stuttgart, a mere three minutes from an autobahn, this small factory is entirely new, the old one having been damaged and requisitioned by military authorities. It was in this original factory that Dr. Ferdinand Porsche had his design and development business, the new factory being built when the construction of Porsche cars began in 1950. Since the death of Dr. Porsche, who was a pure inventor as well as a designer, the firm has been effectively carried on by his son Dr. Ferry Porsche. Apart from car manufacturing, the Porsche concern still do contract design work for all branches of the engineering industry and among the far-reaching effects of the Porsche genius are the new gearboxes on the Grand Prix Bugatti, and experimental B.M.W.s, both of which are built under Porsche patents.

The factory is divided into four departments: machine shop, assembly, service and racing, the last dealing exclusively with competition motoring, the building of the sports/racing " Spyder," the assembly of the 4 o.h.c. Carrera engines and experimental work. When I went to take delivery of my Porsche coupé I took the opportunity of having a look to see how it was made and when I eventually drove away I had already gained a certain amount of confidence in the car. The Porsche is very definitely a hand-built car, the output being in the order of six or seven cars per day, the assembly line running from the front of the factory to the rear, so that when you arrive in the morning you might see a green coupé joining the line and by the end of the day it will be near the end about to receive final adjustments, a continuous flow of about nine or ten cars being on the assembly line. Next door to the Porsche factory is one belonging to Reutter the coachbuilders, and the two are joined by a short private road. This branch of Reutter is occupied solely with Porsche work, and while it is not owned by Porsche it is under their control as far as work is concerned.

There is no chassis in the normal sense of the word, but a flat platform with box-sectioned sides and box structures at the front end and at the scuttle. The whole thing is made of sheel steel pressings which are spot-welded together and it was interesting to see that in some places where the sheet was bent without a former the ripples formed on the surface of the metal were left as they had the same stiffening effect as an intentional corrugation or a pressed-out stiffening channel. At the front are two tubular cross-members to carry the suspension units, another at the rear and a large one across the scuttle joining the rectangular section uprights on which the doors are hung, while these members are used to transmit hot air to the screen ducts. The bodywork, whether the fixed-head coupé, the drophead or the open Speedster, is also of sheet steel and when built is fitted to the platform chassis and welded into place, thus forming a very strong and rigid monocoque. The body is then trimmed, glazed and painted and " undersealed," but as yet there are no mechanical components on the car, but as the platform was built on a one-piece jig all the necessary holes to take bolts, bushes or bearings are finished. This complete body/chassis unit is then taken into the Porsche factory and placed on a three-wheeled trolley, so that it is about three feet off the ground, and it then joins the assembly line. On the base of the trolley are trays containing all the smaller mechanical parts for the chassis, while larger components, such as seats, steering columns and so on, are on racks alongside the assembly line at the points at which they will be required.

Porsches begin life at Reutter (coupe) or Drauze (roadster)

Most of the mechanical components, in the shape of castings, forgings or stampings, are made by outside firms to Porsche specifications and drawings and subject to Porsche inspection before being used, while all machining requiring great accuracy is done at the factory. Engines are assembled by individual fitters, each one being responsible for the whole unit, and the rear axle/gearbox unit is built in the same way. The two major components are assembled on either side of the main line and fitted to the car as complete units. The completed car is removed from its trolley and placed on a special machine on which wheel alignment, castor angles, camber angles, toe-in, etc., are all checked to micrometer accuracy and the car is then given a 60-mile road-test after which any further adjustments required are effected and it is then ready to leave the factory.

There are three basic types of engines built, all having four horizontally opposed air-cooled cylinders, but the main production is concentrated on the normal or " Damen " (the lady) and the Super. These two differ in compression ratio, valve and port sizes, exhaust system and crankshaft, the normal have conventional rods and lead-bronze big-ends and the Super have roller-bearing big-ends with non-splittable big-end eyes in the con-rods, the whole assembly being built-up by the Hirth Company on their patent splined journals and webs. These Super cranks and rods arrive at the factory already assembled, the others being machined and assembled at Porsche. The inlet valves on the normal engine are vertical and the exhaust valves inclined, both operated by pushrod and rockers, a single camshaft centrally placed above the crankshaft having four cams on it which operate the eight valves, each cam working opposed valves. The whole principle of the engine is like the VW, which is not surprising as Dr. Ferdinand Porsche designed that particular vehicle, and the air-cooling is effected by a large fan on top of the engine and driven off the dynamo. This fan blows air through ducts to close-fitted shrouds around the cylinders and heads, the hot air escaping underneath the car. In the main duct an oil cooler is mounted so that the oil is cooled independently of the speed of the car, which is very useful when storming a mountain pass in second gear, for no matter what the road speed the faster the engine runs the more cooling there is to the oil; this also applies in traffic driving. This same layout is followed on the $1\frac{1}{2}$-litre " Spyder " engine, which is now giving 115 b.h.p. at 6,200 r.p.m., but on this unit there are two overhead camshafts to each bank of cylinders. A roller-bearing crank is fitted and from the clutch end there is a gear-drive to a short shaft underneath the crankshaft; this shaft drives two bevel wheels mounted back to back, each in turn driving another bevel gear coupled to another shaft so that the rotation of the main shaft is turned through a right angle in each direction, the secondary shafts running one between each pair of cylinders. When these shafts, enclosed in tubes, reach the cylinder head they drive directly onto a bevel gear mounted in the centre of the exhaust camshaft, which is the lower one on each side of the engine. From this camshaft bevel gear another bevel and short shaft runs upwards to a similar pair on the inlet, or upper, camshaft, this system giving an inclined valve layout in each cylinder. A double-choke carburetter feeds to each pair of cylinders, whereas on the push-rod engines a single-choke carburetter is used, though it is possible to fit double-choke instruments. Twin plugs per cylinder are used on the " Spyder " engine, against single plugs on the normal and Super, and naturally the camshaft engine has a larger cooling fan, still driven by belt with the dynamo mounted on the fan shaft, the whole engine being closely ducted by metal shields. This unit differs from the normal engines by having dry-sump lubrication, with a separate tank and oil cooler in the nose of the car on the racing models.

The production version of this camshaft unit has a slightly lower compression ratio and is known as the " Carrera " engine, so named since its proving-ground was the Carrera-Mexicana or Pan-American road race; Le Mans and Mille Miglia also played a great part in proving the reliability of this engine. Competition is a by-word at the Porsche factory and the Porsche car is a perfect example of a race-bred one, the 1956 models all being available with the Carrera engine. Until the recent Frankfurt Motor Show the push-rod Porsches were sold in 1,100, 1,300 or 1,500-c.c. form, either "Damen" or " Super," the only differences being in the bore and stroke, the rest of the car being the same for all models. Now, however, the 1,100 has been dropped and the 1,500 has been enlarged to 1,600 c.c., that being the International capacity dividing line for Gran Turismo cars, and both sizes are still available in normal or Super form. If you want a car for touring purposes, Porsche recommend the normal engine, the Super being a competition version for rallies or races, and both units being interchangeable a keen owner could have one car and two engines, a " cooking " one and an " eating " one. The " eating " engine being intended for competition, its life is not anticipated at more than 40,000 miles, whereas the " cooking " one is reckoned to do 60,000 miles before worrying about wear and tear. As my use of the car was to tour Europe in reach of motor races I had a 1,500-c.c. normal, " a nice car," said Porsches, " that is reliable and long-living, but rather dull, it does only 95 m.p.h. and 5,200 r.p.m."

Before I made the choice of a Porsche I had to suffer a great deal of barracking with remarks such as " My God, the oversteer," or " they are impossible in the wet," " the fan belt breaks and then where are you?" " it will spin as soon as you see a corner," "you need a bath after changing the plugs," " they are noisy and rough," and " bloody clockwork contraption." I put up with all these because I thought the aerodynamic shape of the saloon looked about right and it was a car I could lean my elbow on (my friends mutter rude things to me about dwarfs when I discuss heights !). I have now completed 30,000 miles of Porsche motoring, all of it spelt with a capital M (see MOTOR SPORT for December, 1954, page 699) and the oversteer I enjoy having learned to drive on a chain-gang Frazer-Nash, the wet petrifies me in any car, the fan-belt is original and has not even needed adjusting, I have only spun it once in the total distance covered, the plugs I changed as a routine every 10,000 miles and the engine keeps so clean I only needed to wash my hands, which I reckon to do within 10,000 miles anyway; I never had occasion to look at a plug while on the road, this being 1955. The noise is outside the car, not in, and the roughness sounds on the Super model but not on the " Damen " and I found my model has a jolly strong spring in its " clockwork mechanism."

The whole essence of driving a Porsche lies in the fact that everything is finger-light; the steering, clutch, gear-change and brakes are all of a light smooth feeling that at first comes as strange after conventional cars. It has a live feel in its manner of going that wants caressing, not taken firmly between clenched fists as on some cars, while this manner of going is something that the driver has to accustom himself to. If you approach a Porsche with a view to driving it like a conventional car you will hate it, but on the other hand if you are prepared to spend say 1,000 miles in learning to drive all over again, you will love it. The Porsche is essentially a sporting car and likes to be driven in a sporting fashion, in fact the harder the better, and you find after a time that there are a number of things about it that you must absorb into your system. One is an appreciation of the rev-counter, for while the engine pulls happily from 1,500-5,000 r.p.m., it pays dividends to keep it between 2,500-4,500 r.p.m., and it doesn't wear out. Another is to realise that the direction in which the nose of the car is pointing is of no importance, providing the driver is convinced of the way he wants to go; and finally, before you start going quickly in a Porsche you must be able to *drive* anyway. I have met lots of people who have tried a Porsche and thought it terrible, and when I have seen them driving a conventional car I understand why; they just cannot *drive* properly anyway. With its low build, trailing-link i.f.s., and swing-axle rear suspension and rear-mounted engine it has an obvious oversteer characteristic, but this is constant and progressive and not changeable and sudden. The worst thing is surely an understeering car that changes its characteristics to violent oversteer in the middle of a fast corner. With the Porsche there are three ways of taking a corner : first at touring speeds, when there is no roll at all and the steering is neutral; secondly at fast road speeds when there is still virtually no roll but a slight oversteer which requires you to unwind the steering slightly before you leave the corner, this unwinding being progressive and varying with radius of the corner. Thirdly, there is the method for *very* fast cornering and this is where the Porsche technique must be applied; if it is not then you find yourself in a classic vintage oversteering slide on full opposite lock and about to turn right round. This special Porsche technique is better described by the acknowledged German expert on this type of motoring, Richard von Frankenberg, and I quote from an article he wrote for the *Sports Car Club of America*. " Often it is said that the Porsche is a difficult car to steer at high speed. In my opinion, this does not hold true. It must be admitted, however, that the Porsche must be driven with a different technique than the normal front-engined car. This ' different ' technique one has, so to speak, to learn. The Porsche is a car which announces in time when it reaches the limit of road adhesion and it is for this reason that I find it easier to drive than a normal car. There are many cars which possess good roadholding characteristics and which one can really drive to the limit of adhesion. Once this limit is crossed by just the slightest margin, these cars break loose and with such force that steering correction will hardly keep them on the road. The Porsche announces the fact that it intends to break loose, a little in advance, by a side wiping of the rear wheels and if one does the correct thing at this particular moment, then the first wiping away of the rear wheels becomes completely harmless. As a matter of fact, you will feel, from prolonged experience, that this is a completely normal and controllable action.

"Pleasure touring in a Porsche car will show little difference in handling characteristics from the normal automobile. However, in driving at really high speed there are two important points to remember. First is the motion on the steering wheel shortly before the turn and at the entrance of the turn itself; one must 'saw' the Porsche wheel. It is important to hold the steering wheel relatively loosely and make small corrective motions before the full centrifugal force has its effect on the car. One does not drive the car around the curve in a simple circular line—instead one drives it in a so-called 'snake-line.' I would repeat that it is important to hold the wheel loosely, so that the 'sawing' motion does not become a jerking one, but remains a small continuous motion. You will find the steering gear of the Porsche helpfully easy and 'soft.'

"The second point is that when driving into a curve at high speed, one does not wait until the Porsche breaks away in a surprising thrust-like manner. On the contrary, intentionally and consciously one brings about the breaking away in the beginning of the curve, a few tenths of a second before the turn itself. This only has sense, of course, when the car is driven really fast, so fast indeed as to cause the car to break away regardless. What you really do is to force upon the car your intention in purposely making it break away, a command the car will follow obediently. After you have set up this situation, you don't have to recover the car as you would do normally by relatively strong counter-steering. The car moves as a whole, the front-end pointing towards the inside of the curve and it literally 'wipes' round the bend; this typical Porsche movement we call 'wischen' (wiping) and it is a state between normal rolling travel and skidding, and one makes the necessary correction by 'sawing' on the steering wheel with an easy hand.

"At the end of this wiping motion, one must watch that the car does not point too much towards the inside. In the ideal situation, the wiping motion runs out into a harmonious roll as one leaves the curve. This results in a high speed at the end of the curve because the whole wiping motion must naturally be a continuous acceleration. This is important because all braking must be completed at the beginning of the curve and you open the throttle earlier than with most cars, driving the entire curve under full acceleration.

"When one has understood this controlled wiping motion, better still, when its mastery has become part of your blood, then Porsche driving becomes enormous fun ! "

The above description, by von Frankenberg, of the Porsche technique gives a very good explanation for the antics of a Porsche that is being driven fast. His remark that the steering is easy and soft is due to every steering box being " run-in " for 24 hours before being fitted to the car. The steering gear is conventional worm and sector running in engine oil, and in the assembly shop is a machine to take five assembled boxes and they are worked through the full range from lock-to-lock by a reversing mechanism driven by an electric motor. The lids are removed from the boxes and a special running-in oil is flowed through them. Day and night the steering box is wound from lock-to-lock and thus the full length of the worm is lapped to the sector, final adjustment being by shims on the sector pivot. This explains to a great extent the lightness of Porsche steering, its constant " feel " throughout its movement and its complete lack of high-spots or harshness, a feature that all who have driven a Porsche must have noticed. The " snake-line " referred to by Frankenberg is well summed up by a friend of mine who described the movement of a Porsche round a curve as a series of chords and tangents. The closing remark, about getting it into your blood, is very true, Porsche driving not only becomes enormous fun but you become a Porsche addict, like the addicts of chain-gang 'Nashes, Bugattis or Bentleys.

In almost exactly eight months of fun I have covered 30,000 miles with my " Damen " and executed every known Porsche antic with the exception of the " ground-level-flick-roll " and I find it hard to extract pleasure from other forms of motoring to the same degree. The performance is not the outstanding thing about the ordinary 1,500-c.c. normal touring Porsche; it will out-accelerate a Zephyr or Mark VII Jaguar, the maximum on English roads is a very honest 90 m.p.h., while given time, as on an autobahn or by-pass, it will do 95 m.p.h. and, under favourable conditions such as a mountain side or a following wind, I have done 103 m.p.h., these figures being rev.-counter readings, the speedo. being 7 m.p.h. fast at maximum. The genuine top speed, such as I would do on the way home from the office every day, if I had to suffer such a journey, is 4,600 r.p.m. in top (95 m.p.h.) and with a maximum-permissible of 5,200 r.p.m. this is a comfortable feeling when a long downhill stretch approaches. These sort of figures are not the real charm of the Porsche That lies in its manner of going, for the suspension gives a very smooth ride, the body makes negligible wind noise, the controls are light, the all-synchromesh gearbox is one of those that will go down in history, and a new standard in lightness, the engine emits a hum like a dynamo at a cruising speed of 4,200 r.p.m. in top, and the seats are comfortable, while the driving position always evokes cries of acclamation from anyone who tries it. It is only natural that a car developed around competition motoring should have an excellent driving position, and as the Porsche saloon is not easy to get into and out of, unless you are fairly agile, it is rather fun to watch an awkward friend struggling to get in and hear the muttered remarks about dwarfs change to satisfied comments as he finds a near-perfect driving position. Visibility, in spite of almost sitting on the ground, is such that even I can see the road eight feet in front of the bumper when adopting a fairly reclining arms-stretched position. If you sit upright, vintage-fashion, this is reduced to six feet. The easy, quiet manner of going and the comfort factor all combine to make it possible to cover more than 600 miles in a day's Continental motoring, driving alone, and yet not feel tired at the end, while 8-10 hours of a consistent average of 55 miles into each hour will show a fuel consumption of 34 m.p.g., the range of the tank being an easy 350 miles. On English roads 400 miles in a day are effortless and do not involve early starts or late arrivals.

Of all the " bogeys " thought up by anti-Porsche types the only serious one is always overlooked; most of the " cracks " at Porsches can be counteracted by the simple remark " When did you last drive a Porsche ? " to which the answer is invariably " Well, I haven't *actually* driven one," so you follow up this with " When were you last taken for a ride in one ? " and you would be surprised how many leaders of the opposition then have to admit that they've never been in a Porsche and they add feebly, " but, I do know that it's a fact, old boy." Even quite well-known rally and racing drivers have been caught out by this counter-play and when they are the central figure of an admiring group they do not like it at all. If these " know-alls " had any experience of Porsches they would quietly ask about the health of the rear tyres and then it would be my turn to look embarrassed, for rear-tyre wear is a slight problem. My best pair lasted 6,500 miles and the worst 4,700 miles, and as I have used various makes there is little point in naming them, except that the best were some much-maligned racing tyres. This excessive wear is entirely dependent on how you drive; if you " wischen " all the time, as I do, then you must pay for it; if you are content to tour then you could do 20,000 miles. The VW is a similar sufferer, one owner needing new rear tyres in 8,500 miles, another **having done 14,000 without a trace of wear. Equally, I knew a man who could never do more than 6,000 miles on his hotted-up Morris Minor without needing new tyres; speed round corners as well as high cruising speeds must be paid for no matter whether you over or understeer.** If you can afford the fun, well why not have it. The Porsche front tyres are very reasonable, they last 12,000 miles.

As to maintenance and reliability I have few grumbles, for maintenance has consisted of routine oil changes every 1,500 miles, new Fram filter element every 10,000 miles and regular greasing. Reliability is such that I never stopped on the road for any " mechanical " reason in those 30,000 miles, though I did suffer some troubles. At 5,000 miles some of the grease in the speedo cable worked its way into the instrument and being of the magnetic-drive type it was converted to hydraulic drive, which meant that it indicated 120 m.p.h. most of the time, but as the mileometer was mechanical and continued to work I did not bother about the free replacement until I returned to the factory at 16,600 miles, the reasons for this return being manifold. I had got the hang of " wischen " motoring and had been warned that if I indulged in it on bad road surfaces the gear-lever would give a violent judder and the rear-end would be subject to abnormal strain and the gearbox mounting might crack. I did what I was told not to do all over the Italian mountains, through the Massif Centrale of France, the Pyrenees and the Portuguese mountains and on the return from Lisbon there was an ominous " click " each time I lifted my foot. This was after 16,000 miles, so I could hardly complain and, anyway, the only effect that this broken gearbox mounting had on the car was that it jumped out of top gear on very bad bumps at over 80 m.p.h. In addition I had a cracked windscreen collected from flying stones when overtaking another car, and I felt it was time the engine was looked at, while the rear shock-absorbers were worn out and I wanted new heavy-duty " competition ones " fitted.

While at the factory I agreed to let the Service Department give the car a routine 15,000 check, but when I suggested a decoke and valve grind they roared with laughter. I had to admit that it was still doing its 4,600 r.p.m. in top, used a pint of oil between changes, and ran as smoothly as when I left the factory, but being old-fashioned I felt the cylinder heads ought to be removed after 16,600 miles of very hard driving. All the mechanical units were removed from the car, cleaned, checked and replaced, though nothing was opened. The engine was checked for compression, timing, valve clearances (they had been done once, at 10,000 miles) and new plugs and ignition points fitted, but that was all. The brake linings were renewed and the drums checked for truth and skinned where necessary and new stub-axle assemblies were fitted. The brake linings and stub axle and suspension bushes were replaced as a matter of course, on an exchange plan, not because they were worn out but because the next check was not anticipated before 30,000 miles and by then the original ones might have worn a little and as the Porsche is a car meant to be driven fast, the Service Department like to know that everything is 100 per cent. While this work was being done I was able to see the new gearbox mounting, which is incorporated in the 1956 cars and will avoid the trouble I had, and also the new saloon with the Carrera engine. At the same time I had the opportunity to try a Speedster, the cheaper open two-seater, with normal 1,500-c.c. engine. Being more spartan it was considerably lighter, my car weighing 17½ cwt. in normal road trim, covered with odds and ends such as extra lamps, radio, tools and so on, and being really fully equipped for comfortable touring, so that this Speedster together with its slightly lower axle ratio was a very lively car. As most of the weight saving arose from it being open it resulted in a lower c.g. and 90 per cent. of this weight removal was from the rear-axle loading, being roof, windows and mechanism, rear window, rear-seat squab and lighter bucket seats and as a result there was quite a marked difference in handling, the " wischen " cornering not being so pronounced, but as it was a sporting two-seater it had all the failings of such models such as unlockable doors, flapping hood at 90 m.p.h., continual indecision about hood-up or hood-down, and while being great fun as a " dicer " it was not what I would have liked for motoring 1,000 miles a week continuously, that is, when the normal saloon Porsche is the available alternative. After all, one of the most pleasing things about the Type 356 saloon Porsche is its aerodynamic body, which spells efficiency and a sense of keeping abreast of the times; it is difficult to justify an open car for long-distance high-speed touring.

While doing the routine Service Schedule, every little detail on the car was checked, even to fitting a new grille in the ash-tray; I had discarded the original as being a non-smoker I used the ash-tray for toffee-papers. Thrown in as a matter of courtesy was a check for alignment of the machine in the assembly department, tightening and a better fitting of the extra lamps I had mounted myself and a wash and polish, inside and out. The steering had required a 40 thou. skim to satisfy the meticulous Porsche standards and the car was given a 20-mile road test before being handed over for me to drive like a lunatic for another 15,000 miles over Europe's best and worst roads, conditions that would never prevail in England.

After a visit to Sweden I returned to Germany and competed in the Rhineland Rally, a wonderful event consisting of leaving the car in the open all night and from a 7 a.m. start covering 22 laps or 380 miles round the entire Nurburgring, using the Grand Prix circuit and the old Southern loop as well. The only stipulation was a maximum time for the whole distance and in the 1,600-c.c. Gran Turismo category the schedule was aimed to make a Porsche " Damen " hustle along a bit, though easy enough for a Super 1,500 c.c. Those who qualified then competed in a timed hill-climb on one part of the circuit. By now I had covered 21,000 miles and " race " preparation consisted of a new set of racing Dunlops, an oil change, and removal of all my luggage. After 17 laps around an average of 60 + m.p.h. I suffered a choked main jet, probably from the open refuelling churns used, and the time lost in locating the trouble after a slow return to the pits was more than I had in hand, so that was that. However, it was a good dice while it lasted.

Returning to duty motoring, the end-of-season trips brought the total to 28,000 miles and two weeks in England made up the round 30,000. Passing through Stuttgart on my way to England I paused to have new rubber bushes put in the front anti-roll bar as it was rattling when going over cobblestones and I again suggested a decoke, or new piston rings or something. The chief tester took the car out on the autobahn and could not see why I was complaining —well, I wasn't exactly complaining, I just thought . . . They took the clutch adjustment up a notch, clicked the brake adjusters a couple of notches each and I left thinking " I suppose they know best." On the way from Stuttgart to Cologne I put 210 miles in three hours, did 77 miles in the first hour, held 4,800 r.p.m. in top for at least three minutes on the Dormstadt-Heidelberg stretch that used to be used for record breaking, all at 33 m.p.g. with the radio playing, and realised that perhaps Dr. Ferry Porsche and his men do know something about building nice touring cars.—D. S. J.

WEBER CARBURETOR SPECIFICATIONS		
Engine	1600 GS/692/3	2000 GS/587/2
Carb.	40 DCM 2	46 IDM 2
Venturi	38 P-3.5A	40 P-3.5A
Mainjet	1.30	1.65
Air Corr.	1.9	2.4
Idling Jet	50 x 45	60
Idling Air	1.2	1.2
Pump Jet	.45	.40
Needle	3.0	3.0
Mixture Tube #	F4	F20
Float Wt.	67g	20.5g

Solex Carburetor Specifications

Engine	1600S-90	1500 GS/547/1	1500 GS/692/0	1600 GS/692/1
Year	1960	1955-58	1958	1958
Carb	40 PJJ-4	40 PII-4	40 PII-4	40 PII-4
Venturi	32	30	34	34
Main Jet	115	102.5	110	110
Air Corr.	180	200	180	180
Idling Jet	57.5	50	50	50
Idling Air	1.8	1.5	1.5	1.5
Pump Jet	50	50	50	50.
Needle	1.75	2.0	2.0	2.0
Mixture Tube #	25	33	21	21
Float Wt.	7.4g	10g	10g	10g
Engine		1600 GS/692/2	1600 GS/692/3A	2000 GS/587/1
Year		1958-59	1960	1962-63
Carb.		40 PII	44 PII-4	40 PII-4
Venturi		34	38	36
Main Jet		110	140	130
Air Corr.		220	220	180
Idling Jet		55	60	60
Idling Air		1.6	1.6	1.6
Pump Jet		50	50	50
Needle		2.0	1.75	1.75
Mixture Tube #		25	25	25
Float Wt.		10g	10g	10g

Electrical Diagram Type 356 A

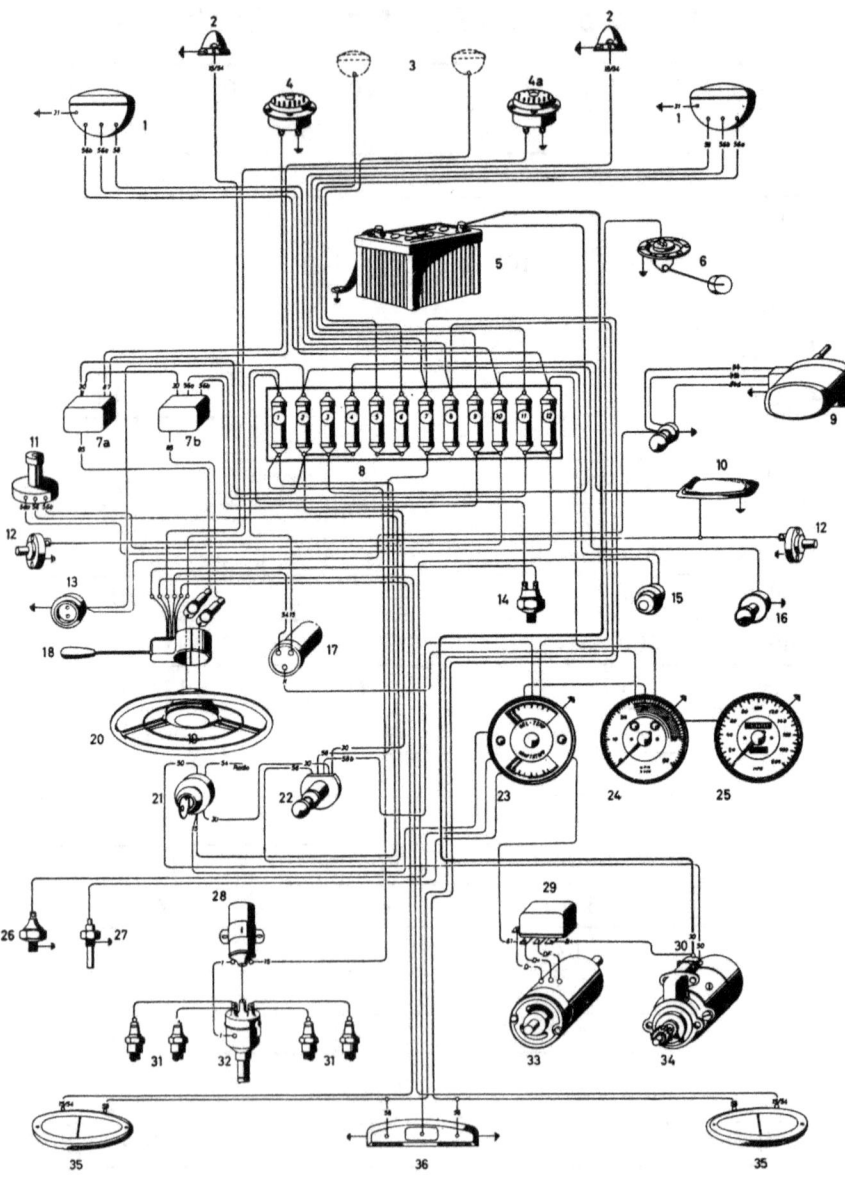

Electrical Diagram Type 356 C

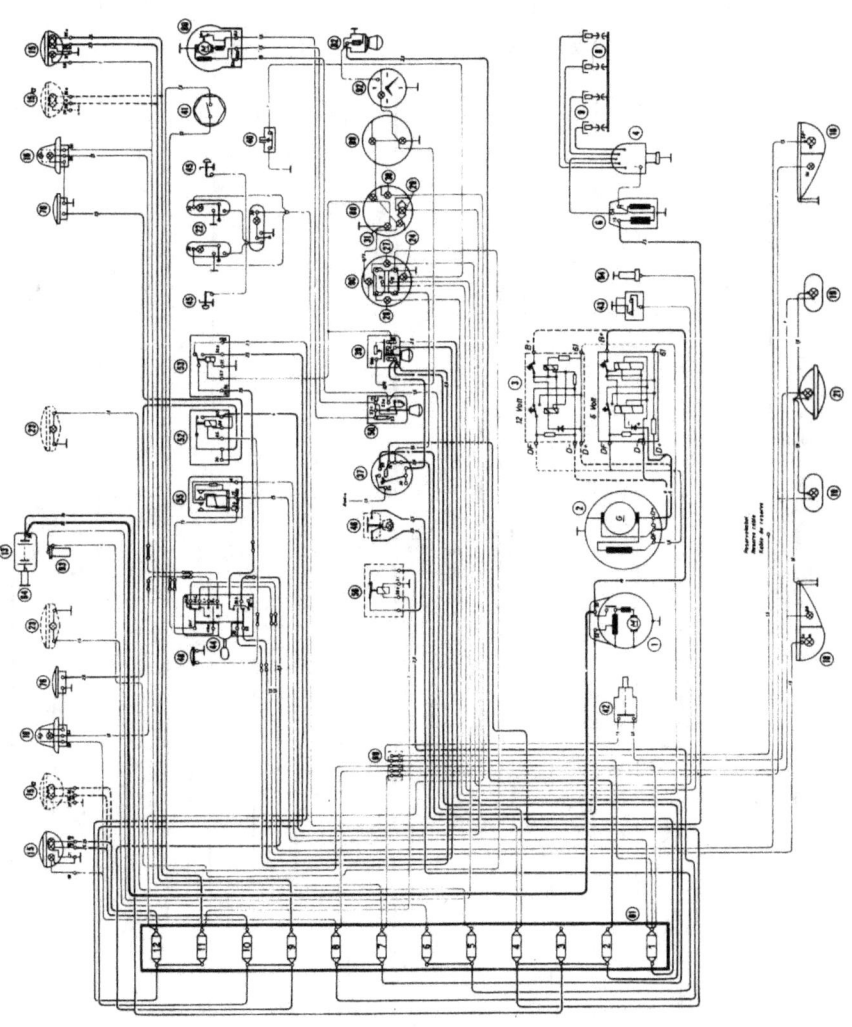

Porsche Engine Specifications

Engine	1100	1300	1300A	1300S
No. Cyl.	4	4	4	4
Bore & Stroke	73.5 x 64	80 x 64	74.5 x 74	74.5 x 74
Displacement	1086	1286	1290	1290
Comp. Ratio	7:1	6.5:1	6.5:1	8.2:1
B.h.p. @ R.p.m.	40 @ 4200	50 @ 4500	50 @ 4500	71 @ 5700
Torque	52 @	59 @	59.5 @	65 @
Ft. lbs. @ R.p.m.	2800	2800	2800	3600

Engine	1500/527	1500/546	1500S	1600
No. Cyl.	4	4	4	4
Bore & Stroke	80 x 74	80 x 74	80 x 74	82.5 x 74
Displacement	1488	1488	1488	1582
Comp. Ratio	7:1	7:1	8.2:1	7.5:1
B.h.p. @ R.p.m.	70 @ 4800	64 @ 4800	82 @ 5400	70 @ 4500
Torque	75.2 @	78.1 @	79.6 @	81 @
Ft. lbs. @ R.p.m.	3000	2800	3600	2800

Porsche Engine Specifications
Spyder & Carrera

Engine	1600S	1600-S90	1500 GS	1600 GS	1600 GS/GT	2000 GS
No. Cyl.	4	4	4	4	4	4
Bore & Stroke	82.5 x 74	82.5 x 74	85 x 66	87.5 x 66	87.5 x 66	92 x 74
Displacement	1582	1582	1498	1587	1587	1966
Comp. Ratio	8.5:1	9.0:1	9.0:1	9.5:1	9.7:1	9.5:1
B.h.p. @ R.p.m.	88 @ 5000	102 @ 5500	110 @ 6200	105 @ 6500	115 @ 6500	152 @ 6200
Torque	86 @	89 @	87.6 @	88.9 @	99.8 @	131 @
Ft. lbs. @ R.p.m.	3700	4300	5200	5000	5000	4600

Porsche Aircraft Engine

Type 678/1   Type 678/3   Type 678/4

One of the more interesting by-products of the Porsche works is an aircraft engine, (or, to be more specific, three aircraft engines, types 687/1, 678/3, and 678/4). Basically a 1600 Super in major components, the Porsche is not merely a converted automobile but one engineered specifically for the job of powering light two-place planes requiring 50 to 75 take-off horsepower.

Modifications which set it apart from the sports car powerplant are dual ignition by magneto or distributor, preheated carburetor and variations in cowling. The propeller is driven from the flywheel end of the crankshaft through reduction gearing. Three years of dynamometer and flight testing have gone into the three engine types and all are certified by the Official German Aviation Research Center at Brunswick. Fitted to several light planes, the performance and low-wear characteristics match those encountered in operation of the Porsche automobile.

The two-place sports plane "Elster" built by Alfons Putzer in Bonn, W. Germany powered by a Porsche 678/3 aircraft engine.

Porsche aircraft engine nestles snugly under cowl of trim "Elster".

Experimental Marine Corps Helicopter with aircooled opposed engine by Porsche.

Rear engined light planes are fitting companions for 1600 Convertible.

"Birdcage" frame of rear-engined lightplane supports aircraft engine with automobile-type forced-draft cooling arrangement.

ARE YOU:
INTERESTED IN EUROPEAN, IMPORT & EXOTIC AUTOMOBILES?

DO YOU:
DO YOUR OWN MAINTENANCE?

If you answered yes to either of these questions, then you should check out our automobile books and manuals. We have included a sample listing of some of our featured marques. However, for complete details and the most up-to-date information, please visit our website.

—— www.VelocePress.com ——

The fastest growing specialist USA publisher of niche market automotive books and manuals.

All VelocePress titles are available through your local independent bookseller, Amazon.com or direct from VelocePress. Wholesale customers may also purchase direct or from the Ingram Book Group.

AUTOBOOKS WORKSHOP MANUALS

ALFA ROMEO GIULIA 1300, 1600, 1750, 2000 1962-1978 WSM
AUSTIN HEALEY SPRITE, MG MIDGET 1958-1980 WSM
BMW 1600 1966-1973 WSM
BMW 2000 & 2002 1966-1976 WSM
BMW 2500, 2800, 3.0 & 3.3 1968-1977 WSM
BMW 316, 320, 320i 1975-1977 WSM
BMW 518, 520, 520i 1973-1981 WSM
FIAT 1100, 1100D, 1100R & 1200 1957-1969 WSM
FIAT 124 1966-1974 WSM
FIAT 124 SPORT 1966-1975 WSM
FIAT 125 & 125 SPECIAL 1967-1973 WSM
FIAT 126, 126L, 126 DV, 126/650 & 126/650 DV 1972-1982 WSM
FIAT 127 SALOON, SPECIAL & SPORT, 900, 1050 1971-1981 WSM
FIAT 128 1969-1982 WSM
FIAT 1300, 1500 1961-1967 WSM
FIAT 131 MIRAFIORI 1975-1982 WSM
FIAT 132 1972-1982 WSM
FIAT 500 1957-1973 WSM
FIAT 600, 600D & MULTIPLA 1955-1969 WSM
FIAT 850 1964-1972 WSM
JAGUAR E-TYPE 1961-1972 WSM
JAGUAR MK 1, 2 1955-1969 WSM
JAGUAR S TYPE, 420 1963-1968 WSM
JAGUAR XK 120, 140, 150 MK 7, 8, 9 1948-1961 WSM
LAND ROVER 1, 2 1948-1961 WSM
MERCEDES-BENZ 190 1959-1968 WSM
MERCEDES-BENZ 220/8 WSM
MERCEDES-BENZ 220B 1959-1965 WSM
MERCEDES-BENZ 230 1963-1968 WSM
MERCEDES-BENZ 250 1968-1972 WSM
MERCEDES-BENZ 280 1968-1972 WSM
MG MIDGET TA-TF 1936-1955 WSM
MINI 1959-1980 WSM
MORRIS MINOR 1952-1971 WSM
PEUGEOT 404 1960-1975 WSM
PORSCHE 911 1964-1973 WSM
PORSCHE 911 1970-1977 WSM
RENAULT 16 1965-1979 WSM
RENAULT 8, 10, 1100 1962-1971 WSM
ROVER 3500, 3500S 1968-1976 WSM
SUNBEAM RAPIER, ALPINE 1955-1965 WSM
TRIUMPH SPITFIRE, GT6, VITESSE 1962-1968 WSM
TRIUMPH TR2, TR3, TR3A 1952-1962 WSM
TRIUMPH TR4, TR4A 1961-1967 WSM
VOLKSWAGEN BEETLE 1968-1977 WSM

BROOKLANDS BOOKS & ROAD TEST PORTFOLIOS (RTP)

AC CARS 1904-2009
ALFA ROMEO 1920-1933 ROAD TEST PORTFOLIO
ALFA ROMEO 1934-1940 ROAD TEST PORTFOLIO
BRABHAM RALT HONDA THE RON TAURANAC STORY
BUGATTI TYPE 10 TO TYPE 40 ROAD TEST PORTFOLIO
BUGATTI TYPE 10 TO TYPE 251 ROAD TEST PORTFOLIO
BUGATTI TYPE 41 TO TYPE 55 ROAD TEST PORTFOLIO
BUGATTI TYPE 57 TO TYPE 251 ROAD TEST PORTFOLIO
DELAHAYE ROAD TEST PORTFOLIO
FERRARI ROAD CARS 1946-1956 ROAD TEST PORTFOLIO
FIAT 500 1936-1972 ROAD TEST PORTFOLIO
FIAT DINO ROAD TEST PORTFOLIO
HISPANO SUIZA ROAD TEST PORTFOLIO
HONDA ST1100/ST1300 PAN EUROPEAN 1990-2002 RTP
JAGUAR MK1 & MK2 ROAD TEST PORTFOLIO
LOTUS CORTINA ROAD TEST PORTFOLIO
MV AGUSTA F4 750 & 1000 1997-2007 ROAD TEST PORTFOLIO
TATRA CARS ROAD TEST PORTFOLIO

VELOCEPRESS AUTOMOBILE BOOKS & MANUALS

ABARTH BUYERS GUIDE
AUSTIN-HEALEY 6-CYLINDER WSM
BMW 600 LIMOUSINE FACTORY WSM
BMW 600 LIMOUSINE OWNERS HAND BOOK & SERVICE MANUAL
BMW ISETTA FACTORY WSM
BOOK OF THE CARRERA PANAMERICANA - MEXICAN ROAD RACE
DIALED IN - THE JAN OPPERMAN STORY
FERRARI 250/GT SERVICE AND MAINTENANCE
FERRARI 308 SERIES BUYER'S AND OWNER'S GUIDE
FERRARI BERLINETTA LUSSO
FERRARI BROCHURES AND SALES LITERATURE 1946-1967
FERRARI BROCHURES AND SALES LITERATURE 1968-1989
FERRARI GUIDE TO PERFORMANCE
FERRARI OPP, MAINTENANCE & SERVICE H/BOOKS 1948-1963
FERRARI OWNER'S HANDBOOK
FERRARI SERIAL NUMBERS PART I - ODD NUMBERS TO 21399
FERRARI SERIAL NUMBERS PART II - EVEN NUMBERS TO 1050
FERRARI SPYDER CALIFORNIA
FERRARI TUNING TIPS & MAINTENANCE TECHNIQUES
HOW TO BUILD A FIBERGLASS CAR
HOW TO BUILD A RACING CAR
IF HEMINGWAY HAD WRITTEN A RACING NOVEL
JAGUAR E-TYPE 3.8 & 4.2 WSM
LE MANS 24 (THE BOOK THAT THE FILM WAS BASED ON)
MASERATI BROCHURES AND SALES LITERATURE
MASERATI OWNER'S HANDBOOK
METROPOLITAN FACTORY WSM
MGA & MGB OWNERS HANDBOOK & WSM
OBERT'S FIAT GUIDE
PERFORMANCE TUNING THE SUNBEAM TIGER
PORSCHE 356 1948-1965 WSM
PORSCHE 912 WSM
SOUPING THE VOLKSWAGEN
TRIUMPH TR2, TR3, TR4 1953-1965 WSM
VEDA ORR'S NEW REVISED HOT ROD PICTORIAL
VOLKSWAGEN TRANSPORTER, TRUCKS, STATION WAGONS WSM
VOLVO 1944-1968 ALL MODELS WSM

VELOCEPRESS MOTORCYCLE BOOKS & MANUALS

AJS SINGLES 1955-65 350cc & 500cc (BOOK OF)
ARIEL 1939-1960 4 STROKE SINGLES (BOOK OF)
ARIEL MOTORCYCLES 1933-1951 WSM
ARIEL PREWAR MODELS 1932-1939 (BOOK OF)
BMW M/CYCLES R26 R27 (1956-1967) FACTORY WSM
BMW M/CYCLES R50 R50S R60 R69S (1955-1969) FACTORY WSM
BSA BANTAM (BOOK OF)
BSA OHV & SV SINGLES - 250cc 1954-1970 (BOOK OF)
BSA OHV & SV SINGLES 1945-54 250-600cc (BOOK OF)
BSA OHV SINGLES 350 & 500cc 1955-1967 (BOOK OF)
BSA PREWAR MODELS TO 1939 (BOOK OF)
BSA TWINS 1948-1962 (BOOK OF)
BSA TWINS 1962-1969 (SECOND BOOK OF)
DUCATI 160cc, 250cc & 350cc OHC MODELS FACTORY WSM
HONDA 50 ALL MODELS UP TO 1970 (BOOK OF)
HONDA 90 ALL MODELS UP TO 1966 (BOOK OF)
HONDA MOTORCYCLES 125-150 TWINS C/CS/CB/CA WSM
HONDA MOTORCYCLES 250-305 TWINS C/CS/CB WSM
HONDA MOTORCYCLES C100 SUPER CUB WSM
HONDA MOTORCYCLES C110 SPORT CUB 1962-1969 WSM
HONDA TWINS & SINGLES 50cc TO 305cc 1960-1966 (BOOK OF)
LAMBRETTA ALL 125 & 150cc MODELS 1947-1957 (BOOK OF)
LAMBRETTA LI & TV MODELS 1957-1970 (SECOND BOOK OF)
MATCHLESS 350 & 500cc SINGLES 1945-1956 (BOOK OF)
MATCHLESS 350 & 500cc SINGLES 1955-1966 (BOOK OF)
NORTON 1938-1956 (BOOK OF)
NORTON DOMINATOR TWINS 1955-1965 (BOOK OF)
NORTON MOTORCYCLES 1957-1970 FACTORY WSM
NORTON PREWAR MODELS 1932-1939 (BOOK OF)
ROYAL ENFIELD 736cc INTERCEPTOR FACTORY WSM
SUZUKI 50cc & 80cc UP TO 1966 (BOOK OF)
SUZUKI T10 1963-1967 FACTORY WSM
SUZUKI T20 & T200 1965-1969 FACTORY WSM
TRIUMPH MOTORCYCLE 1935-1939 (BOOK OF)
TRIUMPH MOTORCYCLES 1937-1951 WSM
TRIUMPH MOTORCYCLES 1945-1955 FACTORY WSM
TRIUMPH TWINS 1956-1969 (BOOK OF)
VELOCETTE ALL SINGLES & TWINS 1925-1970 (BOOK OF)
VESPA 1951-1961 (BOOK OF)
VINCENT MOTORCYCLES 1935-1955 WSM

www.VelocePress.com

www.ingramcontent.com/pod-product-compliance
Lightning Source LLC
Chambersburg PA
CBHW050139240426
43673CB00043B/1726